Reconstructing
Pastoral Theology

Reconstructing Pastoral Theology

A Christological Foundation

Andrew Purves

Westminster John Knox Press
LOUISVILLE • LONDON

© 2004 Andrew Purves

Scripture quotations, unless otherwise indicated, are from the New Revised Standard Version of the Bible, copyright © 1989 by the Division of Christian Education of the National Council of the Churches of Christ in the U.S.A., and used by permission.

Scripture quotations from the Revised Standard Version of the Bible are copyright © 1946, 1952, 1971, and 1973 by the Division of Christian Education of the National Council of the Churches of Christ in the U.S.A. and are used by permission.

Scripture quotations from *The Jerusalem Bible*, copyright © 1966, 1967, 1968 by Darton, Longman & Todd, Ltd., and Doubleday & Co., Inc. Used by permission of the publishers.

Quotations from Calvin's *Institutes of the Christian Religion* are reproduced here from *Calvin: Institutes of the Christian Religion* (Library of Christian Classics) edited by John T. McNeill. Used by permission of Westminster John Knox Press.

Book design by Sharon Adams
Cover design by designpointinc.com

First edition
Published by Westminster John Knox Press
Louisville, Kentucky

This book is printed on acid-free paper that meets the American National Standards Institute Z39.48 standard. ⊚

PRINTED IN THE UNITED STATES OF AMERICA

04 05 06 07 08 09 10 11 12 13 — 10 9 8 7 6 5 4 3 2 1

Library of Congress Cataloging-in-Publication Data

Purves, Andrew, 1946–
    Reconstructing pastoral theology : a Christological foundation / Andrew Purves—
1st ed.
        p. cm.
    Includes bibliographical references and index.
    ISBN 0-664-22733-3 (alk. paper)
    1. Pastoral theology.   I. Title.

    BV4011.3.P874 2004
    253—dc22

2004050880

Dedicated to my three children
with love and deepest respect

Brendan
Gordon
Laura

Contents

Preface

What is not assumed is not healed.
Gregory of Nazianzus

The above quotation expressed Gregory's concern that in the incarnation Jesus had a fully human as well as divine mind. That debate from the fourth century may seem to be very far removed from the concerns of pastoral work today. Yet there is something of underlying importance in the concept that I want to apply to our understanding of ministry. I take the doctrine of sin seriously. I also take seriously that only in and through Jesus Christ, and through our union with him, which is the gift and work of the Holy Spirit, can we approach the Father and serve the Father in righteousness and truth. Thus we must say that Jesus Christ is not only the Word of God to, for, and with us, but he is also the truly human one, who has assumed our whole response to God into himself and who now continually offers in his own name the worship and work of his people. The combination of these two classical doctrines—union with Christ and his dual ministry from and to the Father—has been a kind of Copernican revolution in my thinking. Putting them together has released the floodgates in my theological work, and this book is one result. This has led to the conclusion, firmly fixed now in my mind, that the ministry that is not assumed by Jesus Christ is the ministry that is not healed, but that languishes in the pride of our own attempts to storm heaven.

I have often said to students that the problem with their theology is that they have not yet thought radically enough concerning Jesus Christ. They impose restraints upon the thoroughgoing demands of Jesus Christ and of his reality upon their thinking, usually in order to leave some room for human autonomy. They seem to assume that some areas of human experience do not need to be healed by Christ and can therefore stand independently of him. I reject that assumption. The point is simply this: in what follows I am trying to think radically concerning Jesus Christ and to understand pastoral theology in such a context, guided by the twin doctrines of union with Christ and our participation in his ministry from the Father and to the Father. This is pastoral theology that is thoroughly christologically grounded.

I have been trying to write this book for a long time. It germinated in a graduate thesis written while I was a student at Duke University, during the 1974/75 academic year. The topic then was a Reformed approach to pastoral theology. I have long lost that manuscript—thankfully, perhaps. My doctoral work was a comparative study of political theology and the theology of pastoral care, with special reference to Jürgen Moltmann and Seward Hiltner. Some of that work, nearly thirty years later, is incorporated into the present work, for the theological criticism of liberal pastoral theology and the establishment of the relationship between eschatology and pastoral care remain largely undeveloped. Through four and a half years of pastoral ministry and now in my twenty-first year on the faculty of Pittsburgh Theological Seminary, through many books read and written, and, most importantly, through classes taught, I have kept in view that long-held desire to write a full-scale pastoral theology that was truly theological and that would include an eschatological aspect. This is the goal now finished.

As a student in Edinburgh, and throughout the years since I left with my Ph.D. in hand in 1978, sometimes with intentionality at the front of my mind, at other times pushed to the back but still in play, have been the teaching and influence of James and Tom Torrance. They were teaching together in the department of Christian Dogmatics at New College, the Faculty of Divinity in the University of Edinburgh, Scotland. The theology I was taught got under my skin when I was a young student studying for my bachelor of divinity degree, and I have scratched ever since. In fact, I did not study under the Torrances directly for more than two years. But their legacy throughout the years of both my parish ministry and my seminary teaching has been a gift and a burden; in my mind and through their writings they have been constant companions who provoked, nagged, insisted, questioned, guided, and challenged me to take Jesus Christ very seriously indeed. I have tried very hard to do just that.

James and Tom Torrance gave me the theological categories by which to pursue my own work. My debt is enormous. Especially I have learned from Tom Torrance's amazing productivity as a scholar, and returned again and again to his considerable, passionate, and at times very difficult, huge, and dense published body of work, catching an ever-deeper glimpse of the depth and brilliance of his theological program. I think too that I catch a glimpse even of his astonishing and reverent intuition of God. I hope it is not too pious or silly to say that he strikes me as a man transformed by the renewing of his mind (Rom. 12:2). Certainly he argued often enough, following the fourth-century Greek fathers, that the theologian must do everything before the face of the divine glory and majesty. Those who know his work will recognize an overtone from one of his books in my title. As a summary statement of this theology, and as the launching statement for what follows, perhaps no better than this can be offered: "For us to be in the Spirit or to have the Spirit dwelling within us means that we are united to Christ the incarnate Son of the Father, and are made through union with him in the Spirit to participate, human creatures though we are, in the Communion which the Father, the Son, and the Holy Spirit have among themselves and are in themselves."[1]

I need to mention one other point. While finishing the first draft of this book I was diagnosed with colon cancer. The book received its final form following surgery and during subsequent chemotherapy. One thing I know for sure: what follows is the only hope I have for faith and ministry. I follow only where Paul would take me: "My grace is sufficient for you, for power is made perfect in weakness. So, I will boast all the more gladly of my weaknesses, so that the power of Christ may dwell in me. Therefore I am content with weaknesses, insults, hardships, persecutions, and calamities for the sake of Christ; for whenever I am weak, then I am strong" (2 Cor. 12:9–10). This I am discovering; it is not pious rhetoric, but the thing itself. This theme is especially developed in chapter 9. This book and the experiences at the time of its completion are fused together.

A number of people deserve special mention. My thanks for abiding friendship and encouragement go to Charles Partee of Pittsburgh Theological Seminary, Mark Achtemeier of Dubuque Theological Seminary, and more generally to the wonderful faculty at Pittsburgh Theological Seminary who were there for me in a way that was quite marvelous, and that should be shouted from the rooftops. Is this not how it should be? It is also appropriate to acknowledge my gratitude to Stephanie Egnotovich for her editorial competence, encouragement, and advocacy of my work.

---

1. Thomas F. Torrance, *The Christian Doctrine of God: One Being, Three Persons* (Edinburgh: T. & T. Clark, 1996), 148.

This is my third book under her guidance, and the books are so much the better for her sharp eye and good sense.

Finally, I wish to acknowledge the love, faith, and strength of my wife, the Reverend Catherine Purves. There are no words in my vocabulary by which to express my gratitude and love. She has been my companion in the heights and in the depths. What a gift of God!

Introduction:
Building a New Foundation

The priests of old, I admit, were estimable men; but our own High Priest is greater, for He has been entrusted with the Holy of Holies, and to Him alone are the secret things of God committed. He is the doorway to the Father, and it is by Him that Abraham and Isaac and Jacob and the prophets go in, no less than the apostles and the whole Church. For all these have their part in God's unity. Nevertheless, the Gospel has a distinction all its own, in the advent of our Saviour Jesus Christ, and His Passion and Resurrection. We are fond of the prophets, and they indeed point forward to Him in their preaching; yet it is the gospel that sets the coping stone on man's immortality.

Ignatius
Early Christian Writings: The Apostolic Fathers [1]

Jesus Christ "is the history of God with man and the history of man with God."

Karl Barth, *Church Dogmatics* [2]

Theology is the Greek word for thinking about God. [3] According to H. R. Mackintosh, "theology is simply a persistent and systematic effort to clarify the convictions by which Christians live." [4] Theology is

---

1. Trans. Maxwell Staniforth (New York: Penguin, 1982), 114.

2. Karl Barth, *Church Dogmatics*, IV.1, ed. G. W. Bromiley and T. F. Torrance, trans. G. W. Bromiley (Edinburgh: T. & T. Clark, 1956), 158.

3. I found this very simple phrasing in James W. Leitch, *A Theology of Transition: H. R. Mackintosh as an Approach to Barth* (London: Nisbet, 1952), vii.

4. H. R. Mackintosh, *The Christian Experience of Forgiveness* (New York and London: Harper and Brothers, 1927), 4.

thereby also the clarification of convictions by which Christians engage in ministry. Therefore, God is the principal subject matter of pastoral theology, though from a pastoral perspective or more generally, a theology concerned with action. If God were not the subject of pastoral theology, it would not be theology. To render pastoral theology intelligibly requires almost a complete outline of theology.[5] This is my task.

Much that follows will be distinguished from the dominant pastoral theology published during the last fifty or sixty years. The discipline has tended to organize around a psychological interpretation of human experience and to begin its so-called theological reflection from there. In 1953 Seward Hiltner, the father of the modern pastoral theology movement in the United States, wrote that "the study of concrete experiences like those of pastoral care should lead to a branch of study known as 'pastoral theology,'"[6] and since then the discipline has moved in a distinctly clinical, psychotherapeutic, or, more generally, social-scientific direction rather than a theological or doctrinal direction.[7] There is no doubt that much has been learned from this shift, but it has also had two negative consequences. The first is the loss of Christology, soteriology, and the Christian doctrine of God in the pastoral theology and pastoral practice of the church. Where in recent times have Christology, and therefore the doctrines of salvation and the Trinity, occupied a central role in pastoral theology? The second, and a consequence of the first, is the tendency for pastoral work, when it lacks adequate theological foundation, to be given over to control by secular goals and techniques of care.[8] From this the question arises: What makes pastoral work Christian?

This much is obvious and generally known, whether one is for or against the prevailing model of pastoral theology. What may not be as obvious, however, is that if pastoral theology is indeed a theological discipline, then there is a place within its work for raising directly the question of God. Hiltner also made this claim, but as we will see, his theological method pulled

5. See ibid., 4.

6. Seward Hiltner, "What We Get and Give in Pastoral Care. What We Get: Theological Understanding," *Pastoral Psychology* 4 (June 1953): 14.

7. John Patton offers the threefold distinction within pastoral theology: confessional, clinical, and contextual, but the problem with this is the confusion of content and function. See *Pastoral Care in Context* (Louisville, Ky.: Westminster John Knox, 1993). In what follows I do not see what Patton calls the confessional approach to be an option for pastoral theology, but rather the thing itself.

8. For this wording on this second point, see William H. Willimon, *Pastor: The Theology and Practice of Ordained Ministry* (Nashville: Abingdon, 2002), 60.

in the opposite direction to that which I develop in this book. In either case, the question is, What happens when we look to pastoral theology precisely as theology, expecting from it truthful and coherent speech concerning God? Thus it is valid not just to ask what makes pastoral work Christian, but also to ask what pastoral theology, when it addresses that question, has to teach about God that otherwise might not be known or be understood as clearly. One may make the case that by fulfilling its explicitly theological responsibility to speak concerning God, pastoral theology can be much more than the theory of a churchly pastoral praxis. This is what I intend when I insist that God is the subject matter of pastoral theology.

This book will lay the ax to the root of much that has borne the name of pastoral theology in recent times and offer a totally different perspective on pastoral theology than that conventionally taught in the mainstream of Protestant theological education; this one is explicitly developed out of the evangelical, catholic, and ecumenical theology of the Christian faith. In its basic intention as theology, this pastoral theology is not a newly minted perspective on the task, however, but one whose long tradition faded only with the advent of the modern pastoral care movement in the 1920s, which flowered through the teaching and writing of Seward Hiltner of Princeton Theological Seminary in the 1950s and 1960s. A reading of the major texts from the history of pastoral theology, from the Greek fathers through the Reformation to the Puritan age, however, proves beyond doubt that the content of Christian faith and the understanding of the practice of ministry were hitherto held together to provide a theological framing of pastoral work that was coherently and distinctively Christian.[9] It did not exclude a psychological understanding of human experience—see *Pastoral Care* by Gregory the Great, for example. Gregory is a prime example of a pastor who understood human experience, but who included that understanding within the larger theological, indeed doctrinal, framework in such a way that pastoral theology clearly remained identifiably a Christian theological discipline with the closest possible connection to the content of Christian faith. Neither did Gregory exclude a contextual understanding. In fact he wrote his pastoral theology precisely in part because he was aware of the context of his times, when the Roman Empire was in its last days, when famine and plague wreaked havoc upon the citizenry of Rome, and when invading armies threatened the security of the Holy City.

---

9. See Andrew Purves, *Pastoral Theology in the Classical Tradition* (Louisville, Ky.: Westminster John Knox, 2001), for a discussion of this point with regard to Gregory of Nazianzus, John Chrysostom, Gregory the Great, Martin Bucer, and Richard Baxter.

The main point of difference between what I propose and what has obtained in recent years may be seen in the sense that I take from the citation of Romans 6:17 as applied to ministry: pastoral work is understood according to the "form of teaching to which you were entrusted." Paul does not have it backward. One might think that doctrines are to be entrusted to believers, but believers are entrusted to doctrines, meaning by this the reality of God in Christ for us. It is the gospel that possesses ministry, not ministry that possesses the gospel. To put that in different terms, the meaning of which will become clearer as we progress, the actuality of the gospel is the basis for the possibility of our ministry. It is not Jesus Christ who needs pastoral work, it is pastoral work that needs Jesus Christ. Just as faith lives not by human effort, but solely by the grace of God in, through, and as Jesus Christ, and through our incorporation into his life, so also ministry must be understood to be built not upon human striving for growth, well-being, and health but upon the grace of God, which is understood now as a participation in the life and ministry of Jesus Christ, on earth, in heaven, and as the one who will come again. The focus of pastoral theology, then, is on God's extrinsic grace in Jesus Christ, on the gospel that is a *verbum alienum*, a Word from beyond us, and to which gracious Word and to that Word alone pastoral theology and pastoral practice must submit in order to be faithful to the gospel.[10]

Understanding this takes us immediately beyond the seeming but inadequate basic intention of pastoral theology to provide a basis for churchly praxis interpreted in *pragmatic* terms. For to provide a basis for pastoral work on the ground of the gospel, as I do in this book, is to explicate precisely the inherently practical theological fact of the gospel, that God was in Christ reconciling the world to himself. The gospel is God's act-in-history, not a theory of God or ethical principles of action. In other words, pastoral theology can only meet its basic task to speak concerning God by grounding pastoral work in God's ministry through attention to the act of God in, through, and as Jesus Christ in such a way that it draws out the basis for all Christian ministry as a Spirit-enabled participation in the praxis of God.

Why do I want to redirect pastoral theology in such a total manner, not with a slight touch on the rudder, but with a complete change of direc-

10. For this paragraph I am entirely indebted to Professor James R. Edwards of Whitworth College, Spokane, Washington, whom I heard in a lecture make the point from Rom. 6:17 in the context of his remarkable insight into the meaning of *homothymadon* in the book of Acts. For a technical discussion of issues, see Robert A. J. Gagnon, "Heart of Wax and a Teaching that Stamps: *typos didaches* (Rom. 6:17b) Once More," *Journal of Biblical Literature* 112 (1993): 667–87.

tion? Why such a categorical rejection of the immediate past and present construction?[11] I am not here merely raising the issue of what is wrong with various recent and contemporary constructions of pastoral theology; these are addressed shortly in this introduction. I wish, rather, to ask a much deeper and more elusive question: What forms the *question* in the first place that forces one to wonder about something and subsequently to posit a hypothesis, to be tested in due course? A full answer would take us farther afield into epistemology than we would care to travel in an introduction, but this at least I can say: a question arises when something important does not seem to fit a received or prevailing hypothesis.

The lack of fit is this: a huge space appears to have been opened up between the faith of the church, seen from the perspective of the New Testament and the primary councils and confessions (indicating that I refer to a catholic, ecumenical, and evangelical understanding), the so-called *consensus fidelium*, and what is broadly identified as pastoral theology and pastoral care today. It is reasonable to expect that pastoral theology would in its own way express what Christians believe about God and the gospel of Jesus Christ, and do so more or less in an explicit, simple, and coherent manner that identifies it precisely as *Christian*. Thus the question, What makes pastoral care Christian? has now particular and even poignant relevance, for to ask that question is to ask who God is and what it is that one can rightly expect from this God. Or to put that differently: What does pastoral work have to do with incarnation and atonement, resurrection, ascension, and eschatology; with the Christian doctrine of God as Father, Son, and Holy Spirit, one being, three persons; with the teaching and ministry of Jesus; with the theology of Paul, and the author of Hebrews, and so on? My broad concern is the seeming lack of connection between exegesis of the Scriptures and the central Christian doctrines, on the one hand, and the theology and practice of ministry today, on the other. This seeming lack of connection suggests that something has gone seriously awry.

The question also arises because important bits of the Christian story do not seem to fit in with much pastoral theology scholarship today, and much pastoral theology seems to be developed without explicit regard for the biblical and doctrinal heritage of Christian confession and so has almost nothing to say as theology. Pastoral theology, in my view, has largely abandoned the responsibility to speak concerning God.

---

11. The manner of treating this question in the way that follows arose directly in my thinking while reading N. T. Wright, *The New Testament and the People of God* (Minneapolis: Fortress Press, 1992), chapter 2.

Pastoral theology, I believe, must be developed specifically as *Christian* pastoral theology, rooted explicitly and actually within, arising out of, and accountable to the doctrinal or dogmatic content of Christian faith. God, as the principal subject matter, is to be apprehended from within the event—past, present, and coming—of Jesus Christ, and this event, as we shall see, is itself to be understood in a quite definite way in accordance with the mind of the church as given in the mainstream of Nicene and Reformation theology.[12] Thus Christian pastoral theology, I argue, must be developed in a way that is at once Trinitarian, insofar as we must speak concerning God, and christological, soteriological, and eschatological, insofar as we must speak concerning God with us and for us in the flesh of Jesus, son of Mary, Lord of all. In this way pastoral theology is understood properly first of all as a theology of the care of God for us in, through, and as Jesus Christ; as such it is an expression of the gospel of revelation and reconciliation. There is more to pastoral theology than William H. Willimon's suggestion that because ministry is first of all an act of God, what keeps ministry Christian is obedience to God expressed as vocation.[13] Willimon is not wrong as far as he goes; but he does not develop his point fully enough by giving systematic doctrinal content to his reflection on ministry as an act of God. Jesus Christ as the mission of God to and for us is the ground of and the basis for the church's ministries of care—the content of this is discussed at length in later chapters, but may be summed up in the benediction, "The grace of the Lord Jesus Christ, the love of God, and the communion of the Holy Spirit be with all of you" (2 Cor. 13:13). Only secondarily, derivatively, and above all, participatively, as we shall see, is pastoral theology an account of the pastoral work of the church. When we define pastoral theology in this way, the interconnections among the Christian doctrine of God, the person and ministry of Jesus Christ, and the life and ministry of the church are demonstrable. This is the broad subject of the book that follows.

Others, of course, have tried to identify what it is that makes pastoral theology and pastoral care Christian. The answers given within the broad stream of the discipline today are in general, though usually tacitly or implicitly, developed within a functional unitarian theological worldview in which Jesus Christ as mediator and savior as well as the Christian doc-

---

12. For a masterful summary of what this entails see the opening paragraph to Thomas F. Torrance, "Introduction," *The Christian Doctrine of God: One Being, Three Persons* (Edinburgh: T. & T. Clark, 1996), 1.

13. Willimon, *Pastor*, 15.

trine of God are mostly absent from the discussion. The contemporary shape of the discipline is largely developed in spite of the central claims of Christian faith, that is, without considering the historicity of the incarnation, atonement, resurrection, ascension, and coming again of Jesus of Nazareth as God for and with us, and the presence of the Holy Spirit sent from the Father through the Son as the actual and continual involvement of this same God in time and space precisely in terms of the meaning and consequence of the incarnation, atonement, resurrection, and ascension. Pastoral theology has as a result been largely and interrelatedly ethically, symbolically, and functionally framed. This is not an adequate or faithful expression of the gospel for three reasons.

First, views of human wholeness and competent functioning seem to dominate. Operative views of human well-being as a kind of ethical anthropology function implicitly to guide the hand of pastoral care. The resulting gains for pastoral practice have been enormous, for a seemingly value-free psychotherapy is a myth, and it would be wrong to suppose that we should ever again devise a practice of pastoral work that did not have an ethical perspective, with norms of human well-being and competent functioning. But the losses, too, have been significant in that much if not most pastoral theology and pastoral practice have operated from a diminished view of the Christian doctrine of God, ignoring en route both the understanding of revelation and salvation in, through, and as Jesus Christ and the hope that is a participation in his bodily resurrection. The elevation of ethics into the heart in what is largely construed as Protestant liberal theology completes the Kantian project in which the distinctive Christian knowledge of God is deemed to be epistemologically invalid. Christianity cannot, however, be fully or faithfully developed as an ethically oriented response to the gospel in which Jesus Christ or the Christian faith are understood according to norms of being human that are largely derived from outside Christian faith. Instead, Christianity, and therefore pastoral theology, must first be worked out in christological, soteriological, and eschatological terms, in response to which an ethical and, if necessary, normative framework can be developed as appropriate.

Second, the modern pastoral care movement within the North American Protestant theological academy is by and large shaped by psychological categories regarding human experience and by symbolic interpretations regarding God. A relatively comfortable synthesis results in which pastoral theology and, consequently, pastoral practice in the church have become concerned largely with questions of meaning rather than truth, acceptable functioning rather than discipleship, and a concern for self-actualization and self-realization rather than salvation.[14] This synthesis entails the loss of the transcendence, objectivity, and reality of God, and especially the loss of a christological and soteriological clarity, and the insistence today that talk of God is to be assigned to the realm of myth and meaning. The understanding of humanity standing before God today, from this perspective, is given only in terms of expressions of collective experience or states of inner consciousness.[15] The question for us here again is the nature of pastoral theology in the light of the explicit reality, truth, and knowability of God given in, through, and as the gospel of Jesus Christ.

Third, pastoral work today is understood largely in functional terms. In part this arises from the pragmatic cast of the American mind, for scholars from the United States dominate the modern pastoral care movement. The fruit has been a vast increase in "how to" knowledge. Thus Seward Hiltner, in his immensely influential *Preface to Pastoral Theology*, published in 1958, set the discipline as oriented to the tasks of healing, sustaining, and guiding—with reconciling later added to complete the fourfold task of pastoral work in recent times.[16] In an attempt to wrestle the discipline back to its historical roots, Thomas C. Oden published his encyclopedic *Pastoral Theology: Essentials of Ministry* in 1983. He nevertheless set his presentation within the functionalist paradigm, even defining pastoral theology in terms of what the minister does. The only significant exception to this trend, which proves the rule (and it came from Europe!), was the now much neglected *Theology of Pastoral Care* written by Eduard Thurneysen and published in English in 1962.

In this book, in contrast, I argue that pastoral theology guides the practice of the church in speaking forth and living out the gospel by bringing to expression the meaning of our life in union with Christ, who is both God's Word of address to us and the fitting human response to God. As such, pastoral theology has both a prescriptive and a self-critical responsibility explicitly in the light of the gospel. This claim takes us to the evangelical, ecumenical, and catholic heart of all that is confessionally Christian, namely, that in the one person of Jesus Christ God and human being are

14. Note the subtitle to E. Brooks Holifield, *A History of Pastoral Care in America: From Salvation to Self-Realization* (Nashville: Abingdon, 1983).

15. Ellen T. Charry, *By the Renewing of Your Mind* (New York: Oxford University Press, 1987), 6.

16. Thus William A. Clebsch and Charles R. Jaekle, *Pastoral Care in Historical Perspective: An Essay with Exhibits* (New York: Harper Torchbooks, 1967), 4. Seward Hiltner, *Preface to Pastoral Theology* (Nashville: Abingdon Press, 1958), 89–172.

inseparably united, as, according to Athanasius of Alexandria, "He was very God in the flesh, and He was true flesh in the Word."[17]

To insist that God, or, more accurately, the ministry of the Father through the Son and in the Holy Spirit, is the subject matter of pastoral theology means then that there is no faithful content to speaking forth and living out the gospel pastorally apart from knowledge of and sharing in the mission of the God who acts savingly in, through, and as Jesus Christ and in the Spirit precisely as a man for all people. It is important to emphasize the reality of our union with Christ, for without that all pastoral work is cast adrift from the actuality of God's ministry. If it gets God wrong, or more specifically fails to appreciate that knowledge of God is always and only a knowledge of a God who acts, and who acts in, through, and as Jesus Christ, and into whose action and life we, by the Holy Spirit, participate through our union with Christ, the church gets its saying and doing wrong also. Knowledge of God and God's mission is the only critical perspective from which or by which we can judge our own pastoral actions. Thus the introduction to and the most important part of pastoral theology is a presentation of the doctrine (or better, the practice) of God in christological, soteriological, and eschatological terms. This involves no less than the knowledge of the inseparable relation between what the Greek fathers called the *oikonomia* and the *theologia*, between God as he is for us in, through, and as Jesus Christ, and God in the eternal communion of the Holy Trinity. This is to be followed, derivatively, by a presentation of the life and ministry of the church as a sharing in the ministry of the Trinitarian God who acts through, in, and as Christ and in the Spirit. This means that the doctrine of God and the practice of the church must be explicated according to the actual practice of God in human history and therefore available for faith as a Trinitarian practice through Jesus Christ and in the Holy Spirit, and not speculatively or according to some scheme of ethics regarding human well-functioning that is available only to reason or the phenomenology of human experience.

I must now ask a critical question.[18] To what extent is my proposal a reaction to subjectivism in pastoral theology? In response, while I argue that mine may be a legitimate and timely reaction, we must beware of driving

17. Athanasius, *Four Discourses Against the Arians* 3.41, in *The Nicene and Post-Nicene Fathers*, ed. Philip Schaff and Henry Wace, 2d series, vol. 4 (reprint, Edinburgh: T. & T. Clark; Grand Rapids: Eerdmans, 1998).

18. The following is indebted to Emil Brunner, *The Divine-Human Encounter*, trans. Amandus W. Loos (London: SCM, 1944).

the turn toward the object so hard that subjectivity is lost, for the result would be a twofold God-dishonoring consequence: (1) the loss of the work of the Holy Spirit within us, and (2) a damaging discounting of the human as the subject of God's acts. Thus Calvin, in a hinge chapter at the beginning of book III of the *Institutes* that has profound epistemological consequences for theology, insists that "as long as Christ remains outside of us, and we are separated from him, all that he has suffered and done for the salvation of the human race remains useless and of no value for us. Therefore, to share with us what he has received from the Father, he had to become ours and to dwell within us" (3.1.1). Thus both the objective and subjective poles of faith and knowledge are held together in response to the one act of God. That my argument pulls strongly toward God, focusing on the God in whom we believe rather than on the experience or faith of the believer, must not be interpreted to mean that there is no value in or place for human experience or for the study of this experience. It is to make the claim rather that the former and not the latter is definitive and as such is the proper ground and subject matter of pastoral theology.

Pastoral textbooks tend to use the designations "pastoral theology" and "theology of pastoral care" interchangeably, which suggests there is little difference between them. While pastoral theology and the theology of pastoral care obviously share a family similarity within the broad spectrum of practical theology, a sharper distinction is helpful. Pastoral theology, as I intend it, is principally concerned first with the practice of God, that is, with what God does as a result of who God is. Second, it moves to reflection on the participative practice of the church within that theological perspective through our union with Christ. The theology of pastoral care, in contrast, while surely never either somehow purely practical or, even worse, applied theory, is principally concerned with theological reflection on actual churchly practice, and to that end is likely to move into appropriate conversation with auxiliary disciplines like psychology, psychotherapy, sociology, anthropology, and so on. Neither discipline is exclusive, for the one implies the other. Yet the principal focus is different. Without clarity about the principal task of pastoral theology, namely, the doctrine of the practice of God and the understanding of the church's sharing in that practice through union with Christ, the theology of pastoral care will tend to spin off into a discipline normatively and effectively controlled by something other than the church's Trinitarian knowledge of the practice or mission of God.

Pastoral work today confronts the danger that it is increasingly at home responding to the demands of private and personal interests. The pastoral counseling movement within pastoral care is a case in point. Only when pastoral care is properly theological and as such rooted in the ministry of God in, through, and as Jesus Christ is it liberated from anxious concerns over its place in church and ministry in the world, to be itself in the freedom and authority of the gospel. The issue is not whether skills for ministry taught by the social sciences are to be learned and applied. It is a far deeper problem that we confront, but it is one with which we are already familiar: What makes ministry Christian? There are also practical concerns: On what basis is ministry possible at all, and what is the nature or content of that ministry? The answers are not immediately self-evident, and when we do find them, these answers will have to be theological.

Pastoral theology as I understand it is not an attempt to take over the tasks of systematic and dogmatic theology, both of which, with pastoral theology, share a family similarity within the broad spectrum that is theology as such. As is often noted, especially within Reformation tradition, all theology is rightly practical, and pastoral care is not to be regarded as some kind of "third thing" alongside Word and sacraments, or even worse, as an applied theology. Systematic theology, however, also explores the systematic integration of all doctrines, in faithfulness to the God who is theology's own reward.[19] Pastoral theology, we might say, while sharing in this legitimate goal, is also consciously altruistic, having as its reward the service of the church as we live and act faithfully always and only in union with Christ. The relationship between systematic/dogmatic and pastoral theology, then, is utterly complementary, because they have the same content and are really only distinguishable for the sake of convenience and task.

The Book

Through our union with Christ we share in the ministry of Jesus Christ with, to, and for us, through the Holy Spirit, to the glory of the Father. Two doctrines, then, occupy central place in the development of my argument: (1) the mission of God in and as Jesus Christ in history (chapters 3 and 4), in his heavenly session (chapter 6), and at his coming again (chapter 7); and (2) union with Christ (chapter 5). Union with Christ, which is the principal work of the Holy Spirit, is the functional condition for all Christian life and the mediatorial ministry of the Lord Jesus, once on

---

19. Robert W. Jenson, *Systematic Theology*, vol. 1, *The Triune God* (New York: Oxford University Press, 1997), 11.

earth, eternally in heaven, and at his coming again, is the material condition, in which, again drawing on the formulation of Athanasius, he ministers the things of God to us and the things of humankind to God.[20] James B. Torrance puts it in succinct form: "As Christ was anointed by the Spirit in our humanity to fulfil his ministry for us, so we are united by the same Spirit to share his ministry."[21] Thus in Jesus Christ, in his one person, we have to do with an ontologically unique twofold soteriological mediation from above to below *and* from below to above (as it were), which is both the revelation of God and reconciliation with God. He is at once *both* God's address/act to us in, through, and as a man *and* humankind hearing, responding, and obeying that address/act in perfect communion with God in, through, and as that same man, Jesus of Nazareth.[22] Christ's ministry from and to the Father through his vicarious humanity we call, in abbreviated form, the ministry of the priesthood of Christ. We will see that the church's ministry is conformed throughout to a Trinitarian reality in which we participate, and that its material content is determined by Christ's own ministry on earth, while it is empowered by the heavenly priesthood of the ascended Christ in which ministry he graces the church for faithfulness, joining the church to share in his communion with the Father, interceding for the church, and sending upon the church the gift of the Holy Spirit. What follows then is a pastoral theology of our participation in the priesthood of Jesus Christ.

While our topic is a pastoral theology, it supplies the dogmatic or scientific theological framework for a properly conceived practical theology, for all theology, all knowledge of God, is inherently a practical theology or a practical and soteriological knowledge, by virtue of the subject matter: God with and for us in, through, and as Jesus Christ, in the power of the Holy Spirit. Two points can elucidate this general statement. First, while God is not reducible to our knowledge of God, or to our theological words about God, theology is nonetheless *knowledge* of God, who is active in creation, revelation, and the work of salvation, in the divine

---

20. Athanasius, *Four Discourses Against the Arians* 4.6. We will return to this Athanasian position more fully in due course.

21. James B. Torrance, "The Vicarious Humanity of Christ," in *The Incarnation: Ecumenical Studies in the Nicene-Constantinopolitan Creed A.D. 381*, ed. Thomas F. Torrance (Edinburgh: Handsel, 1981), 145.

22. See, for example, Thomas F. Torrance, *The Christian Doctrine of God* (Edinburgh: T. & T. Clark, 1996), 144; and idem, *The Trinitarian Faith: The Evangelical Theology of the Ancient Catholic Church* (Edinburgh: T. & T. Clark, 1993), 149ff., and elsewhere throughout Torrance's published works.

economy, within the frame of human history and experience. Knowledge of God is knowledge of the relationship: God—world—us.[23] There is no knowledge of God that excludes the empirical component of the world and God's engagement with us (this is why the theology-science conversation is important and why the theology of pastoral care must find a place for the social sciences in its discussions).

Second, because Jesus Christ, as God in our flesh, is where God defines himself, we can say that who God is for us and toward us in, through, and as Jesus Christ, God is eternally and antecedently in himself. God is in himself who and what he is toward us in, through, and as Jesus Christ; and who and what God is toward us in, through, and as Jesus Christ God is eternally in himself. Thus, although God is never reducible to our words about God, we have a true knowledge of God in, through, and as Jesus Christ. My point is that knowledge of God in, through, and as Jesus Christ leads to a Trinitarian way of thinking about God; and a Trinitarian theology is inherently practical theology in that it is a knowledge of God's action grounded in God's being. The doctrine of the Trinity is the basis for Christian practical theology.[24]

Practical theology is theology that is concerned with action: first, with God's action, the *missio Dei*; and second, with the action or praxis of the church in its life and ministry in faithful communion with the God who acts, the mission of the church. But God's acts are always first, and our acts, the church's acts, are always second, and even then, I argue, our acts are but a participation in the Holy Spirit in our Lord's human response on our behalf to the prior act of God. Even in response we find ourselves within the sphere of God's prevenient grace and the functioning of the Holy Trinity.

This book is not a full-orbed practical theology, for it is not my concern to develop a complete account of Christian action; the argument nevertheless will pull in that direction and will be suggestive for a systematic practical theology as the understanding and development of pastoral theology falls ever more fully under the sway of the gospel. In this way I seek to develop appropriate structures of thought that function as heuristic devices by which we can feel our way forward toward a theologically coherent and faithful knowledge of the practice of the Trinitarian faith.

23. Thus Thomas F. Torrance, *Reality and Evangelical Theology: A Fresh and Challenging Approach to Christian Revelation* (Philadelphia: Westminster, 1982).

24. For a full discussion see Andrew Purves, "The Trinitarian Basis for a Christian Practical Theology," *International Journal for Practical Theology* (1998): vol. 3, 222–39.

My goal is to apprehend more clearly the economic and Trinitarian pattern of God's actual ministry toward us in, through, and as Jesus Christ as they are given in the gospel,[25] and to develop the practice of the church accordingly in view of the fact that our Lord by the Holy Spirit has taken us into union with himself, not only to share in his Word as God's Word, but also to share in his Word as our human word heard by and acceptable to God "for Christ's sake." Thus what follows will greatly enlarge the Trinitarian, christological, soteriological, and eschatological framing of pastoral theology by way of the doctrine of the vicarious humanity of Christ. This will bring it more into line with dogmatic theology, while not yet offering a fully developed statement of practical theology in its own right.

One may already have noted that the discussion sometimes moves from the conventional language of scholarly discourse to the first person plural. This is by way of correspondence to the subject matter. There is no neutral knowledge of God. Christian theology inevitably, therefore, must bring to expression God *for us*. Pastoral theology, with Christian theology in general, is a personal knowing of God, and its language must reflect this fact.

Obviously, then, what follows reorders pastoral theology according to certain explicit theological categories. Pastoral theology will be developed as a theological thought experiment according to the apostolic framing of Christ as the apostle and high priest of our confession (Heb. 3:1) in which by the Holy Spirit we share, through union with him, in his apostolic and priestly mission for the sake of the world.

Shepherding: The Nonutility of a Metaphor for Ministry

In order to continue setting the scene it is helpful to examine briefly the dominant metaphor for pastoral care found in the last half century. A building can only be as large as the load-bearing capacity of the cornerstone will allow. Pastoral theology and pastoral care as we know it today, both as taught in the majority of Western seminaries and as practiced perhaps by very many pastors, is built upon a shaky foundation. The crisis is intellectual and is caused by a twofold inadequacy of approach. The first inadequacy relates to the prevailing theological metaphor that casts pastoral care in a particular manner; the second relates to theological method and to the nature of theology itself.

The metaphorical cast that has shaped pastoral theology over the last half century is of God or Jesus as the Good Shepherd, of ministers as

25. See Torrance, *Christian Doctrine of God*, 91–92.

undershepherds or pastors, and of the ministry as pastoral care. But when pastoral care is formed almost entirely in terms of this metaphor, it is increasingly unable to be a faithful witness to the gospel in its fullness. This is because the figure of Jesus as the Good Shepherd—while a biblical figure, undoubtedly helpful and appropriate as far as it goes—fails to bring to expression the full meaning either of his person and work, or of the ministry of the church. An inadequate controlling metaphor leads inevitably to a reductionist pastoral practice.

Metaphors help us to describe the world; they also define the practice of living in the world. Especially as they pertain to aspects of experience that defy easy definition (arguably often those parts of our experience that really matter to us), metaphors assist in the process of understanding by enabling an imaginative construal that opens up the world in hitherto undisclosed meaning. Unlike literal use of language, which sees language as a "mirror" of reality (itself a metaphor!), or a simile, which operates by the process of likeness, metaphorical use, because inevitably indirect, opens up our understanding to deeper awareness as definitions that rigidly mark boundaries give way to understanding as insight. A metaphor "works" when a word or image is "retooled," imported from one context to be used in another in such a way that is still faithful to the object of reference. It carries the force of persuasion and conviction. A metaphor "dies" or outgrows its utility when it is no longer able to sustain understanding and practice.

To a certain extent casting pastoral work within the theological framework of Jesus as the Good Shepherd is metaphorical theology at its best, for it has opened up paths of understanding in ministry that served the church well. Pastoral care came to be understood as poimenics or shepherding (*poimen*, shepherd). Even the names given to the practice of care, *pastoral* care, and to the caregiver, *pastor*, take their identity from this rural and agricultural metaphor.

"Shepherding" appropriately connects the identity and work of God and the caring work of the church. It has been remarkably successful in its clarity and endurance, and for good reason. Its biblical base and history in the life of the church ensure that a place will always have to be found for understanding God as our Shepherd, and for ministry as shepherding or pastoring. Jesus will always be understood as the Good Shepherd who laid down his life for his flock, fleshing out soteriologically the meaning of Psalm 23. Nevertheless, four problems arise from this metaphor, all of which are closely linked, that raise a serious theological uncertainty today and require the reconstruction of pastoral care on an alternative theological foundation.

1. We note the increasing nonutility of a once appropriate though limited metaphor. Such has been the historic power of the shepherding metaphor in ministry that it abides, despite the ontological distinction between the shepherd and the sheep as different species. When the metaphor is applied to God and humankind, a good case can be made for continued use, but applied to ministry that ontological distinction gets carried over. The metaphor of shepherding is more at home amid the kind of Neoplatonically derived ontological distinctions between priest and parishioners proposed by, for example, John Chrysostom in the fourth century, than for Protestantism in the twenty-first. Further, most North American Christians have never seen a sheep, much less a nonmetaphorical shepherd. All too easily, naivete and sentimentality sneak into the picture. It is forgotten perhaps that shepherds farm sheep in order to kill and eat them! As the rural landscape diminishes and the urban and suburban landscapes expand, the connections between what is nonmetaphorically and metaphorically pastoral suffer increasing strain. How much distance can be placed between metaphor and experience and metaphor and truth before the metaphor no longer works? A metaphor that loses touch with praxis becomes worthless.

2. The framing of pastoral work as shepherding led in modern times to the functionalizing or professionalization of ministry in which the gap between shepherd and sheep, clergy and people, has become institutionalized. The tendency of much recent pastoral care theory flies in the face of the basic Reformation principle: the care of all for the souls of all, of *Seelsorge aller an allen.* This professionalizing or specialist tendency in much modern pastoral care has moved away from the liturgical and theological community of Word and sacraments, away from the congregation. The question still arises whether shepherding as the controlling metaphor has the theological capacity to control the trend of the last fifty years and ground ministry adequately in the gospel of Jesus Christ in its fullness.

3. Most modern approaches to pastoral care are notable for their departure from biblical and theological tradition and stand over and against the kind of pastoral theology developed in Reformation tradition—for example, by Martin Bucer, Richard Baxter, and Eduard Thurneysen—with its overriding concern to understand ministry biblically, and in which ministry is thought through on the grounds of a vigorous Christology, soteriology, and eschatology. Behind this departure, of course, lies the ambiguity that the church now seems to feel regarding both the place of Scripture for life and ministry and the person and work of Jesus Christ. Cast off from a serious engagement with the Bible and the theological heritage of the church, the modern pastoral care tradition has separated its

appropriation of Jesus as the Good Shepherd from his person and work understood on a broader theological front. One illustration of this is the virtual eclipse of the Christian doctrine of God as Holy Trinity in pastoral theology. Borrowing from James B. Torrance, who wrote with regard to worship,[26] we can ask similarly with regard to pastoral care: Are pastoral theology and pastoral care Trinitarian or unitarian?

Whatever metaphor for or model of ministry is employed, surely there is the strongest connection between what Christian faith confesses about God, revelation, reconciliation, eschatology, and so on, on the one hand, and the care of God's people, on the other. Theologians have known too that the faith confessed by the church is the rich material to be molded and shaped by the person-sensitive pastor so that it applies appropriately to the situations of life and death that pastoral work must confront daily. Of course, a pastor must develop interpersonal skills and understand emotions, human development, and the complexities of human relationships and family systems. But none of these supplies the ground, the basic content, that gives pastoral work its specific identity as Christian. That identity is given by the content of faith itself, for it is the grace of God in Christ for us that exposes the depth of the human condition in its separation from God in a way that science cannot. And this same grace offers a remedy that leads to healing, blessing, and salvation to eternal life in union with Christ. This means there is the strongest possible connection between pulpit and counseling room, and between the study of Christian theology and the practice of pastoral care. One cannot be a pastor without also being a theologian, one who speaks and lives knowingly out of the center of the ecumenical, catholic, and evangelical faith of the church.

Whatever the case was in the past, in modern times a rift has opened up between being a pastor and being a theologian, as if a person could be one without the other. While I recognize the danger of generalization, I detect today both a lack of confidence among pastors in the efficacy of Word and sacraments to effect healing and blessing and a failure among theologians to present the gospel in a manner that allows pastors to discern directly the pastoral power of the Word of God.[27] Pastoral work is

26. James B. Torrance, *Worship, Community and the Triune God of Grace* (Carlisle: Paternoster, 1996).

27. Jaroslav Pelikan notes that from 100 to 600, most theologians were bishops; from 600 to 1500, in the West they were monks; and since 1500, they have been university professors! Jaroslav Pelikan, *The Emergence of the Catholic Tradition (100–600)* (Chicago: University of Chicago Press, 1971), 5. I found this reference in R. A. Krupp, *Shepherding the Flock of God: The Pastoral Theology of John Chrysostom* (New York: Peter Lang, 1991), 3.

concerned always with the gospel of God's redemption in, through, and as Jesus Christ, no matter the presenting problem that someone brings. Pastoral work by definition connects the gospel story, that is, the truths and realities of God's saving economy, with the actual lives and situations of the people. In other words, pastoral work is at all points guided by biblical and theological perspectives, and these biblical and theological perspectives, properly rooted in the gospel of salvation, are discovered to be inherently pastoral.

4. Shepherding has been developed as an imitative rather than as a participatory approach to ministry. This approach follows the example of Jesus in some regards—*imitatio Christi*—without having at its core a vital way in which the church's ministry shares in Christ's continuing personhood and ministry—*participatio Christi*. It builds on a reductionist Christology that limits Jesus to a moral influence because it finds no place for a complete understanding of his person and work, and in particular, for his vicarious humanity and continuing priesthood. The effect is to cast the pastor back upon his or her own resources—thus it can be defined as pastoral Pelagianism, a ministry by works rather than a ministry through grace. This is the most serious of all the problems, the result of a defective or limited Christology.

Buried within this tendency in pastoral theology to think about Jesus in ethical terms is a corresponding loss, first, of God, and second, of Jesus himself. If Jesus only illustrates God, and is not understood as the incarnate Son among us in the flesh of his humanity, then God remains hidden behind the back of Jesus—a point made often by the Greek fathers of the fourth century. The loss of ontological connection between Jesus and God leads also eventually to the loss of Jesus in and as himself, and to his replacement by an ethical Christ-principle separated from him. It is by this route that Christianity tends toward becoming a philosophy of abstract nouns—inclusivity, hospitality, justice, love, and so on that have an independent character such that they can even be turned back against Scripture and Christian tradition.[28] This twofold loss of the Christian doctrine of God and Jesus leads to the fundamental crisis of identity for pastoral theology, for it is no longer clear how it is to be regarded as theology, or even as Christian.

Shepherding is a good theological metaphor for ministry as far as it goes, but it ill serves the church today when it is employed as the dominant or controlling metaphor for pastoral ministry.

---

28. For a brief discussion see Mark Achtemeier and Andrew Purves, "Introduction," *A Passion for the Gospel: Confessing Jesus Christ for the 21st Century* (Louisville, Ky.: Geneva, 2000).

The "Preface" That Formed a Movement

Some of the issues I raised in passing in the discussion of shepherding arise quite directly in the discussion of pastoral theological method. The best way into this question is through a presentation and critique of Seward Hiltner's approach in his immensely influential *Preface to Pastoral Theology*, a book, I suspect, that is rarely read by pastors today but that has shaped the mind of Protestant pastoral theologians, especially in North America, more than any other text. More recent attempts at constructing pastoral theology have built on Hiltner's foundation in one way or another. Thus there is virtue in going to the source.

Although only designated a "preface," Hiltner's major text is a fairly full-orbed pastoral theology. I will not here present and criticize the whole thing, for that would take us too far afield; his basic positions, however, can stand in for the whole.

As noted, *shepherding* is a key term. He defines it not as an office of ministry, however, but as a perspective on ministry. This is a helpful insight on pastoral care. Shepherding is in some degree present in everything a minister does, even if only present in readiness. The essential meaning of shepherding is given in the parable of the Good Samaritan. The mode of response to need is appropriate to the situation; thus when healing is required, shepherding is an appropriate response. The biblical base is secured for Hiltner by the illustration of the shepherd who goes in search of the one sheep that is lost. Central to shepherding is tender, solicitous care directed toward healing in some regard.

Hiltner has a theory of the organization of the body of divinity—one he discovered, he claims, not one he invented. According to his view, there are two forms or areas of theological inquiry: logic-centered theological inquiry and operation-centered theological inquiry. The body of divinity consists of the interrelationship and intercommunication between these two areas. Logic-centered theological inquiry consists in inquiry that is oriented to the logical organization of subject matter. Thus doctrinal theology, for example, is organized logically according to the relations of doctrines to one another. This is a very narrow basis for theology concerned with the content of Christian faith. There is surely more to such theology than the logical (what does this mean with regard to theology?) arrangement of doctrines (according to what criteria?). Operation-centered theological inquiry is organized from reflection on acts or events or functions from a particular perspective. The three areas are shepherding the needy, communicating the gospel, and organizing the fellowship.

What is the significance of this? First, Hiltner insists that operation-centered theological inquiry is theological inquiry, every bit as theological as, say, biblical or systematic theology. It exists as a branch of theology in intercommunication with every other branch of theology, using, as all do, the common currency of the faith. Second, pastoral theology is not thereby applied theology, existing in a deductive relationship with logic-centered theological inquiry. It has its own task as theological inquiry within the broad fold of theological studies. It deals with the theological theory of the shepherding perspective.

Hiltner, as noted, argues for two-way communication at all points within the body of divinity. This means a rejection of the kerygmatic approach, found, for example, in the theology of Karl Barth. Hiltner's theology is constructed ostensibly upon *both* biblical base*s* *and* reflection upon acts and events of ministry, when theological questions are asked of them. It is, however, especially constructed upon reflection on acts and events, with a notable *absence* of biblical and classical theological references and content. The Word of God, Hiltner believes, is found in many areas of inquiry into human experience, and especially from inquiry into psychological and psychotherapeutic processes. He develops what we might call an immanentalist pastoral theological method that is heavily influenced by the empirical theology movement that came out of the University of Chicago, and a precursor of process theology, and Paul Tillich's method of correlation. Thus, according to Hiltner, the theological study of Anton Boisen's notation of "living human documents"—people, in other words—is the study not merely of psychology but also of theology when theological questions are put (what this means is not defined). The method of correlation, which Hiltner actually advanced beyond Tillich to anticipate by about twenty years David Tracy's own correction of Tillich, states that there is a correlation between our deepest existential questions and the answers of faith. It allows for culture to raise questions and for Christian faith to show its relevance by answering them. According to Hiltner, the correlation must also go the other way, from questions raised by faith to answers found in human experience. Thus Hiltner opened the way for a profound dialogical relationship between the personality sciences and pastoral care under the rubric of pastoral theology. This was a remarkable achievement, for he offered a systematic construal of pastoral theology that has guided the practice of care for two generations of ministers.

Hiltner's understanding of the actual practice of shepherding is the grist for his pastoral theological mill. Shepherding describes a perspective on ministry, one of tender and solicitous care of those who are in need.

Thus the basic attitude of the Christian shepherd is genuine interest in and concern for the sheep. Attitude is everything. No amount of technique can cover up a wrong or uncaring attitude. Even so, good attitude and the expression of genuine concern must harness sound technique. Principally, Hiltner leans on a program of acceptance of feelings devised by Carl Rogers, accepting en route the philosophical assumption that it is the motivation of inner resources that leads toward the worthy goal of self-actualization. Only on this basis can the pastor help the parishioner move to clarification of feelings and judgment and decision accordingly. The goal is healing, though healing almost entirely defined in terms of feelings. It involves restoration to functional wholeness in terms of possibilities opened up by pastoral counseling in an eductive mode, one that draws out the feelings for examination and decision and that relies on the parishioner's inner resources for healing and well-being.

What can be said of this significant proposal that I have here briefly outlined? Four initial observations may be made. First, Hiltner's approach is functionalist. Pastoral theology exists as an operation-centered inquiry. It has a function, a task, and a goal, namely, shepherding the flock. There may be nothing wrong with that as far as it goes. The question is: Is his pastoral care inclusive of the whole sweep of Christian theology? In fact, his vision is reductionistic when seen in the light of the whole body of divinity, in spite of his good intentions. Second, Hiltner stands within the liberal Protestant tradition, a position he characterized by spirit and attitude rather than by content.[29] He advocates an unchaining of the mind so as to allow Christianity to encounter modern knowledge. His position implies a doctrine of continuity between creation and redemption that in his case suggests almost no distinction between salvation and health. Third, Hiltner's pastoral perspective is largely individualistic. Recent developments in pastoral thinking have moved away from this position to advocate the need for a contextual awareness.[30] Nevertheless, might it not still be said that pastoral care tends largely to be seen and practiced in terms of one-on-one conversations? And is there still not a psychotherapeutic overlay on pastoral care? Fourth, Hiltner's anthropology is developmental. The human has within the self the capacity for movement toward health and salvation, only to be unfolded. Sin is, for Hiltner, movement away from self-fulfillment. Thus Hiltner is attracted to developmental psychology.

29. James Luther Adams and Seward Hiltner, eds., *Pastoral Care in the Liberal Churches* (New York: Abingdon, 1970), 222.

30. See, for example, Patton, *Pastoral Care in Context.*

In the last analysis, pastoral care for Hiltner means pastoral counseling. Rather than seeing pastoral counseling as a category within the broader framework of pastoral care, Hiltner sees pastoral care within the specific category of pastoral counseling. This brought in its train the assumptions, explicit and implicit, and practices of the psychotherapeutic community. These were taken over largely uncritically, and only slowly have critical voices been raised.

From "Preface" to Pastoral Dogmatics

In what follows I attempt to reconstruct the foundations of pastoral theology. In this I will move away from Hiltner's *Preface to Pastoral Theology* altogether by the development of what might be called "pastoral dogmatics." By this I intend that we think of pastoral work in a rigorous way out of the dogmatic or doctrinal content of Christian faith: our minds must be conformed to this way of thinking, for at its center is God as revealed and self-declared, rather than we ourselves. The result is pastoral theology defined and developed precisely and systematically in explicit use of christological, soteriological, Trinitarian, and eschatological categories as they have been developed and understood within the *consensus fidelium*. This may be claiming too much, for the sense of the faith throughout confession within a catholic, evangelical, and orthodox expression is huge and beyond our reach. But I do claim to stand *within* this confession and to represent it, however poorly. Thus pastoral theology is brought home, as it were, to its proper foundation within the Christian faith, to find there, one trusts, a new rootedness, generativity, and liveliness that faithfully bears witness to Jesus Christ, God with us and God for us, and our only hope of glory.

The book is divided into two parts. In part one, chapters 1–6, I present the constructive theological argument: Jesus Christ is the mission of God. In chapter 1 I consider the nature of Christian doctrine and its role in constructing pastoral theology. In chapters 2–6 I develop the particular doctrines required for the task. In chapter 2 I develop an understanding of the ministry of God. In chapter 3 I explore the meaning of Jesus Christ the Apostle and High Priest (Heb. 3:1) in his twofold ministry from God and to God. This chapter and the next provide the essential building blocks for the whole project. They develop the key theological categories. In chapter 4 I deal with union with Christ by means of which we participate in his twofold ministry. In chapter 5 I consider the heavenly priesthood of Christ by which he empowers the church for ministry. And in chapter 6 I reflect on the relationship between eschatology and ministry and what it means that the church ever lives within the horizon of expecting Christ's return.

In part two, chapters 7–10, I develop the subsequent shape of ministerial practice. This is not the application of theological theory but thinking through the content and meaning of sharing in Christ's apostolic priesthood at four points of concrete ministry. In chapter 7 I construct the ministry of the Word of God, and I am concerned significantly with preaching. In chapter 8 I go to the heart of the ministry of the grace of God and the meaning of ministry in the light of forgiveness. In chapter 9 I examine the ministry of God's presence, especially as that is understood by way of Paul's practical theology of comfort. Finally, in chapter 10 I reflect on the ministry of the reign of God in which Christian hope is the significant topic.

Part One

Jesus Christ: The Mission Of God

In part one I lay out the basic theological structure for pastoral theology. There are two primary categories. The first is christological, derived in part from Athanasius, in which Jesus Christ is understood to be both the Word and act of God addressing us *and* the word and act of humankind addressing God. The second is Calvin's doctrine of our union with Christ. By the work of the Holy Spirit we are joined to Christ's mission from and to the Father, thereby to share in his ministry. Thus the ministry of God in, through, and as Jesus Christ is the proper foundation for the understanding and practice of ministry. This is not a new idea, but rather the classical teaching of the church. It stands over and against more recent perspectives in pastoral theology that begin with the human experience on its own terms.

Such a recasting of pastoral theology does not fit neatly into a "theology from above," however. For to ground pastoral theology at all points in the ministry of Jesus Christ as he is attested for us in Scripture is to insist that we approach the subject matter both "from above" insofar as Christ is the incarnation of God ("the word became"), and "from below" insofar as he was truly human ("flesh"). Thus we understand human experience christologically rather than phenomenologically through the social sciences, but it is nevertheless human experience that is apprehended in Christ.

The focus is on God's ministry, which was and is and ever will be actual, and therefore relevant and appropriate because of what it is. The church's ministry is a participation in that ministry, not something new of the church's invention to meet some present need or circumstance, or a vague imitation of Jesus Christ but doomed to failure because we are not messianic. It is not an ideal ministry yet to be made practical; it is the actual ministry of God, rather, that makes our ministries practical, relevant, and appropriate.

Chapter 1

Doctrine and Pastoral Care

Introduction: Ministry Is What God Does

While, loosely speaking, pastoral work is what pastors do, this is true only derivatively. Pastors do what they do because of who God is and what God does. Or more precisely, before it is the church's ministry all ministry is first of all God's ministry in, through, and as Jesus Christ in the power of the Holy Spirit. In a primary sense, then, pastoral theology is conducted by reflecting on ministry—God's ministry.[1] The acting subject of pastoral work is not the pastor or the church but Jesus Christ in his coming as God and in his obedience to the will of the Father. Pastoral work has no subject other than Jesus Christ, and no content other than "the faith that was once for all entrusted to the saints" (Jude 3).

Some may view this claim as counterintuitive because we are so used to thinking of pastoral work as the work that pastors do. In fact, ministry today is skill-driven rather than theology-driven, and seems to incorporate little of the dynamically practical nature of theology insofar as it speaks about who God is and what God does. There is, however, no knowledge of a God other than the knowledge of a God who acts in such a way that we can know him; therefore, as we will explore at length, all theology is inherently practical theology, and all church practice is properly understood as sharing in God's practice. Thus it is only true derivatively that pastoral work is what pastors

---

1. This point was already made some years ago by Ray S. Anderson in an important essay, but seems not to have had the significant influence upon the general subject of practical theology that it deserved. Ray S. Anderson, "A Theology of Ministry," in *Theological Foundations for Ministry: Selected Readings for a Theology of the Church in Ministry*, ed. Ray S. Anderson (Edinburgh: T. & T. Clark, 1979).

3

do. Rather, pastoral theology has to apprehend as its first and highest responsibility the God who acts for us in, through, and as Jesus Christ. The derivative nature of pastoral work is worked out through our union with Christ and through his gracing of the church for ministry in his heavenly session; I attend to this important point of my argument in chapters 4 and 5.

The ministry of the church is, by the Holy Spirit, a sharing in God's ministry to and for us in, through, and as Jesus Christ. The task at hand, then, is to focus on the profound interrelationship that must obtain between, on the one hand, those truths and realities about God that the church brings to expression through Christian doctrine and, on the other hand, pastoral care. The reason for this focus is basic to the task of pastoral theology: the direct connection between pastoral work and the mission of God, which can be stated as God in and through the gospel of Jesus Christ, active, at work, and involved savingly in human existence. If the meaning of Jesus Christ clothed with his gospel is not understood clearly or is inaccurately or inappropriately developed, pastoral work becomes unhinged from its true ground in the actual ministry of God and inevitably loses its way. The pastoral theologian, then, must give primary attention to understanding God in and as Jesus Christ as the source of life and hope, meaning and value, and everything that should follow from this attention for the church's ministries of care. The implications of the gospel must be developed and made explicit in order to remind the church that Jesus Christ is the pastor who guides us to streams of living water, who forgives us our sins and saves us, who heals all our hurts, who brings life out of death, and in whom alone we have union and communion with God.

Pastoral theology, then, before it is a theology of what the church or the pastor does, is axiomatically and first of all a theology of the pastoring God, a theology of the living gospel of Jesus Christ. That is why at the end of the introduction I spoke of our task as pastoral dogmatics. Only as pastoral theology engages in this task is it equipped to be a theology also of what the pastor does. As a theology of the pastoring God, pastoral theology is inherently therefore a practical theology, a theology concerned with action, defined and shaped at all points by the acts of God in Christ given in and as the gospel.

In this chapter I offer a general discussion of the relationship between doctrine and pastoral care. This prepares the way for the doctrinally cast chapters that follow on the ministry of God, the twofold ministry of Christ, the meaning of our union with Christ, the ascended Christ's gracing of the church for ministry, and the relationship between eschatology and pastoral care. But first it is helpful to offer some general introductory remarks on the consequences of the lack of relationship between doctrine and pastoral care.

Because pastoral work today is often only loosely attached, if at all, to the gospel-given understanding of the pastoring God, it tends to have a formal identity through a relationship with an auxiliary discipline. Thus pastoral care is commonly defined in terms of the psychological and contextual processes of caring rather than in terms of a disciplined theological understanding of the gospel. As I have noted, pastoral care becomes pastoral counseling and social work (students and ministers in the vast majority still tend to refer to pastoral care as pastoral counseling), and it is largely therapeutically construed and practiced.[2]

The questions (once again) are: if its identity is taken from psychology or social work, what then makes pastoral care pastoral or Christian, and what makes pastoral theology theological? Behind these questions lurks the realization that in the prevailing assumptions in pastoral theology we have become the subject. Human autonomy is assumed. God has become existentially dependent on us for the ministry of care. It is no misjudgment to say that this invites in its wake an approach to ministry in which we are cast back upon ourselves because everything is now up to us.

This shift in the church's understanding and practice of pastoral care is in large part the result of the great turn toward subjectivity that characterized the European Enlightenment. The thinking and experiencing self rather than the acting God in Jesus Christ came to occupy center stage in the formation of the modern pastoral consciousness. For pastoral care this shift meant a steady drift away from the defining connection with the gospel of Jesus Christ as the act of God. The stage was set for the transmutation of pastoral work into a discipline able to respond to the ubiquitous claims of the experiencing self *on its own terms*. In the United States at least, from the 1920s, pastoral care came to be cast in a psychological and therapeutic, rather than a theological and liturgical, framework. While attempts have been made to think theologically about pastoral work and about the relationship between theology and psychology, these have been made largely on the basis of an a priori, immanent, and panentheistic view of God that assumes God and humankind are in some kind of relationship of mutuality—a pleasant thought, but one that quite neglects the sovereignty and holiness of the Lord God. There is, in fact,

2. For a completely different approach, rooted in the Greek Orthodox theological heritage, see the bishop of Nafpaktos, Hierotheos, *Orthodox Psychotherapy: The Science of the Fathers*, trans. Esther Williams (Levadia, Greece: Birth of the Theotokos Monastery, 1994).

a vigorous anticonfessionalism in much writing on practical theology. The eclipse of doctrine from pastoral theology is bound to happen when by dint of method in theology we begin with ourselves and our experience of being in relationship with God in some oblique but unknowing way, faithful to the end to Enlightenment epistemological proscriptions. As such, we remain indifferent to the salutary pastoral consequences of doctrine.

Another indicator of the shift in the basis for pastoral work today has been the lack of obvious connection between pastoral care and the worship, fellowship, and mission of the church in many of the standard contemporary texts. It has become largely an open question whether there is any serious material connection at the point of ministerial churchly practice between kerygma (proclaiming the gospel) and *didache* (teaching the gospel), on the one hand, and *diakonia* (the "serving ministry" of the gospel), on the other. What is pastoral care when it is separated from or only loosely connected to the doctrinal center of Christian faith?

Lost in the turn toward subjectivity is the recognition that the singularly significant theological basis for ministry lies in the unique vicarious priesthood of Jesus Christ, the ministry that he exercises in the flesh of his humanity on our behalf. When we fail to understand ministry through union with Christ as a sharing in the priesthood of Christ by the grace of the Holy Spirit, all things are cast back upon us, and every issue depends on the pastor's ability to work his or her skills successfully. The work of the pastor replaces the work of God. This approach to pastoral care has fueled the publication of skill-related books and programs for clergy, which are not wrong or unhelpful in themselves, but which leave pastoral ministry open to all kinds of muddle stemming from doctrinal disconnectedness and theological incoherence.

The maturing of the modern age has meant an irreversible cosmological revolution in our self-understanding. Premodernity is not a legitimate intellectual option. But neither is it necessary to follow Kant's proscription and posit an inviolate chasm between faith's object and faith's experience. In part the legacy of twentieth-century pastoral care is the continuing need to find ways by which the content of Christian faith (not always the same as theology!) and psychology may be properly related. If in some sense or other the human soul retains a meaning other than the merely metaphysical, pastors have to be psychologists to some extent. Yet even as the psychophilosophical world of the West changes from the subjective certainty of modernity to the epistemological and moral relativism of postmodernity, as it moves from a worldview centered on the experiencing self to one represented by the deconstruction of the self and even of truth itself, the church continues to assert—albeit sometimes hesitantly today—a confessional faith. Christians recite the creeds (in the jargon of today, a "meta-narrative"), and to some extent presumably make sense of them, not bowing fully either to the subjectivist certainty of modernity or to the relativizing pluralism of postmodernity. In plain sight of both, Christians still assert the central confessional affirmation—Christ Jesus is Lord!—and mean by this not just a statement of truth but also a relationship with the living God given to us through the gospel.

Practical Theology, Doctrine, and Pastoral Care

As a broad and inclusive category, *practical* theology is theology that is concerned with action. Yet the meaning of the term is not obviously cogent, combining as it does the noun *theology* with the adjective *practical*.[3] Is not theology associated with ideas and arguments that seek to present eternal truths, while the practical tends to be associated with the mundane, "where the rubber hits the road"? The adjective seems to qualify the noun in an odd way. It is precisely this way of thinking, however, that has led theology to be thought of as "pure" and therefore impractical, and "practical theology" to be thought of as the functional, pragmatic end of the curriculum, where the theory of theology gets applied in churchly work. Even if, with Schleiermacher, we think of practical theology as the crown of the theological enterprise, it remains a discipline struggling to develop a theory.

So, in what way does it make sense to speak of *practical* theology? Practical theology is practical because it is theological: it has to do with God. All theology, all knowledge of God, by virtue of the subject matter—the acting God—is inherently a practical theology or a practical knowledge of God. Axiomatically, knowledge of God is knowledge of God creatively, redemptively, and eschatologically active in the world and in human history through Jesus Christ. Aside from the specific history of revelation and redemption, we would not know God.[4] Knowledge of God is knowledge of the *missio Dei*, of Jesus' ministry to the glory of the Father, in the power of the Holy Spirit, for the sake of the world. Revelation and the mission

3. The following was sparked by Jaroslav Pelikan's discussion of a similar problem posed for historical theology in *Historical Theology: Continuity and Change in Christian Doctrine* (Philadelphia: Westminster, 1971), xiii–xiv. See also my article, "The Trinitarian Basis of a Christian Practical Theology," *International Journal for Practical Theology* 2 (1998): 222–39.

4. Emil Brunner, *Dogmatics*, vol. 2: *The Christian Doctrine of Creation and Redemption*, trans. Olive Wyon (Philadelphia: Westminster, 1952), 198.

of God for reconciliation are held together christologically for the church as practical knowing: "All things have been handed over to me by my Father; and no one knows who the Son is except the Father, or who the Father is except the Son and anyone to whom the Son chooses to reveal him" (Luke 10:22); "I have come down from heaven, not to do my own will, but the will of him who sent me" (John 6:38). Because there is no knowledge of a God absent from history, or of an uninvolved God, there is no such thing as impractical theology, which would be the knowledge of a God notable exactly as a God who is not revealed and who does not act in human history.

Two points concerning the consequences of this view of theology as inherently practical are equally true and therefore must be held in tension. First, as T. F. Torrance has repeatedly observed, one major significance of the Nicene phrase *homoousios to Patri* ("of one substance with the Father," referring to Jesus Christ) is that God is in himself always and reliably what he is toward us through his son, Jesus Christ.[5] God is none other as God than who God is in revelation and reconciliation, and when we look into the face of Jesus Christ it is indeed the face of God that we see. This theological affirmation is critical to the truth of the gospel as gospel, for it means that when we deal with Jesus Christ we are dealing with God. We do not appeal to a hidden God behind the back of Jesus Christ. Thus in summary, "We believe that what [Jesus Christ] is toward us, with us and for us in his incarnate mission from the Father he is antecedently and eternally in himself, the eternal Son of the Father. . . . By living his divine Life within our human life as real human life and addressing us within it, God has revealed to us something of the innermost secret of his own divine personal life not otherwise possible."[6]

Second, while our knowledge of God is dependent on God's self-revelation, God is not only God in relationship with us.[7] While we know God only insofar as God is self-revealed in the divine economy of salvation, and God is none other than who he is in his revelation, this does not mean either that we must thereby limit God to God's being with us or that our knowledge of God has no reference beyond our self-reference. That would leave no place for God existing *a se* (God's being from himself), and

5. See, for example, T. F. Torrance, *The Christian Doctrine of God: One Being, Three Persons* (Edinburgh: T. & T. Clark), 149.

6. Ibid., 142–43.

7. For the following I am indebted to the clarifying essay by Paul A. Molnar, "Toward a Contemporary Doctrine of the Immanent Trinity: Karl Barth and the Present Discussion," *Scottish Journal of Theology* 49, no. 3 (1996): 311–12.

pushes so hard toward agnosticism that in the end it would lead to the loss of God as such, in which we cannot separate God from our own experiences. Although there is no knowledge of God that does not include the fact that it is we who know God, that knowledge of God is not a conceptual construction derived deductively from reflection upon ourselves and our experiences of God. While all knowing involves a subject who knows, true knowledge of God demands that God, not we ourselves, is the subject of our knowing. It is *God* who acts in the economy of salvation, and while God acts as God is, we must beware of applying a "vice versa" in such a way that our understanding of God collapses into the human experience of God in history.

Aristotle called practical knowledge *phronesis*, practical skills applied to moral ends. A Christian *phronesis*, Christian practical knowledge, is concerned with true knowledge of the living and acting God and the living and acting practice of that knowledge day by day. It is not we by our actions who make theology practical (the old notion of practical theology as applied theology), but it is God, by virtue of what God does, who makes knowledge of God inherently a practical knowledge. This means that churchly practice arises out of our sharing in the practice of God, and it is only properly and appropriately practical insofar as it does this. Nothing could be more practical than the teaching about who God is and what God does in relation to us, on the one hand, and the concern to live in that relationship as the fundamental or constitutive basis of what it means to be a human being and the church, on the other. This point is significant for my argument in this book.

Theology that truly refers to God as the revealing and acting God in, through, and as Jesus Christ, and that the church through due process confirms, is known as doctrine. Doctrine is practical theology because it is church theology. With doctrine the church bears witness to the ministering God in the language of our knowing, to the acting God who reaches out in saving and serving love in Jesus Christ, not only in revelation but also to bring us into the joy of reconciliation and relationship with God. The subject of doctrine is God known through the *missio Dei*, the reaching-out ministry of God in Jesus Christ for our salvation, in which the person and act of God in Jesus Christ are held together in such a way that the one cannot be understood without the other. At the constitutive level, the ministry of the church, therefore, has no content apart from the content of the gospel of Jesus Christ to which the doctrine of the church bears witness and on which it depends for its truth and reality. Were not the deepest connection maintained in our minds between the gospel and kerygma, *didache* and *diakonia*, ministry would be severed from that which gives it identity and truth in the first place. Doctrine exists as the church's witness to the primary ministry of God in, through, and as Jesus Christ and as such has its source in the freedom and love of God to be God for us.

We can speak, therefore, of the dogmatic or doctrinal constitution of ministry by which I mean that reality of the gospel of Jesus Christ without which Christianity cannot exist and which gives the church's ministry its defining content and reality as sharing in the *missio Dei*. The ministry of the church is our participation in the continuing ministry of Jesus Christ, to the glory of the Father, in the power of the Holy Spirit. There is in this the closest possible connection between doctrine as the church's expression of the God who acts and what the church and pastors do. Therefore pastors are encouraged to make a fundamental connection between the doctrines of covenant and promise, incarnation and atonement, the Christian apprehension of God as one being and three persons, the resurrection and ascension of Jesus and of his coming again, and the day-by-day work of pastoral care. Otherwise, they are best advised to demit the ministry of the gospel. There is a difference between helping someone therapeutically and leading that person to Jesus Christ.[8]

Thus defined, doctrine can be properly understood pastorally (although not only so), and pastoral work doctrinally (in this case, without qualification). While doctrine is the church's disciplined way of keeping in mind who God is and what God does, this knowledge is by its nature practical rather than theoretical or abstract. Pastoral work, then, is not some churchly activity apart from that to which doctrine refers, not something apart from who God is and what God does in, through, and as Jesus Christ.

The primary issue for pastoral theology is not the nature of the relation between theology and psychology, important as that is, or, more broadly, between theology and theological and psychosocial anthropology. The primary issue is, rather, understanding the nature of the relation between the gospel and kerygma, *didache* and *diakonia*. In its preaching, teaching, and serving, the church depends on the acts of God in Christ. To borrow from and rephrase Karl Barth, it is not Jesus Christ who needs pastoral work, it is pastoral work that needs Jesus Christ. The relation between God's ministry in, through, and as Jesus Christ in the power of the Holy Spirit and the ministry of the church is the proper concern. Because pastoral care is at all points both a ministry of God and a ministry of the church, it is tied to the gospel given in Word and sacraments. Func-

8. See T. F. Torrance, *Theology in Reconciliation* (London: Geoffrey Chapman, 1975), 275.

tionally, this means that as a ministry of Word and sacraments pastoral care is tied also to Christian worship and community, discipleship and mission. To bring Calvin's notion to mind, pastoral care is not a third thing alongside Word and sacraments.

One final point needs to be made about the general nature of practical theology as it bears on the relationship between doctrine and pastoral care. Practical theology in general, and pastoral theology in particular, are hermeneutical disciplines. What pastors do interprets situations in reference to the being and acts of the *living* God. In pastoral listening as also in ministries of presence, in interpretation of experience as also in ministries of proclamation and worship, in acts of compassion as also in ministries of discipline and repentance, it is the presence and power of God in the gospel of Jesus Christ that reveals and interprets the reality of the human situation and heals, sustains, reconciles, and guides. It is the actuality of the gospel, the presence of the living Christ clothed with his saving works, that defines and enables the pastoral ministry of the church, giving it a power from beyond itself. The gospel is not doctrines, of course, but the saving power of God at work in and among the lives of people, to which actuality, however, doctrines make coherent and accurate witness. Pastoral care, then, is the interpreted meanings of baptism and Eucharist, Christology and soteriology, Trinity and the presence of the Holy Spirit, sanctification by the power of the Holy Spirit and eschatology, and so on, in the lives of actual people, insofar as these doctrines disclose the human condition and bear witness to the saving and blessing actuality of Emmanuel.

Insofar as pastors interpret the lives of their people before God in the light of the love of God in Jesus Christ, they are able to bring doctrine to a deeper and more faithful articulation on the basis of their pastoral work. Take, for example, one of the greatest books on the doctrine of the atonement, John McLeod Campbell's *The Nature of the Atonement*, published in Scotland in 1856. Here a pastor was engaged in a Herculean theological effort to wrestle the understanding of the central aspect of the atonement away from the dominant (Westminster Confession) penal view of atonement to a view rooted in the love of God, because of his gospel-derived, evangelical concern for his people's assurance of their salvation. It was McLeod Campbell's reflective pastoral engagement with his people in the context of his understanding of the gospel at the deepest level that led to his reassessment of doctrine. A critical analysis of a cruel and theologically inadequate doctrinal view of God and the atonement conjoined with an explicit pastoral concern led to the reformation of doctrine in the Church of Scotland and the restoration of pastoral preaching and practice rooted in the gospel. Pastoral work is part of the dispensation of grace necessary for the healthy development and understanding of Christian doctrine. When doctrinal theologians and pastors are separated from one another, both suffer.

Just as the pastoral practice of the faith is possible only as we develop a deep practical wisdom rooted in a graced participation in God's missional reality in, through, and as Jesus Christ, knowledge of God too is illumined and clarified by the study of situations and events where the gospel is preached, taught, and lived out. In other words, doctrine and practice in the life of the church interpret one another. While it is right to insist that doctrine shapes pastoral work insofar as it discloses the human situation and bears witness to the pastoring God, which is the content of the gospel, it is right also to insist that reflection on pastoral practice leads to the interpretation of Scripture and the reformation of doctrine. Because of the work of the Holy Spirit, God is active through the Scriptures but also surely in situations of human experience. The basis for the interpretation of the latter is given by the former, and the meaning of the former is found as a lived reality in the latter. It is the present and continuing mediation of Jesus Christ through the Holy Spirit in and through Scripture *and* in and through the experiences of life that opens up Scripture as the hermeneutic of the church's pastoral practice, and the church's pastoral practice as a necessary aspect of the interpretation of Scripture. A two-way relation exists between the church's knowledge of the acting God and the ministry of the church, the results of which are the ministry of pastoral care and continuing interpretation of Scripture and the development of doctrine as the true and appropriate interpretation of God and human experience. Might it not be said rightly that in this we have drawn upon Seward Hiltner's concept of two-way communication and brought it into a different frame of reference?

The Utility of Doctrine

The intent of Christian doctrine is to give true and precise expression to God's identity and acts as they are revealed through the gospel of Jesus Christ. As Alister E. McGrath puts it, "Christian doctrine is not primarily concerned with the insights of Jesus of Nazareth but with the insights of the community of faith concerning him."[9] Two points arise from this statement. First, doctrine assumes the community of the church and expresses this community's faith concerning God. Second, doctrine moves

9. Alister E. McGrath, *The Genesis of Doctrine: A Study in the Foundations of Doctrinal Criticism* (Oxford: Blackwell, 1990), 2.

beyond the mere recitation of biblical texts, but not away from Scripture, to make statements concerning God to which the texts bear witness, and to do so in a coherent and systematic manner.

Doctrine arises in the church out of the movement of apprehension and thought to grasp more deeply the meaning of the apostolic witness so that in and through its semantic references and arrangements it really is God who is known.[10] Neither individual doctrines nor the system of doctrine, however, substitutes for God and the gospel, for doctrine does not have a reality and truth independent of that to which it refers. Two points help to explain what I mean.

1. Christian faith is not a theory about God. It is not at its heart a series of ideas or arguments, as if faith were foundationally cognitive and discursive. While faith involves a cast of mind (Rom. 12:2), that mind is formed through a relationship with God in, through, and as Jesus Christ. The truth of doctrine does not lie in its nature as a semantic or cultural language game. The truth of doctrine does not lie in the coherence of its concepts and statements as such, or even in its capacity to specify rules for Christian speech and action. Truth lies in the reality of God to which doctrine refers. Doctrine is true when it refers appropriately to the substance of the faith, to the God-event of the gospel of Jesus Christ. It is in this way that doctrine is descriptive, for its subject is the identity and acts of God;[11] and it is prescriptive insofar as the identity and acts of God constrain all Christian believing and acting.

2. Christian faith is not ultimately about believing Bible stories. Christians after all were believing, praying, worshiping, and living the life of disciples before the New Testament was written, before the biblical canon was settled (the first complete list of books found in the New Testament is given in Athanasius's Easter Letter in 367), and before councils published their creeds. At 1 Thessalonians 2:13, for example, Paul gives thanks "that when

10. I disagree with Emil Brunner, who appears to insist upon an absolute and irretrievable distinction between the development of the doctrines of the Trinity and the hypostatic union on the one hand, and the apostolic proclamation on the other. Brunner's concern is that doctrine as such led to the subject-object split that belonged to the Greek concept of knowledge. This is not what is intended here. Brunner seems not to appreciate how doctrine is related to Scripture and the rule of faith, nor does he grasp the role that doctrine plays in protecting the mind of the church in order precisely to be faithful in proclamation. A discussion of Brunner's thesis may be found in *Dogmatics*, vol. 3: *The Christian Doctrine of the Church, Faith, and the Consummation*, trans. David Cairns (Philadelphia: Westminster, 1962), chapter 15.

11. This is different from saying that doctrine is only descriptive of the beliefs of the church. On one level this is true. On a deeper level, God, not the church, is the subject of doctrine. Yet as doctrine, it remains a doctrine of the church, and cannot be confused with God.

you received the word of God that you heard from us, you accepted it not as a human word but as what it really is, God's word." What was the word of God that was preached before Scripture was written? What norm formed Christian identity pre-Scripture? What did Christians confess before Nicea, in 325? At the end of the second and into the third Christian centuries, Irenaeus and Tertullian, for example, going beyond the emerging canon of Scripture in support of their arguments against the gnostics, spoke respectively of the "canon of truth" and the "rule of faith," meaning in each case the living tradition of Jesus Christ passed on through the church, enshrined in Scripture, fluid in form, and fixed in content that set out the key points of God's revelation and reconciliation in Jesus Christ. Later, in the fourth century, Basil of Caesarea noted the great unwritten apostolic tradition that guided the church, mentioning, among other actions, signing with the sign of the cross and praying facing east.[12]

Of course, the Bible stories and the ideas and arguments of doctrine give coherent expression to the substance of faith, and test and interpret the speaking and living of faith in accordance with the truth of the gospel. But the sense of faith in Jesus Christ, a faith with real content, as something alive that radically changes people, existed from the beginning as a core deposit once for all delivered to the saints. This was a dynamic faith that would be thought through in an elastic way, so that while it was necessary to record the apostolic witness, that was never understood to reduce the faith to a repetition of its words. This faith would lead to an exegetical method in which the church could rightly and necessarily stretch beyond Scripture without abandoning Scripture. It took the church almost three centuries to bring this witness to closed canonical expression, and four centuries to bring it to an adequate conciliar articulation, although the process is never ending for the church on earth where we do not yet see God face-to-face (1 Cor. 13:12).

The point here is subtle and elusive, but nonetheless true: there is a deep source of knowledge of Jesus Christ to which the canon of Scripture and doctrine bear witness. Theologians distinguish between doctrine and "dogma." "Dogma" refers to the God-given content of faith, God's Word, Jesus Christ, heard and believed in faith certainly, systematically expressed in church doctrine undoubtedly, but itself the truth of revelation and reconciliation upon which the church in faith and doctrine depends at every turn. God is the subject of dogma. Dogma is "all that the Lord has commanded [the church] to

---

12. Basil, *On the Holy Spirit* (Crestwood, N.Y.: St. Vladimir's Seminary Press, 1980), 98–99.

say" (Acts 10:33), the deep tradition to which the Scriptures and doctrines bear witness, and on which they depend for their truth.

In contrast, doctrine (sometimes called the confessional teaching of the churches) is the church's later reflection on revelation and reconciliation by which the deposit of faith is brought to coherent articulation through the years. Doctrine is a teaching of the church. A good example is the *doctrine* of the Trinity, which is the church's way of speaking faithfully about God as a result of the revelation of God in the gospel of Jesus Christ. The church had to learn to think about God in a new way on the basis of Jesus Christ, a process that took about three hundred years. The Trinity is a *theologoumenon*, a doctrine of the church. God is not reducible to our words about God, to the *doctrine* of the Trinity, yet the doctrine of the Trinity stands in a faithful relation to God, for it was formed in the mind of the church by the pressure of the gospel forcing the church to express in a coherent and faithful way what it believes and lives by.

A dialectic exists between Scripture and doctrine. Scripture and doctrine arise out of the living faith of the church, the sacred deposit laid by the Lord Jesus Christ, to which they are accountable. Yet the living of faith will go astray without them, for there is no other guide to Christian growth and faithfulness than Scripture and doctrine, and the faith of the church is embodied in them. Colossians 2:7 refers to Christians being "established in the faith, just as you were taught." Similarly, doctrine will go adrift when it is detached from Scripture as the norm by which it is judged, and when it no longer faithfully articulates the deposit of faith upon which the church depends and which it must guard for its very life. Doctrine, then, is the considered reflection on the gospel by the church, judged according to the norm of Scripture, which itself depends for its truth on the sacred deposit given by Christ and the apostles, by which the church brings to expression the gospel of the Lord Jesus Christ.[13]

Four points concerning the Christian understanding of doctrine should be noted.

1. Doctrine is basic to the development of Christian faith as a way of life in obedience to God and as an intellectual system of meaning, value, and truth that has enduring power to inform and guide. Christianity voided of doctrine makes no sense. There is no possibility of an adoctrinal faith, a faith that only experiences, that is formless, that does not rest on and in turn shape fundamental axioms that give coherence and cogency

---

13. For a discussion of these issues see Paul M. Blowers, "The *Regula Fidei* and the Narrative Character of Early Christian Faith," *Pro Ecclesia* 6, no. 2 (spring 1997): 199–228.

to what otherwise would be discrete but uninterpretable data of apparent religious experience. The faith of the church is not only the experience of being in relationship with God, but also the mind transformed in its knowing of God and the life transformed in its service of God. Faith gives rise to and is also marked by a cognitive and conceptual relation to God that is expressed as doctrine, and that has continuity with the apostolic and postapostolic traditions that arose around Jesus of Nazareth. Indeed, without doctrine, Christian faith must inevitably lose hold of Jesus Christ, for he slips away from present experience as merely adventitious, not the thing itself, collapsed into a metaphor of our own devising.

2. There is no neutral knowledge of God, no sense in which Christian doctrine apart from faith in and relationship with God in Jesus Christ could exist as an independent item of information that did not stake an absolute claim upon us. This is the impact of Peter's declaration at John 6:69: "We have come to believe and know that you are the holy One of God." Doctrine is not a theory about the fact that we have union and communion with God in and through Jesus Christ, as if the fact of Jesus Christ could be just an idea, even a Christian idea, something other than an act, and a continuing act, of the truth of the living God. The person of the man Jesus in his identity as God, indeed as the incarnation of the "I am" of God, and the church's continuing sense of being in relationship with God in and through him, give rise to doctrine. There is no ecclesiastical or moral compulsion. Protestantism has no magisterium to stand behind the doctrines of the church and insist upon compliance. One should hardly comply with a doctrine of faith if one neither believed it or did not experience for oneself the truth, love, and power of God to which it refers. But the reality of Jesus Christ is theologically compelling insofar as the Holy Spirit seals that knowledge in our hearts and minds in the gift of faith.

3. Like Scripture, doctrine is a two-edged sword that cuts and divides.[14] Operating externally, in the context of other truth claims, doctrine expresses what the church believes and marks out the boundary of Christian faith, in terms of both belief and discipleship. Doctrine drives toward *exclusivity* regarding what is to be believed, and toward *inclusivity* only on the basis of Jesus Christ. Operating internally, doctrine separates off those understandings of the gospel that are not considered adequate. It defines heresy as that understanding of the faith given from within the faith that is not an adequate or faithful expression of the faith. To some extent partial truths about the gospel forced the church to clarify what was properly

14. See McGrath, *Genesis of Doctrine*, 37–38.

to be believed.[15] For the church, doctrine implies self-definition, though not on the basis of self, but on the basis of God. This is most strongly the case when the church is in danger of losing its identity, as many argue is the case today within mainline Western Protestantism.

4. All doctrines are important, but not all doctrines are equally important and not all doctrines have the same power to shape the pastoral mind of the church. This important view can be found in Scripture itself.[16] The Gospel of Mark is more authoritative for Christian doctrine than the Letter of Paul to Philemon, although the latter is not thereby rejected as an unimportant document. The Letter of Paul to the Romans arguably is of more value to Christian theology and faith than 1 Chronicles. Similarly, John 3:16 has played a more impressive role in the shaping of the Christian mind than Paul's injunction to Timothy to drink wine for the sake of his digestion (1 Tim. 5:23). While we must not use this argument in a cavalier manner, its truth seems to be self-evident. There is always danger, then, when doctrine is developed in a lopsided manner, relying on a text here or there, selected for a priori reasons, but cut off from the mainstream of biblical teaching. Similarly, there is great danger when there is no metanarrative to guide in the interpretation of Scripture, no overarching, epistemic, and integrative frame of mind, no explanatory theory, by which the various data of Scripture can be interpreted. Because Scripture is read as a theological text, and not just as an historical text, there must be the closest hermeneutical relationship between doctrine and Scripture.

The church has long distinguished fundamental from secondary doctrines. The hierarchy of doctrines suggests that there are some doctrines so central that their denial means the betrayal of Christianity. To reject them is to place oneself outside the church and away from Jesus Christ. Below this cluster of nonnegotiable doctrines are a spread of variously important doctrines, but about which there can be disagreement without forfeiting one's Christianity. Philipp Melanchthon, the German reformer, called these secondary doctrines *adiaphora*, likening them to an outer ring of faith; they do not define a person as a Christian as such, but their acceptance or rejection defines one as one sort of Christian or another. Thus Protestants, Catholics, and Orthodox all believe in the full divinity and humanity of Jesus Christ—that makes us Christians. The nature of

---

15. William J. Abraham, *Canon and Criterion in Christian Theology* (Oxford: Clarendon, 1998), 36.

16. I found this idea in R. P. C. Hanson, *The Continuity of Christian Doctrine* (New York: Seabury, 1981), 78.

Christ's presence in the sacraments divides us, however, both Protestants from Catholics, and Protestants from Protestants—and that shapes our denominational affiliations to some extent.

The Authority of Doctrine

Doctrine has truth, power, and authority for Christians when it teaches truthfully about Jesus Christ as God with us (Emmanuel), as past event, present experience, and future hope, and as it is able to contend for the truth of God by bringing the gospel to a coherent and faithful expression in each generation. Doctrine refers to a living, experienced, personal reality in our lives, and not to a deposit of ideas independent of the experience and truth of the living Christ. Doctrine is a living expression of faith, not propositions that are timelessly true in any single mode of expression, even though there is a long history of doctrinal continuity that marks the expressed faith of the church. Properly understood, doctrine is not in any sense just a dead proposition.

Christian doctrine did not drop out of the sky, formed and sealed once and for all, passed on from Jesus to the church. While this is to say the obvious, it reminds us that doctrine is organic, a living, historically grounded reflection on the acting God given in and through the gospel to which the Scriptures bear witness. The alternative notions of doctrine as static and fixed, whether read off the pages of Scripture or propounded by a holy magisterium or as always in flux and therefore fluid, are wrong. The conservative (Catholic) view is that doctrine is to be identified, according to Vincent of Lerins in the fifth century, as *quod ubique, quod semper, quod ab omnibus creditum est*, "In the Catholic Church itself, every care should be taken to hold fast to what has been believed everywhere, always and by all."[17] Even Vincent, however (followed by John Henry Newman in the nineteenth century), understood this developmentally and biologically in a way analogous to the growth of the body from infant to adult. The problem with the biological growth metaphor is that it does not deal satisfactorily with discontinuities or even with reductions and reversals in the development of doctrine. On what basis is a new doctrine promulgated—for example, the ordination of women to the ministry of Word and sacrament—and an old doctrine quietly dropped from the faith of the church? What are the criteria?

---

17. Vincent of Lerins, *Commonitories*, trans. Rudolph E. Morris, in *The Fathers of the Church*, vol. 7 (New York: Fathers of the Church, 1949), 2.270. For a recent discussion of Vincent's role in theological thinking today, see Thomas C. Oden, *The Rebirth of Orthodoxy: Signs of New Life in Christianity* (San Francisco: HarperSanFrancisco, 2003), chapter 11.

The conservative (Protestant) view of *sola scriptura* can be interpreted to mean that the church should adhere only to doctrine deduced from the plain meaning of Scripture, and that the development of doctrine is to be treated with grave suspicion and even resistance. The problem with this view is that the church then needs an authoritative method of interpretation in order to decide what it means by the plain meaning of Scripture. This is where the arguments begin. Protestants have usually used confessional statements as subordinate standards by which to interpret Scripture, but even these move in and out of theological fashion, and have today an uncertain hermeneutical authority. Interpreted by the likes of Calvin and Barth, however, *sola scriptura* means going beyond the mere reiteration of biblical texts to develop our theology on the foundation of the prophets and apostles as a witness to the truth of the gospel today. The complexities that confront the conservative side of the ledger—Roman Catholic and Protestant—are significant.

The liberal Protestant view, at least as interpreted in the church today, is that doctrine is to be understood in the light of *Ecclesia reformata, semper reformanda*, "the church reformed, always reforming." Contemporary expressions of this can be found in the view that doctrine is appropriately normless, expressing the current mind of the church as it reads the Bible, worships, and goes about its business. This is the "continuing activity theory" of doctrine. The sense of a vague, indefinable center of the faith is hardly likely to produce a vigorous Christianity, however, as most North American mainline denominations are now finding out, to their cost. This seventeenth-century statement is not an invitation to freewheeling change in doctrine but is to be understood as the church reformed and reformable only according to the Word of God. And we are back with the problem of what "according to the Word of God" means.

Openness and constraint, development and tradition, continuities and discontinuities, all mark the nature of the Christian doctrinal process. It is in the resulting tensions—not the least of which is that it was a process of trial and error, and error not only on the part of those condemned as heretics—that doctrine is understood properly in a dynamic yet stable way. In a sense doctrine is a process as much as it is a transmitted and received tradition.

There is a deeper point to be made, however, that takes us into the heart of the nature of the authority of doctrine. It is the nature of doctrinal statements that they have a twofold character. Because the faith of the church rests upon the truth of God given in, through, and as Jesus Christ, that faith is expressed in such a way that doctrinal statements are, as T. F. Torrance has put it, at once bounded yet open-ended, closed at one end yet open at the other. This can be explained in the attention of theological method to the kataphatic (with images) and apophatic (without images) nature of theological statements.[18]

On the one hand, doctrine is kataphatic, having a positive intent; that is, there is appropriate content to our talk about God. God's truth in Jesus of Nazareth has taken form in time and space in a precise and actual way. Our statements must reflect a given historicity, and we dare not bypass that history lest we cut the anchor of incarnation that grounds Christian faith in Jesus, and Jesus with the idea of Christ. The Apostles' Creed rehearses the empirical scope of the gospel: "suffered under Pontius Pilate, was crucified, died, and was buried," though the tendency to reduce the life of Jesus to a comma is hardly acceptable. Because the Word became flesh, we cannot turn Jesus into a timeless Lord with no historical context without doing our understanding of him very serious damage indeed. Further, as noted, under the pressure of obedience to the truth of the gospel given in Jesus Christ, the faith of the church came to evangelical expression in core doctrinal statements that have the significance of setting aside any other gospel and any other approach. This came to early expression at Galatians 1:9: "If anyone proclaims to you a gospel contrary to what you received, let that one be accursed!" In the fourth century, the Nicene Creed brought Christian faith to expression in such a singularly important way that the church henceforth came to recognize that in its affirmation of the consubstantiality of the Son with the Father it had in documentary form a reliable and authoritative guide for the interpretation of the Scriptures, the proclamation of the faith, and the protection of the gospel. In the *homoousios to Patri*, the deepest truth of Christian faith as a gospel of salvation was brought to expression. As such, the Nicene Creed has played, and continues to play, a doctrinally and liturgically normative role in the life of the church. In such ways the church makes doctrinal assertions that have guided the people of God in Christian faithfulness through the centuries.

On the other hand, doctrine is apophatic, having a negative intent; that is, our talk of God is never adequate to its subject. We must "think away" from the words and concepts that we use in order to apprehend the living God through and beyond the words that we use. To think otherwise is idolatry. A timely and controversial example is the doctrine of the father-

---

18. The notion that doctrine is closed at one end, and open at the other, is a concept developed particularly by T. F. Torrance. See especially *The Trinitarian Faith* (Edinburgh: T. & T. Clark, 1993), 18–19, which helped in the framing of these comments.

hood of God. This was never intended by the fourth-century Trinitarian theologians, for example, to be the projection of concepts of human fatherhood onto God. To suggest such is disingenuous. There was, in fact, a strongly asserted apophatic element that involved "thinking away" all that was inappropriate. Explicitly this meant not thinking of God in biological or sexual terms. The *imago Dei*, after all, is not reversible. Rather, God's fatherhood was to be thought through in terms of God's relationship with and revealed act in Jesus Christ, that is, relationally as a communion of self-giving love. In this way doctrine, properly understood, is not objectified faith, but the living expression of faith. As such, there are limits to doctrine, and there is always the danger of trying to say too much. It is, however, an avoidable danger, for doctrine is necessary in order for the church to mark out the boundaries of faith.

The truth of doctrine resides in the reality of God to which doctrines refer, in that objective truth of God that transcends all that the church says, even in its most profound doctrines, and not in the meanings given to or the arrangements of the words. Doctrinal statements have an open-endedness, functioning iconically, as it were, with a reversed perspective, pointing away from themselves in their bearing witness to an immeasurable truth that cannot be limited to the attempts to bring it to expression.

In sum, while we must "guard the deposit" (1 Tim. 6:20) and "contend for the faith that was once for all entrusted to the saints" (Jude 3), what this means for Christian faith and life continues to be a matter of discussion, although properly so only on the gospel's own terms, and according to appeal to Scripture. We are compelled, time and again, to bring to light the inner theological connections inherent within the gospel in order the more deeply and faithfully to understand, love, and serve the living God. Yet we do so aware that our doctrinal formulations always fall far short of the truth of the living God. We see in a mirror, dimly (1 Cor. 13:12), and knowledge of God remains something we cannot get our minds around. But let it not be forgotten that while we are confronted with the majesty and transcendence of God, the church nevertheless claims truth for its doctrines when that to which they refer is the truth of the living God disclosed in Jesus Christ clothed with his gospel.

Chapter 2

The Ministry Of God

Ministry—from the Father, through the Son, and in the Holy Spirit

Pastoral theology begins as a theology of the ministry of God for us in, through, and as Jesus Christ, and as such brings to expression the gospel of revelation and reconciliation. Jesus Christ as the mission of God to and for us is the ground of and the basis for the church's ministries of care. To insist that the ministry of the Father through the Son and in the Holy Spirit is the primary subject matter of pastoral theology means that there is no faithful content to speaking forth and living out the gospel pastorally apart from knowing and sharing in the mission of the God who acts in and through Jesus Christ and in the Spirit precisely in and as a man for all people.

I begin in this chapter with a discussion of the ministry of God in, through, and as Jesus Christ for our redemption, a huge topic.[1] The first organizing theological category by which I present the ministry of God is Jesus Christ, the mission of God. I intend that the presentation of the ministry of God in, through, and as Jesus Christ will reflect an ecumenical, catholic, and evangelical theology of the church. I then consider the ministry of God in the light of the doctrine of the Trinity as given for us in the apostolic benediction.

Jesus Christ, the Mission of God

According to Christian faith the ministry of Jesus Christ is the direct act of God: "I do as the Father has commanded me" (John 14:31). Jesus comes

---

1. See Andrew Purves and Mark Achtemeier, *Union in Christ: A Declaration for the Church —A Commentary with Questions for Study and Reflection* (Louisville, Ky.: Witherspoon, 1999).

with a job to do, with a saving purpose in view. That saving purpose is his work, for which he is sent from the Father, conceived by the Holy Spirit, and born of Mary. This means much more than saying that Jesus embodied or carried out the mission of God to the world and for the world. To say that Jesus Christ embodied the mission of God could imply that such a mission was a separate entity, standing potentially on its own apart from the particular person known to us as Jesus of Nazareth. It would introduce the possibility that other historical figures or movements (Muhammad, Buddha, the labor movement, etc.) might similarly embody or carry forward the mission of God. Thus we cannot consider the meaning of the mission of God apart from or independently of the person of Jesus Christ. He is in his own person the mission of God to and for the world, and any sense in which some person or movement might subsequently become identified with the mission of God is possible only on the basis of sharing in Christ's mission. For this reason I emphasize in chapter 4 the doctrine of our union with Christ, which is the work of the Holy Spirit.

Further, we want to avoid the danger that we become more interested in what Christ has done for us than in Christ himself, so that Jesus Christ slips away. To safeguard against such abstractions and problems, the personal particularity of Jesus Christ must be maintained, namely, that Jesus is God's mission to the world and for the world, and that his work or ministry—what he said and did—may not be understood independently of who he is. With regard to Jesus Christ, his being and act, his person and work, must be held tightly together lest in unhinging the meaning of the mission of God from the person of Jesus we lose altogether the actual event of that mission *as Jesus Christ* and turn it thereby into an abstract idea or moral principle. There is simply no talking about God's mission to and for the world apart from the historical figure of Jesus of Nazareth, and no validity in the attempt to understand it in a merely instrumental way apart from Jesus' actual person, as if the mission of God were only incidentally attached to him.

Thus Jesus is not just a messenger of God or a prophet like Isaiah, Jeremiah, or John the Baptist. He comes as Emmanuel, as God with us in human flesh, God in our midst as a particular human being. As Athanasius put it clearly, "He was not a man, and then became God, but He was God, and then became man, and that to deify us."[2] In the fourth century,

---

2. Athanasius, *Four Discourses Against the Arians* 1.39, and also many places throughout, in *The Nicene and Post-Nicene Fathers*, ed. Philip Schaff and Henry Wace, 2d series, vol. 4 (reprint, Edinburgh: T. & T. Clark; Grand Rapids: Eerdmans, 1998).

the church codified this central affirmation of faith in the Nicene Creed's assertion that Jesus is "of one substance with the Father" (*homoousios to Patri*). This was the church's formal way of confessing that Jesus in the flesh is God incarnate as Mary's son who was conceived by the Holy Spirit, God with, among, and for us. The *homoousion* is the core confession of the church that has guarded the mystery of the incarnation, without which there would be no Christian faith, and apart from which there is no ground for understanding the mission of God. The irreducible singularity of Jesus Christ as the only begotten Son of God become incarnate for us and for our salvation is both the foundation and the totality of what is meant by the mission of God. He is the one place given by God where the mission of God comes to full and complete expression and fulfillment. The mission of God is thereby christologically grounded in a thoroughgoing and controlling way so that everything in Christian faith and life flows out from this center and toward this center. The corollary of the affirmation of God incarnate by the Holy Spirit, of course, is the Christian doctrine of God as one being, three persons, the doctrine of the Holy Trinity.

The incarnation of the Word of God becoming flesh as Jesus of Nazareth is identified as the mission of God. It is a gracious sending and becoming, because as God with us he comes as God for us, to do for us in the flesh of our humanity what must be done to restore us to union and communion with the Father. The whole doctrine of the atonement can be assumed here, for he comes not just as Emmanuel, but as Emmanuel and Savior. He comes not just into the world, but also for the world. The theme of reconciliation is woven into the fabric of the gospel because it is woven into the being of the Savior and takes place within his incarnate person, not outside or adjacent to him in an instrumental way.[3] Thus, Karl Barth insists that God "is amongst us in humility, our God, God for us, as that which He is in Himself, in the most inward depth of His Godhead. . . . The truth and actuality of our atonement depends on this being the case. The One who reconciles the world with God is necessarily the one God Himself in His true Godhead. Otherwise the world would not be reconciled with God."[4] The issue is whether *God* has in, through, and as Jesus Christ taken up the cause of the world. For Christian faith, everything is at stake in the affirmation that God has so acted.

One aspect of the atonement that runs like a thread through much that follows is theological anthropology, for it is an important aspect of pastoral

---

3. T. F. Torrance, *The Trinitarian Faith* (Edinburgh: T. & T. Clark, 1988), 155.
4. Karl Barth. *Church Dogmatics*, IV.1, ed. G. W. Bromiley and T. F. Torrance, trans. G. W. Bromiley (Edinburgh: T. & T. Clark, 1956), 193.

theology. As God with us and for us, Jesus reveals what it means to be the truly human one. As Lord of all, in the ontological union of his divinity and humanity, he also totally remakes human nature to be now fully conformed to the image of God. He is thus "the firstborn of all creation" (Col. 1:15). In Jesus we see what a human being was intended to be in the purposes of God; we see the power of his life to reveal human being in its fullness. His love, his purposeful ministry, his relationships, his God-centeredness show what being human really involves and stand over and against the claims of our culture's proponents of self-fulfillment. Autonomy is unbelief.[5] Thus true humanity is not found in the accumulation of wealth or acquisitiveness, in power, or in self-indulgence, but in Jesus Christ through participating in his life. As, for example, the medieval monastics well knew, spiritual enemies were to be dealt with through their vows of poverty, chastity, and obedience. In contemporary terms, our union with Christ leads us to confront the accommodations we have made to money, sex, and power. The New Testament is replete with Jesus' teaching on these and other issues involved in Christian faith and life.

Because our deepest identity as human beings is found in union with Christ, who is the truly human one, the core of who we are is defined not by our achievements, possessions, personalities, natural endowments, or even our religious associations and experiences. We find and claim our own authentic personal humanity in the fact that God has been gracious to us and become one with us in Jesus Christ, and by the Holy Spirit made us one with him. Our union with Christ is the ontological basis of true humanity. It is the real meaning of faith—not that it is a psychological disposition or spiritual virtue, but that it is given by God from beyond us as the ground for a true humanity. It takes but a little stretch of the imagination to see immediately the significance of this for pastoral work, for here we are dealing with the stuff of real human existence, both its loss and its regeneration through union with Christ, the human one.

But this does not mean that Jesus' humanity is only to be imitated, for the atonement is more radical in its implications for human being. We discover and live the fullness of our humanity only when we live in union with Christ, God as the man with and for us. Redemption takes place within the mediatorial life and person of Jesus Christ. Our salvation takes place in the inner relations of the mediator in the unity of his person as wholly God and wholly human, and not just in Christ's external relations

---

5. See Emil Brunner, *Dogmatics*, vol. 3: *The Christian Doctrine of the Church, Faith, and the Consummation*, trans. David Cairns (Philadelphia: Westminster, 1960), 140–41.

with God and with humankind. It was because of his "inhomination" (*enanthropesis*), his becoming a man, that the Son of God made what we are his own so that what he is by nature as a human person in communion with God, as God becomes ours in him by grace through our union with him. Here the patristic principle, taken from Irenaeus, Origen, and Gregory of Nazianzus, finds its place: what is assumed is redeemed. The stress in atonement is rightly placed first of all on the Word becoming flesh, and thus for all flesh, before it is placed on the cross.

In order to protect this mystery the Greek fathers, under the influence of Cyril of Alexandria especially, developed the twin doctrines of *anhypostasis* and *enhypostasis*. The hypostatic union, the doctrine that Jesus Christ was to be understood in terms of the personal and particular union of God and humankind, is the personal union that takes place when the one person of the Son assumes human nature into himself and thus into his divine nature. The union of divine and human natures is entirely the act of God in becoming a man. The result is that the Son of God exists as the man Jesus, son of Mary, in the integrity of his human agency. Apart from this act of God in becoming human, however, Jesus would not have existed at all. Thus the fully human life of Jesus must be regarded as grounded in the act of the Word of God becoming flesh. The human life of Jesus does not have an independent existence apart from the divine *assumptio carnis*. The doctrine of the anhypostasis asserts that Christ's human nature has its reality only in union with God, having no independent existence or subsistence apart from the incarnation. Christ's human personhood is human nature, therefore, in communion with God, human being as it was intended by God to be.

The doctrine of the enhypostasis asserts that Christ's human nature was nevertheless a real and specific existence in which Jesus had a fully human mind, will, and body. This means that we must think of the incarnation in terms not of God in humankind, but of God *as* a particular man, yet not ceasing to be God even while being wholly and actually that man. In sum: the human nature of Jesus Christ was enhypostatic in the Word. Jesus Christ the Word of God was really human, a man, at once the one and the many. In traditional language (inclusive language does not allow the point to be made as clearly), he was both man and a man, representing all humanity in the singularity of his specific, individuated manhood.[6] Thus we must not speak of the incarnation and the atonement as two actions, one of God and the other of the man Jesus. We must speak rather of the

---

6. See T. F. Torrance, *Conflict and Agreement in the Church: Vol. 1, Order and Disorder.* (London: Lutterworth Press, 1959), 238–62.

one action of the "God-man," maintaining the unity of his person, in which grace is understood in terms of Christ's human as well as his divine nature.[7] This means that the hypostatic union is to be understood not just in terms of incarnation, but also soteriologically in terms of the reconciliation between God and humankind in the unity of his person, while reconciliation is to be understood not just in terms of the cross, but also in terms of the incarnation.[8]

Consequently, everything has changed because God has come to us as a particular human being, into whose humanity we are incorporated through union with him. What does that involve?

1. His authority is primary. As such, Jesus Christ the Lord casts down every idolatrous claim to ultimate authority. There is no power in the world, no regime, no religious or political authority, no economic order, no worldly dominion, and no claim to an equal saving revelation of God that stands above Jesus Christ and his lordship. None can claim from us a loyalty that supersedes, contradicts, or compromises our loyalty to Christ. Humanness, we can say, is to be found nowhere else than in Jesus Christ. According to the Theological Declaration of Barmen: "Jesus Christ, as he is attested for us in Holy Scripture, is the one Word of God which we have to hear and which we have to trust and obey in life and in death."[9] We, the church, serve Jesus Christ, though his lordship is inclusive in its command "that at the name of Jesus every knee should bend, in heaven and on earth and under the earth, and every tongue should confess that Jesus Christ is Lord, to the glory of God the Father" (Phil. 2:10–11). It is in this service that we have our human identity and destiny: "Those who want to save their life will lose it, and those who lose their life for my sake will find it" (Matt. 16:25). It is on this ground, and on this ground alone, that there is a basis for ministry that is properly grounded in the reality and truth that it attests.

2. The incarnation of Jesus Christ discloses the only path to God, and he is thus alone our human destiny. John 14:6 has been taken very seriously by the church in its reflection of the mediation of Christ: "No one comes to the Father except through me." This is both an absolute claim and a singular statement of authority and access. In the face of today's religious

---

7. T. F. Torrance, *Theology in Reconstruction* (Grand Rapids: Eerdmans, 1965), 183.

8. For a fuller statement of these points in a wider christological context, see Andrew Purves, "The Christology of T. F. Torrance," in *The Promise of Trinitarian Theology: Theologians in Dialogue with T. F. Torrance*, ed. Elmer Colyer (Lanham, Md.: Rowman and Littlefield, 2001), 51–80.

9. The Theological Declaration of Barmen is found in *The Book of Confessions*, Presbyterian Church (U.S.A.), 2002, 8.11.

pluralism this affirmation may seem offensive. We should certainly respect all religious viewpoints and treat all persons of whatever creed with dignity. But Christian faith as expressed through the creeds and confessions of the church makes a singular claim for Jesus Christ that cannot be compromised without undoing the gospel itself—because of who he is. Here we must speak of truth. He alone is the mediator between the Creator and the creation, between God and a sinful humanity; he reveals the Father and does God's work for us and among us; and at the last he brings us home to communion with the Father in union with himself through the Holy Spirit. All other paths to God, no matter how apparently pious, are inadequate, are ultimately not saving, and, indeed, are ultimately deadly, leading to judgment. This singular claim is not made on behalf of the church, or any theological school, or system of doctrine, but is made by the New Testament on behalf of Jesus Christ, who makes it for himself. Especially in the *ego eimi* claims, for example, Jesus appropriated the name of God given to Moses at Exodus 3:14: "I am the light of the world"; "I am the bread of life"; "I am the resurrection and the life"; "I am the vine"; "I am the way, the truth, and the life"; and so on. Supremely at John 14:10, "I am in the Father and the Father is in me," we see that the "I am" of Jesus is grounded in the mutual indwelling of the Father and the Son in one another.[10] It is on the basis of this mutual indwelling that the incarnate Son is, in the flesh of his humanity, the way to the Father through our union with him. It is precisely this incarnational soteriological grace of the gospel that the *homoousion* of the Nicene Creed was inserted to protect.

In view of this christological concentration one might object that knowledge about God does come to us on occasion through our experience of God's works in the created order. Paul, for example, claims that "ever since the creation of the world God's eternal power and divine nature, invisible though they are, have been understood and seen through the things he has made" (Rom. 1:20). Confessing Jesus' incarnation and atonement as the only path to God is not to deny the existence of partial intimations of God outside Jesus Christ. Our experience of living in the world will surely reflect something, however dimly, of this world's creator, but intimations are no substitute for the saving proclamation of the gospel, and that in Christ we encounter the definitive revelation of God by which we are able to sort out truth from falsehood in these other dim and partial apprehensions. John Calvin, for example, paints a vivid picture of the way the bibli-

---

10. T. F. Torrance, *The Christian Doctrine of God: One Being, Three Persons* (Edinburgh: T. & T. Clark, 1966), 124.

cal testimony to Christ clarifies and sorts out the blurred confusion of prior intimations of God:

> Just as old or bleary-eyed men and those with weak vision, if you thrust before them a most beautiful volume, even if they recognize it to be some sort of writing, yet can scarcely construe two words, but with the aid of spectacles will begin to read distinctly; so Scripture, gathering up the otherwise confused knowledge of God in our minds, having dispersed our dullness, clearly shows us the true God.[11]

3. Jesus' death reveals the depth of God's love for sinners. The gospel is about the love of God. Too often, we have placed love behind law, or made the love of God conditional upon our own acts. This is demonstrated, for example, in the Western *ordo salutis* by the primacy of law and nature over grace, and where relationship with God is construed in contractual terms with ensuing legal requirements and conditions.[12] The atonement is not the condition for the love of God, it is the consequence of the love of God. "God so loved the world . . ." (John 3:16). First there is the gospel of the love of God, and only consequently the response that we make. As Calvin so firmly insisted, it is God's forgiveness that conditions our repentance, God's grace that calls for our obedience, and God's love that enables our faithfulness.[13] I will shortly develop the themes of the grace and love of God more fully.

4. Christ's bodily resurrection shatters the powers of sin and death. In the resurrection, life conquers death and vanquishes evil. Even hell itself cannot hold the Lord of life, for he rose again on the third day. The resurrection of Christ is affirmed by the church to be a bodily resurrection. We should not be in doubt that in the bodily resurrection we confront a great mystery. It is spiritual, certainly, for the resurrected body is a *spiritual* body (1 Cor. 15:44). But as such it is the resurrection of the *body*— there is a future for the material life we live on earth. To think of the resurrection only metaphorically is to shatter the gospel, reducing it to an idea only. In the continuity between Christ's earthly body of flesh and blood and his glorious, resurrected body, we discern that God's final plan

---

11. John Calvin, *Institutes of the Christian Religion*, ed. John T. McNeill; trans. Ford Lewis Battles; 2 vols. (Philadelphia: Westminster, 1960), 1.6.1.

12. See Alan J. Torrance, *Persons in Communion: An Essay on Trinitarian Description and Human Participation* (Edinburgh: T. & T. Clark, 1996), 59–60.

13. Calvin, *Inst.* 3.3.20.

is not to discard and abandon this creation, but to renew, perfect, and redeem it in glory. For this reason, Christians take creation seriously even as we look for a new heaven and a new earth. In union with Christ we, in the wholeness of personhood—body and soul and spirit—anticipate in hope the new life in communion with God.

This is surely significant, for both hope and a future for creation are legitimate themes in pastoral theology. As we must take seriously Christ's incarnate particularity as Jesus of Nazareth, son of Mary, likewise we must take the created order seriously as the place where God is really known and where Christian faith is lived out. This important point about the Christian understanding of creation shapes the church's use of knowledge drawn from the experimental and social sciences. It means that pastoral theology cannot elide the social sciences, for Christian faith and ministry never exist apart from or independently of actual people in the world. Pastoral theology must be clear that the gospel and not the social sciences provides the foundation for pastoral work, all the while recognizing that the social sciences have much to teach concerning our understanding of and response to the people in our pastoral charge. It is unacceptable to be in ministry without a working knowledge of people. On what basis, or according to what kind of a relationship, however, do we proceed to speak of Christian faith and social sciences sharing in a common task? Addressing that issue and answering that question remain always part of the subject matter of this discipline.

The Ministry of the Trinity

The doctrine of the Trinity does not just tell us about God. It is the basic framework of meaning within which we live our lives as Christians. Christian speech about God as Trinity attempts to express the mystery of who God is as God is self-given to be known by us in, through, and as Jesus Christ and in the Holy Spirit, and as such it brings us into communion with God. Abstract though our attempts to speak of the Trinity of God sometimes can be, it is important to keep in mind that the subject matter is God in action. The Christian doctrine of God is inherently dynamic, not static; actual, not speculative; relational, not impersonal; historical, not metaphysical. The doctrine of the Trinity is the conceptual framework within which we get a correct theological perspective on Jesus Christ, the *missio Dei*. That is, the emphasis is placed on Jesus Christ as God, and on his significance for our understanding of God and God's acts in him and through him on our behalf. Pastoral theology has in view who God is and what God wills to be for us: God's care of ourselves brought by God into knowledge of God as a God of love, and of our being in intimate relation with God and with one another, the fruit of which is our being as persons. All of this is another way of following the order and meaning of the apostolic benediction: "The grace of the Lord Jesus Christ, and the love of God, and the communion of the Holy Spirit, be with you all." In this we emphasize the economic or evangelical order in which the doctrine of the Trinity is embedded implicitly for our knowing of God, who is known explicitly as the Father, the Son, and the Holy Spirit.[14]

Our exploration of the mystery of human life and experience, the purpose and meaning of faith, and the proper understanding of the call to discipleship are set in the context of the identity, purpose, and acts of God. In this way theology and experience come together in the expression of Christian life. This is not an abstraction but an experienced and known relation of God with us, and of us in God. In this way the doctrine of the Trinity is the grammar of all talk of God, every theological understanding of Christian ministry, and all attempts to apprehend the nature of the Christian life.

Two core theological assertions regarding the doctrine of the Trinity should be made before we discuss the theology of the benediction: (1) Christian knowledge of God is Trinitarian knowledge, and (2) the doctrine of the Trinity has at its core the act of God, and is therefore a practical knowledge of God.

1. The doctrine of the Trinity refers accurately, appropriately, and singularly to God. Without the doctrine of the Trinity there is no Christian knowledge of God as God, and Christian faith, worship, and practice lose all groundedness and coherence in God and fall apart. Karl Barth answered the question: "Who is God?" with the reply: "It is He who gives Himself to humanity as Trinity."[15] Either the doctrine of the Trinity is a true way to speak of God as God—indeed, the only way to speak of God, as God gives himself to be known in and through Jesus Christ—or else we do not know who God is and we have no basis to assume that God is like Jesus. If the latter were the case, Christianity would lose all transcendent reference and be viewed consequently as a speculative or symbolic system of meaning and ethics with no revealed basis in or experience of the reality of God.

---

14. Torrance, *Christian Doctrine of God*, 50ff.

15. Karl Barth, *Church Dogmatics*, I/1, ed. G. W. Bromiley and T. F. Torrance, trans. G. W. Bromiley, rev. ed. (Edinburgh: T. & T. Clark, 1975), 489.

2. Perhaps surprisingly, although I make the point repeatedly in the argument that follows, the doctrine of the Trinity is a *practical* doctrine in the most basic meaning of that word: it has to do with action. It refers us to the acting God, and therefore to a basis for our action in God; or as Paul would more familiarly put it, the Christian life is lived *en Christou*, in Christ. Of particular interest for pastoral theology, we find here a properly rooted basis in God for what it means to live as persons. "Persons" is not a surrogate word for the outmoded generic "man," but rather refers to our being in the image of God as that image is re-created in and through Jesus Christ to be our participation in the communion of love between the Father and the Son in the unity of the Spirit. In general, the doctrine of the Trinity is inherently a practical theology, for knowledge of God is knowledge of the God who acts. If God did not and does not act, we have no way of knowing anything about God, and neither, I must insist, would we know the truth concerning ourselves as other than mere material creatures trapped in the isolation of our autonomy. Thus there can be no Christian practical theology, no theology for Christian action, and no understanding of action in God that is not a Trinitarian theology.

The Grace of the Lord Jesus Christ

Grace and love are the two most dangerous abstract nouns in Christian discourse because they carry so much of the power and truth of the gospel that when misunderstood or misrepresented they have the capacity to damage Christian faith and life. Further, because of their common currency in Western culture, no doubt in large part due to the Christian heritage, it is assumed that we know what each word means when we use these words with regard to Christian faith and life. Dietrich Bonhoeffer taught that grace apart from Jesus Christ is no grace at all, in fact, it is cheap grace, "grace as a doctrine, a principle, a system."[16] By this, Bonhoeffer alerted us to the danger of understanding *grace* as an abstract noun. When not specifically anchored in the actuality of the gospel, grace and love become unhinged from the reality that gives them meaning and truth.

Jesus Christ is the actuality of God—"in him the whole fullness of deity dwells bodily" (Col. 2:9)—and as such he is the reality of grace. But this does not mean that he is to be apprehended over and against the Father and the Holy Spirit. The grace of the Lord Jesus Christ is the grace of

---

16. Dietrich Bonhoeffer, *The Cost of Discipleship*, trans. R. H. Fuller (London: SCM, 1959), 35.

God, from the Father, through the Son, and in the Holy Spirit, and is not something apart from the whole act and being of the Trinity. Grace implies both the whole of God and the full message of the gospel. The grace of the Lord Jesus Christ is the mission of God to save.

God's grace is the key signature of the gospel, the message of the coming of God in the flesh into the world specifically in and as Jesus for a saving purpose. Grace means Jesus; grace is Jesus. He is *Emmanuel*, for he is God with us. But more, he is also "*Yeshua*, meaning *Yahweh-Saviour*, for 'he shall save his people from their sins'" (Matt. 1:21).[17] Thus the incarnation directly implies the atonement, and there is no atonement without the incarnation; otherwise God has not come among and dealt with us, and done so precisely in and as this man. Thus Jesus is worshiped as *Iesous Kyrios*, Jesus Lord. Grace has no Christian meaning apart from this confession.

Coming as Emmanuel who is Savior, Jesus lived the singular human life as it was intended by God in filial obedience and love toward both God and those he came to and lived among, though his own people did not accept him (John 1:11). His life was lived "full of grace and truth" (John 1:14). The manner and nature of his life led to his death. While his was on one level an ordinary though violent human death, on another level, because of who he was and because of what occurred on the third day, his death was quickly seen to be redemptive, as God's act to forgive and to save. While no one account of the atonement has ever been normatively identified in Christian doctrinal history, the vindication of the life and death of Jesus as an atonement for sin was nevertheless a primary meaning of the resurrection. Through the lens of the resurrection, his life and death was read back to be fraught with divine, and therefore saving, significance. As T. F. Torrance has observed: "The confession of the Deity of Christ was soteriologically rooted and evangelically evoked, for the death of Jesus together with his resurrection from the grave showed him to be the power of the living God over life and death and demonstrated his identity as the transcendent Lord and Saviour of the world."[18] Because Jesus is Lord it was seen by the church then that God had really come to earth, becoming passible as he entered into the ghastly plight of our human life unto death under the holy judgment of God.

Because he took on all flesh, and because the range of his atonement includes all things, we, and the creation of which we are a part, having no hope, now have a future that is entirely God's doing. Thus the atonement

17. T. F. Torrance, *Christian Doctrine of God*, 51.
18. Ibid., 52.

has a past and a future reference. For Jesus Christ comes not just as one who forgives, but also as one who restores us to a new relationship with the Father. It is not yet the atonement that our sins are given; we must still be restored to communion with God, to a new and hitherto and otherwise unavailable at-one-ment. In this way the grace of God does a new thing: it opens the kingdom of God, that is, communion with God, to all who are in union with Christ.

Grace, then, is (a) tied specifically to Jesus Christ; and as such (b) understood as the nature of God's operation by which we are saved and restored to communion with God. From this we see that "grace" is inherently a theological word that characterizes God's reconciling, forgiving, and communion-restoring love toward us. Paul therefore testifies to "the good news of God's grace" (Acts 20:24). It is good news or gospel because it is entirely unearned or unmerited, the result of God's sovereign and unconditioned choice to act freely and objectively in Jesus Christ and through the Holy Spirit.[19] According to James D. G. Dunn, Paul's understanding of the gospel as a gospel of grace arose out of his own experience and led to his view of God as generous and forgiving and to his perception of grace as God's free acceptance that transformed, enriched, and commissioned him.[20] Grace is God's saving action in history, meaning in effect "God's purpose of election" (Rom. 9:11) being fulfilled in, through, and as Jesus of Nazareth.

Grace does not leave us passive and without responsibility, however. In grace (*charis*) the Holy Spirit, who is the "Spirit of grace" (Heb. 10:29), gives to each Christian his or her particular grace-gift (*charisma*), which is to be expressed in thankfulness (*eucharistia*) or gratitude in actual Christian service and ministry. The more literal translation of Hebrews 12:28 reads, "Let us have grace [*charin*] [rather than 'let us give thanks'] so that we may offer service well-pleasing to God." John Calvin introduces an indicative rendering of this verse that is congruent with the main idea, taking it to mean that we have been given the grace that enables us to worship and serve God faithfully.[21] Empowered by grace-giftedness, the

---

19. Thus Alan Richardson, *An Introduction to the Theology of the New Testament* (London: SCM, 1958), 283. The discussion at this point is indebted to Richardson's brief review of grace in the New Testament, 278–79.

20. James D. G. Dunn, *Unity and Diversity in the New Testament: An Inquiry into the Character of Earliest Christianity*, 2d ed. (London: SCM, 1990), 190.

21. *Calvin's Commentaries: The Epistle of Paul the Apostle to the Hebrews and the Epistles of Peter,* ed. David W. Torrance and Thomas F. Torrance; trans. William B. Johnson (Edinburgh: Oliver and Boyd, 1963), 203.

Christian life is the thankful response to the glory of God. The goal of the gospel is that we live lives of fruitful and joyful discipleship in the power of the good news. This is the continuing historical significance of grace.

This understanding of the "grace of the Lord Jesus Christ" has two defining implications for pastoral work (I will develop them more fully in chapter 8). First, the indicative of grace means that pastoral work must give the highest priority to the kerygmatic affirmation "You are forgiven." The whole movement of the gospel pulls in this direction. This was Thurneysen's primary point in his *Theology of Pastoral Care*, where he developed an understanding of the pastoral conversation as moving a person from the ground of his or her own human experience to the ground of the Word of God. The conversation does not become pastoral until that shift is made. For Thurneysen, the actual content of this ground was the proclamation of grace, meaning forgiveness of sins through Jesus Christ. The goal of pastoral work, he contended, was a restored communion with God.

Second, pastoral work should be concerned to assist people to identify grace in their lives in its specificity as forgiveness of sins and to equip them to be faithful in the thankful response of Christian discipleship. Far too often pastoral work has been interpreted in terms of responding to needs, hurts, and all kinds of personal problems, and has left out the concern to call people to lives of fruitful and joyful discipleship in the power of the good news. But pastoral work must not only respond to the negative; it must act also as the midwife of the positive, for we have received "grace upon grace" (John 1:16), meaning that all things pertaining to the Christian life are based only on grace. Pastoral work has its marching orders from the great evangelical truths of justification and sanctification, although little contemporary literature in pastoral theology would indicate that this is the case.

The Love of God

The familiar words, "God so loved the world . . ." (John 3:16), characterize the ministry of God, revealing the divine nature and purpose. They express the confidence of Christians in the ground of the gospel in God's love. The ministry of God arises out of God's very being, for "God is love" (1 John 4:16). God's love for us is not a casual or accidental divine virtue, but rather as God's act within history through Jesus Christ, it expresses the being of God who loves eternally within the communion of the Father, the Son, and the Holy Spirit, one being, three persons. Our discussion of the love of God, then, leads us to consider (1) the relations between the

Father and the Son in the unity of the Holy Spirit; (2) Jesus' ministry as the revelation of the love of God; (3) the Christian experience of the love of God through union with Christ; and (4) Christ's love commandment.

1. There is an unbroken and eternal relationship in the Spirit between Jesus Christ and God upon which the New Testament builds. Over and against any thought that the church or human faith should occupy center stage in Christian faith, the New Testament posits the centrality of the Father-Son relationship. Everything in Christian faith and life arises out of this relationship, sealed in the unity of the Holy Spirit. This relationship is described as the *agape* with which the Father loved the Son even before the foundation of the world (John 17:24). Jesus Christ is revealed as *God's* Son, showing thereby that God's fatherhood and Christ's sonship belong to God's eternal being. That is, fatherhood and sonship have an ontological basis, and the relationship between God the Father and God the Son is inseparable. T. F. Torrance makes the point:

> Knowledge of the Son and knowledge of the Father are locked into each other, so that it is in and through the unique Sonship of Christ that the Fatherhood of God is made known as the ultimate Nature and Being of God, and is thus given supreme prominence, even in relation to himself, in all that Jesus proclaimed and taught about God as the one Lord of heaven and earth whom we are bound to love unreservedly with all our heart and soul and strength and mind.[22]

So it is that the Son alone "exegetes" (*exegesato*) the Father, for the Son is close to the Father's heart (John 1:18) and is loved by the Father (5:20), knows the Father as the Father knows the Son (10:15). Indeed, the Father and the Son are one (10:30) so that whoever has seen Jesus Christ has seen the Father (14:9).

The love that flows between the Father and the Son in the unity of the Holy Spirit reveals that God is a God of love within the communion of the Holy Trinity, both loving and being loved. It is this loving and being loved that is the ground of the ministry of God in and through Jesus Christ for our salvation. It is the basis for Christian confidence in God, for who God is toward us in and as Jesus Christ God is antecedently and eternally in himself, the God who loves and is loved. God, therefore, is always the God who loves and is loved within the ineffable mystery of the Trinity, and who loves his creation out of the eternal plenitude of that same self-love, and who can

---

22. T. F. Torrance, *Christian Doctrine of God*, 56.

no more cease to love than he can cease to be God or act toward us in a way other than God has acted toward us in and through Jesus Christ.[23] Nothing, then, "will be able to separate us from the love of God in Christ Jesus our Lord" (Rom. 8:39). This confidence has its ground and basis in the being and acts of God, as the content of the gospel bears witness.

2. Jesus' ministry is the incarnation of God's love. Interestingly, there is only one reference in the Synoptic Gospels to the love of God—at Luke 11:42—yet the Gospel accounts are replete with instances of God's mercy and compassion in Jesus Christ in and through which the love of God is actual and concrete.[24] We need only mention Jesus' healing of the sick, his companionship with those cast out from society and synagogue, his sense of oneness with the poor, and his life laid down for sinners to make the point. He lived what he taught—that he loved them, and that therefore God loved them with a power and authority that brought them into God's company.

We see something of the meaning of this in a brief look at the compassion of Jesus in the Synoptic Gospels. On nine occasions Jesus acted with compassion (*splanchnizomai*—a verb!);[25] on three occasions he used compassion as the turning point in parables.[26] In each case his compassion was not just an emotion of solidarity or shared pain, but involved an act of redemptive ministry, as often as not involving personal physical contact. The accounts indicate that in compassion Jesus broke through the barriers of social and religious convention in order to bring God's healing care to those in need. In doing so, Jesus clearly ministered in a way that was appropriate to each person, circumstance, and context. Just as "Jesus had compassion on them," so he instructed his followers to "go and do likewise."

The love of God is not an abstract ethical theory, but a conclusion rightly drawn from the specific teaching and events of Jesus' ministry. Christian faith asserts, therefore, (a) that God is none other than who God is in Jesus Christ toward us—a God of love; and (b) our experience of God toward us in Jesus Christ as a God of love is who God is eternally as God. There is no other God, no hidden God, no secret God lurking behind the facade of God's love in Jesus Christ, ready to judge us with law rather than love, or even worse, with capricious disregard for justice. For

23. Ibid., 59.
24. For an extended discussion see Andrew Purves, *The Search for Compassion: Spirituality and Ministry* (Louisville, Ky.: Westminster/John Knox Press, 1989), especially chapters 1 and 2.
25. Mark 1:40–45; 6:30–44; 8:1–10; 9:14–29 and parallels; Matt. 9:35–38; 20:29–34; Luke 7:11–17.
26. Matt. 18:23–35; Luke 10:30–37; 15:11–32.

even when we stand under the judgment of God, we do so through the love that God has for us in Jesus Christ, who died for us and rose in power for us to bring many sons and daughters to glory. As the writer to the Ephesians put it, God "has made known to us the mystery of his will, according to his good pleasure that he set forth in Christ, as a plan (*oikonomia*) for the fullness of time, to gather up all things in him" (1:9–10).

3. Next we consider the Christian experience of the love of God. According to Alan Richardson, "in the whole New Testament view the Christian experience of *agape* is the result of man's being taken up into the unity of the Godhead through incorporation into Christ."[27] The Father's love for the Son is the love that Christians share in through their union with Christ. This love is not possible within the natural capacities of human experience and will, but it is entirely the result of abiding in Christ, the true vine (John 15:1–11). The Christian life and its possibility are appropriately summed up in the conjunction of the indicative and the imperative in John 15:9: "As the Father has loved me, so I have loved you; abide in my love." God's love profoundly marks out the framework for understanding and living Christian faith. The ministry of God's love means that through union with Christ we not only stand under grace, but also are to consider ourselves enfolded into the communion of love that flows eternally within and among the Father, the Son, and the Holy Spirit. Through grace we are saved by and for the love of God.

Knowing that we are loved by God, I suggest, is primarily a cognitive recognition that leads to trust rather than a feeling of being loved, though without doubt that is also part of it. The reason for this emphasis is that the truth of our being loved by God lies in what God has done objectively for us in and through Jesus Christ, in which event and its concomitant promises we place our trust, irrespective of any passing affective state. We might put it this way: knowing God's love for us and our abiding in that love are the knowledge of the truth of our baptism.

4. Finally, it is important to note that abiding in God's love is directly related to obeying Christ's commandment that we love one another in a way that is similar to the love Christ has for us (John 15:12). Love, in other words, is most certainly a far greater thing than an emotion; it is an act of will, even of obedience. The only ground for its possibility, of course, is already clear to us, for it is the fruit of our union with Christ. We in turn can be commanded to be lovers because we have been chosen and appointed by Jesus Christ to be fruit bearers (John 15:16). Thus the relationship

---

27. Richardson, *Introduction to the Theology of the New Testament*, 259.

between the Father and the Son in the unity of the Holy Spirit, into which we are incorporated by grace through union with Christ, is the ground for the relationships that must now obtain among humankind. How is this new way of life possible for those who fall short of the glory of God? The grace of the Lord Jesus Christ and the love of God lead irresistibly to the reality and empowerment of the communion of the Holy Spirit in which everything I have said thus far concerning the ministry of God becomes ours in an actual way for and in the living of the Christian life.

The Communion of the Holy Spirit

In the context of the ministry of God, the Holy Spirit is the personal presence of God by whom God brings us into communion with himself through relationship with Jesus Christ. According to Karl Barth, the Holy Spirit "is the power in which Jesus Christ is alive among [people] and makes them His witnesses."[28] Christian doctrine teaches that the work of the Holy Spirit is a Christ-related event; as such it is a God-glorifying, person-empowering, and church/mission-creating event. Because the Holy Spirit binds us to Jesus Christ, we are bound by the same Spirit to share in Christ's communion with and mission from the Father.[29] The Spirit calls the church into existence to be a community of worship and ministry through our union with Christ. Thus to speak of the communion of the Holy Spirit is to refer to the communion-creating work of the Holy Spirit—communion with the Father through our Spirit-led union with Christ, and consequently communion with one another as we are formed into the missionary body of Christ, the church. For this reason we do not speak of communion *in* the Holy Spirit, but the communion *of* the Holy Spirit, meaning by this, communion *in Christ*. There is no dissociating of the Holy Spirit from Jesus Christ; rather, in T. F. Torrance's felicitous image, the Holy Spirit has a diaphanous self-effacing nature,[30] showing us the Son and joining us to him, so that in and through the Son we have communion with and serve the Father.

In reflecting on the communion of the Holy Spirit as a part of our understanding of the ministry of God in the context of the apostolic benediction, we must consider two points: (1) the work of the Holy Spirit in our union

28. Barth, *Church Dogmatics*, IV.2, G. W. Bromiley and T. F. Torrance, trans. G. W. Bromiley (Edinburgh: T. & T. Clark, 1956), 323.

29. This language is taken from James B. Torrance, *Worship, Community and the Triune God of Grace* (Carlisle: Paternoster, 1996), 19.

30. T. F. Torrance, *Christian Doctrine of God*, 66.

with Christ, which means our communion with God; (2) our communion with one another.[31]

1. When the Christian tradition therefore teaches the communion of the Holy Spirit, it means union through the Holy Spirit with Jesus Christ himself. Here I introduce a theme that recurs throughout the book. Union with Christ is not an imitation of Christ, a life of following the example of Jesus. Rather, the Christian life as taught by Paul, for example, is a participation in Christ's righteousness, holiness, and mission through the bond of the Holy Spirit. Through the communion of the Holy Spirit the Christian life is *participatio Christi*, not *imitatio Christi*. Our lives must be redirected and rerelated by God so that our being and becoming Christian is first of all a divine initiative and not something that can be worked out through our heightened religiosity, morality, activity, or spirituality. As in being forgiven, so also in being and becoming saints, God in Christ through the Holy Spirit provides for us. We are conjoined to Christ by the unilateral work of God through the Holy Spirit—in what Calvin called a "mystical union" (*Institutes* 3.11.10). By the bond of the Holy Spirit we become one with him and thereby partake of his benefits.[32] Calvin's term "mystical union" parallels Paul's "in Christ," meaning that God through the Holy Spirit saves us by engrafting us into Christ.

Understanding the Christian life as a union with Christ entails the Spirit-created participation of the saints in his righteousness and holiness. Through the work of the Holy Spirit Christ brings us into union with himself to share in his own life before and from the Father. The Holy Spirit is the "bond"—Calvin's word, ambiguous as it is—by which Christ unites us effectually to himself and enables us to share in that which is his by nature. Our being bonded to Jesus Christ is a miracle wrought by the Spirit of God.

2. By the Spirit, in union with Christ and in communion with the Father, we have communion with one another. Christ cannot be our savior nor God our Father unless the church is our community of faith. The communion of the Holy Spirit means also the communion of the body of Christ, and as such a sharing in Christ's mission from the Father for the sake of the world. To belong to Christ's fellowship means to share in his

31. For a full account see Andrew Purves and Charles Partee, *Encountering God: Christian Faith in Turbulent Times* (Louisville, Ky.: Westminster John Knox Press, 2000), chapter 5, from which some of this material is taken.

32. For discussions see Charles Partee, "Calvin's Central Dogma Again," *The Sixteenth Century Journal* 18, no. 2 (summer 1987): 191–92; and Dennis E. Tamburello, *Union with Christ: John Calvin and the Mysticism of St. Bernard* (Louisville, Ky.: Westminster John Knox Press, 1994).

ministry. Therefore, to share in the communion of the Holy Spirit is to share in the life and ministry of the church.

Pluralistic individuality can confuse our understanding of the church. Theologically, it is wrong to think that communion through the Holy Spirit with the ascended Lord Jesus Christ is possible without being necessarily bonded together with one another as the one, holy, catholic, and apostolic church. To assume one can be Christian without attending church and participating in the life and mission of the fellowship is to misunderstand the meaning of being joined to Jesus Christ. Communion with Christ involves communion with one another and sharing together in Christ's mission to and for the world. While Christianity provides a deeply personal relationship with God, Christianity is not to be construed as individualistic and as an essentially private experience. Christian faith is lived as a communion in the body of Christ. Christians are joined to Christ and to one another at the deepest levels of human existence. The church is not a free association of voluntary individuals, but the joyful community of those whom Christ claims as his own, who in the Holy Spirit joins them to himself, and who live together as disciples under an obedience that is true freedom.

Over forty years ago, Emil Brunner made much of the distinction between what he called "*ekklesia*" (the Greek word for church) and "*ecclesia*" (the Latin word for church).[33] By "*ecclesia*" he intended the church as an institution—the church largely of the West over the last fifteen hundred years; by "*ekklesia*" he intended the church as the fellowship of the saints in fellowship with Jesus Christ—the church of Paul. The *ekklesia* is the true church, according to Brunner, the community that lives from a living experience of Christ and that is determined by its *pistis*, its faith. Ecclesiology is understood primarily in terms of Christology as a community-creating encounter. Brunner is helpful here, although perhaps rather rigid in his bifurcation between fellowship and institution. The point is this: the communion of the Holy Spirit is a dynamic and living relationship with Christ that can never be separated from the fellowship that being in Christ creates. The church as an institution is derivative and exists at the service of the fellowship in faithfulness to Christ.

As the body of Christ the Holy Spirit joins us to Christ to share not only in his communion with the Father, but also in his mission from the Father. The communion of the body is the church that shares in the continuing work of Jesus Christ for the sake of the world. Rooted and grounded in love, and growing up in every way into him who is the head (Eph. 3:17;

33. Brunner, *Dogmatics*, 3:19–20.

4:13), we share also in Christ's ministry from the Father. Since piety and action are intimately related, Christian discipleship is understood both intensively and extensively as communion with God and as service of God in the life of the world. United with Christ through the bond of the Holy Spirit, the church is driven by the two imperatives, to worship and to serve.

At John 17:18 Jesus prays regarding the church, "As you have sent me into the world, so I have sent them into the world." Likewise at 20:21 we read, "As the Father has sent me, so I send you." For John, the founding of the church is deeply bound up with the meaning of the resurrection of Jesus. On the evening of the first Easter, the risen Jesus came to the house where the disciples had locked themselves in for fear of attack and arrest, and appeared to them. This is John's setting for the commissioning of the church. For John, the immediate consequence of Easter is not merely the forming of a religious fellowship that is in communion with the risen Jesus. The risen Jesus appears to give them his peace, but only as a prelude to their great charge of being sent out to continue Christ's ministry in and for the world. Thus there is no proper knowledge of the risen Lord that does not involve a commission to go forth into the world in the name of Jesus. We might put it this way: there is no proper knowledge of the risen Christ that does not involve the commission to be Christ's disciple. The ministry of Christ, sent from the Father, becomes, through the bond of the Holy Spirit that unites us to Christ, the evangelical and missionary ministry of the church. The church of the Easter gospel is also and necessarily the church with a gospel mission. This, then, is part of the meaning of the communion of the Holy Spirit: in union with Christ, the church is given as mission from beyond herself. It is not the world in its own analysis of its needs that sets the agenda for the church, but Jesus Christ in his being sent and sending. In the power of the Spirit and in union with himself, he sends the church out, and the parallel with his own sending by the Father in incarnation and atonement is quite intentional and definitive. God, we can say, is a sending God. It is the job of the church to be the present form of God in Christ in and for the world. It is to this end that the church is given the Holy Spirit, and for this end that the church is the communion of the Holy Spirit. Thus the ministry of God becomes the ministry of the church.

Chapter 3

Jesus, the Apostle and High Priest of Our Confession

Mark well these words: John said, We have presently a sufficient Advocate, whom Paul affirms to sit at the right hand of God the Father, and to be the only Mediator between God and Man. "For he alone (says Ambrose) is our mouth, by whom we speak of God; he is our eyes, by whom we see God, and also our right hand, by whom we offer anything to the Father"; who, unless he make intercession, neither we, neither any of the saints, may have any society or fellowship with God.

John Knox[1]

Introduction: How Is Ministry Gospel?

Given the theological understanding, first, of the nature and content of Christian doctrine and, second, of the ministry of God, what is the ministry of the church? This is the question that drives pastoral theology to its task. Buried within this question, however, is this theological issue: to understand and engage in ministry without that ministry becoming a new law in which everything is cast back upon us to achieve. How is ministry gospel?

Unless we move beyond the view that ministry is something that we do in response to the gospel, ministry becomes our burden, becoming a duty rather than a joy to perform. The perspective I will develop is that we should think about ministry as empowerment for faithfulness that God does in and through us by *joining us to the faithfulness of Jesus Christ*. Within

---

1. "A Declaration What True Prayer Is," *The Works of John Knox*, collected and edited by David Laing, vol. 3 (New York: AMS, 1966), 97, my own translation into contemporary English.

such empowerment there remains obedience to union with Christ, but now obedience is understood as sharing by the Holy Spirit in Christ's obedience.[2] Pastoral ministry is not something that is first of all up to us to do. Jesus Christ is the primary minister (Heb. 8:2), and our ministry, as I suggested earlier, is derivative and best understood as our participation in his apostolic and priestly ministry.

My goal in this book therefore is to map out the contours of pastoral theology and the practice of ministry *precisely as gospel*, in which ministry is understood not as obligation but as gift, as discipleship in which we bear the easy yoke of Christ, learning from him whose burden is light (Matt. 11:29–30). That is, through union with Christ the church's ministry is participative, according to a christological pattern (*hypodeigma*, John 13:15).

This approach cannot properly be addressed by drawing only from general experience or through a pragmatic sense of what needs to be done or by an appeal to churchly practice. The questions still arise: What it is that the church must do and how is that work to be understood as gospel? Clearly, from all that has been said thus far, Jesus Christ is the hinge on which the argument must turn, or, in a different metaphor, he is the hinge to the door that must open and through which I must walk if I would be faithful in ministry (John 10:7–9). Christological specificity is required to take us beyond either pragmatic or ecclesial practice models of pastoral work, to clarify the nature of pastoral work.

The position for which I argue is this: first, Jesus Christ is himself both God's saving Word of address to humankind, *and* the human response of hearing and receiving that Word and acting in perfect obedience toward God (see John 5:17–47; 10:30; and Heb. 3:2 especially, where Christ is faithful—*piston*—to the one who appointed him). This dynamic twofold nature of Christ's ministry is the heuristic truth embedded within the doctrine of the hypostatic union, in which Jesus Christ is understood to be wholly God and wholly human in the union of his one personhood. I will use this classical doctrine as a basic building block in the construction of pastoral theology. From this, we see that the hypostatic union is inherently a practical doctrine: Jesus Christ is the "place" where the Word and action of God and the word and action of humankind meet in oneness, and is therefore "full of grace and truth" (John 1:14).

Second, Christian faith and life in general, and Christian ministry in particular, are our participation through the Holy Spirit in this twofold

---

2. For a discussion see Andrew Purves and Charles Partee, *Encountering God: Christian Faith in Turbulent Times* (Louisville, Ky.: Westminster John Knox Press, 2000), chapter 9.

ministry of Jesus Christ, where the Word of God is spoken, heard, obeyed, and given back to God in its fullness in fulfillment of its purpose (Isa. 55:11). Thus the church's ministry is inherently an apostolic and priestly ministry because it is a sharing in Christ's ministry, which is itself apostolic and priestly, as Hebrews 3:1 insists. Through our union with Christ, ministry is accordingly shaped to the christological pattern. Thus Jesus' statement at John 14:6, "I am the way, and the truth, and the life," is the singular basis not only for piety and faith, but also for life and ministry, for it is in union with Christ that we can walk the way, know the truth, and live the life of those who serve in the name of Christ. In this way we share in his ministry, in which he ministers the things of God to us and the things of humankind to God, to the glory of the Father and for the sake of the world.

Apart from union with Christ, ministry is cast back upon us to achieve. This is a recipe for failure, for we all fall short of the glory of God. The understanding and practice of pastoral work in this case is a burden too heavy to bear and follows a path that denies the gospel. We do not heal the sick, comfort the bereaved, accompany the lonely, forgive sins, raise up hope of eternal life, or bring people to God on the strength of our piety and pastoral skill. To think that these tasks are ours to perform is not only hubris, but also a recipe for exhaustion and depression in ministry.

We must move away from a pragmatic and needs-assessment perspective of ministry—in which we ask, What should I to do in response to the need before me? and How do I do it?—and toward a perspective rooted entirely in the gospel, in which what we do and how we do it are done in the Spirit through sharing in Christ's own speech and action as the one Word of God and in Christ's own response in filial obedience to the Father. This is the reversal of the approach that moves from ministry that God makes possible, with the responsibility to make it actual left up to us and toward the approach that moves from ministry that God makes actual, our sharing in which ministry makes our ministry possible. It is an approach that is entirely theological, and as such, rooted at all points in the grace of the Lord Jesus Christ, the love of God, and the communion of the Holy Spirit.

Let us now view the tasks of ministry with this in mind. It is not at all obvious today that we have a grasp on those tasks of ministry. The reasons no doubt are many and include the pragmatic and codependent consequences of a consumer-dominated approach to religious life. Ministers want to be liked and needed—nothing wrong with that; but when ministry is organized, often covertly and implicitly, around meeting the felt and expressed needs of others and gaining their approval, the scene is set for serious trouble. It is enough to say that what makes ministry Christian is often highly ambiguous. It is in such a context that a christologically grounded approach to ministry must be earnestly advanced.

Such an approach to ministry is twofold. First, with regard to the minister, christologically grounded ministry must understand and incorporate ways of speaking forth and mediating Jesus Christ, the Word of God, to the people for whom one has pastoral responsibility. Without that, ministry collapses into social work. Second, with regard to those who receive ministry, ministry must include a gospel-based understanding of faith and life in order for them to believe and live more clearly and assuredly in Christ. Otherwise all we encourage is self-help. If there is no word from the Lord, there is really no content to the gospel, and ministry has no sure center in God. And if there is no way given by God to respond to a word from God that is spoken or mediated to the people (consider, for example, the sacraments as the Word of God not spoken but mediated), the people are ultimately cast back upon themselves to do the best they can do in their response. This is a cruel, despairing, and unpastoral thing to do, for it defeats the grace of the gospel at the point where it is needed most of all.

We must now give content to the notion that our ministry is a sharing in Christ's twofold ministry from God and to God. This is especially important in part two, where I discuss the necessary content of pastoral work. To provide this content, however, we can hardly jump from the birth to the meaning of the death of Jesus (his ministry as a preface to the passion) in a soteriologically driven orthodoxy and imagine that in doing so we have taken Jesus of Nazareth seriously as the one who ministered the things of God to humankind and the things of humankind to God in the flesh of his own humanity. For example, despite its protests to the contrary, how easily has orthodox Protestantism slipped in a nearly docetic Christ whose life is reduced to a comma: "born of the Virgin Mary, suffered under Pontius Pilate."

I have argued thus far that generally speaking, ministry is our sharing in the mission of God, for ministry is first of all what God does. The methodological significance of this priority of God's ministry for pastoral theology can hardly be overemphasized. The foundation on which to build pastoral theology must bring the *missio Dei* to expression in an explicit way that both opens up the gospel for our understanding in a faithful way and grounds the church's ministry in a sharing in God's saving and serving ministry in Christ Jesus for us. To do this requires us to go beyond the discussion of Jesus Christ as the mission of God (chapter 2) and turn to consider Christ's twofold ministry in his apostolic mediation from the side of God and his priestly mediation from the side of humankind.

I begin with a discussion of the apostolic and priestly ministry of Christ in order to ground the discussion in the New Testament, for it is appropriate and necessary to consider carefully the biblical basis for the proposed argument. The discussion of the apostolic priesthood of Christ is not theologically idiosyncratic or aberrant, but central and necessary. Christ is indeed a real apostolic high priest, both from God and of humankind; the designation is not metaphorical.[3] I then consider the understanding of the apostolic and priestly ministry of Christ in the thought of representative theologians, past and contemporary, in order to situate the argument firmly within the heritage and development of Christian theology.

The Twofold Ministry of Jesus Christ, the Apostolic Priest

The apostolic and priestly ministry of Jesus Christ is the soteriological center of Christian practical theology. By the terms "the apostolic and priestly ministry of Jesus Christ" I mean the double character of priesthood in general as it is found in the Old Testament and carried into the New. Christ is the apostle of God, the one who utters the Word of God. Christ is also the high priest, who responds to this Word and to God on behalf of the people. By emphasizing the apostolic priesthood in this way, we lay the cornerstone both for a radically reconstructed theology of the church and for pastoral care that is able to bear the full load of the gospel as a gospel of salvation. Through union with Christ, pastoral work has a dynamic, participative doctrinal grounding in which emphasis is properly placed on who God is and what God does for us in, through, and as Jesus Christ. Through our participation in Christ's humanity, the practice of ministry is sharing in the apostolic and priestly ministry of the pastoring God. This recasting of pastoral theology as participation in the ministry of Christ gives the perspective developed here a thoroughgoing soteriological character.

Christian ministry is grounded in the twofold character of Christ's ministry in which through his incarnation he took on our human nature and from within it healed it and made it holy in himself, and which he offers up to God in and through himself on our behalf. As Son of God, Christ

3. Thus Barnabas Lindars, *The Theology of the Letter to the Hebrews* (Cambridge: Cambridge University Press, 1991), 58.

represents God to us. He is the Word of God, Emmanuel. As son of Mary, Christ represents humankind to God. He is the appropriate response to God from the body of the flesh. Christ's ministry in this way is determined by who Christ is in the hypostatic union of his incarnate personhood, as wholly God and wholly human, and what God, the Father of our Lord Jesus Christ, wills in and through him that we should be and do. As the "apostle and high priest of our confession" (Heb. 3:1), Christ, in the unity of his personhood, brings God to us and us to God in a saving work of grace that restores to us the gift of communion with God in which we discover the fullness of our humanity. In this dual action of the one work of incarnation and atonement does our Lord's ministry consist.[4] Because of the centrality of Christ's twofold ministry, the understanding of Christian faith, church, and ministry needs to be thoroughly constructed in the light of the theological testimony to the ministry of Jesus Christ exercised through his vicarious humanity.

Two points should be noted briefly. First, the church's faith in this singular ministry of Jesus Christ presupposes the reality of the incarnation, which in turn presupposes the doctrine of the Trinity. It is only as God with us in a singular and unique way that Christ is also the human for God in a saving way. From beginning to end, from God and as God *and* from humankind and as a human person, salvation is God's work. The gospel stands or falls, then, on the singularity of Christ's soteriological apostolic and priestly sonship in the flesh of our humanity, which is, of course, the point made by the *homoousios to Patri* of the Nicene Creed. Second, it is because Jesus is the human for God that the incarnation becomes wholly redemptive through his active obedience in which he offers us up to God in the flesh of his own humanity through his life of worship, obedience, and filial love. Understood in this way, we take seriously the teaching that no one comes to the Father except through Jesus (John 14:6). We are presented to God by the priestly hand of Christ alone. This is not only a completed past event in the body of the flesh, but is the continuing priestly ministry of Christ in his ascended rule at the right hand of the Father, in which he ever intercedes for us (Rom. 8:34; Heb. 7:25), as we will see more fully in chapter 5.

Second, the danger for orthodoxy is likely always to lie in understanding the incarnation—the "downward" act, as it were—as the whole gospel,

---

4. For standard accounts see James B. Torrance, "The Priesthood of Jesus: A Study in the Doctrine of the Atonement," in *Essays in Christology for Karl Barth*, ed. T. H. L. Parker (London: Lutterworth, 1956) 155–173; James B. Torrance, *Worship, Community and the Triune God of Grace* (Carlisle: Paternoster, 1996), 32–57; and T. F. Torrance, *Royal Priesthood: A Theology of Ordained Ministry*, 2d ed. (Edinburgh: T. & T. Clark, 1993), 1–22.

which undercuts Christ's ministry in our humanity in a docetic way.[5] When we do not understand the incarnation in terms that include the priesthood of Jesus' sacrifice of obedience in the flesh of his humanity, we reject the atonement. Salvation means not just that God is in communion with us and that God has acted in Christ for us, but also that we should be in communion with God. For this, Christ must, from the side of our humanity, be our high priest, offering by his own hand vicariously our human sacrificial response to God, confessing our sin, and living the filial life that God requires. In him and through him in his priestly humanity as the Word or apostle of God we have both the holy Word of God to us *and* the righteous response of humankind to God, the response given by God for us.

Taken together, this twofold ministry of Christ constitutes the double character of priesthood in general as it is found in the Old Testament, and in continuity and discontinuity with which the ministry of Jesus Christ is properly understood. Richard Nelson has shown that priesthood in Israel was a complex matter that from the distant perspective of Western Christianity can at best only be partially understood.[6] It is clear that Israel's priests were both ministers of God's Word and ministers of the altar of sacrifice.[7] Mosaic and Aaronic aspects became one in Christ's priesthood, the former being a mediation of God's Word, and the latter a witness and response to the Word. The priests of Israel ministered at the boundary between God and the community, between the Word of God and the human response, bringing God to the people and the people to God. Having access to holy space and holy tradition, priests also acted both as insulators, protecting the people from God, and as connectors, mediating between the people and God, making religious life possible.[8] Of importance here, as Torrance makes clear, is the subjection of the response to the Word: "The continuance of the sacrificial priesthood of Aaron is dependent on the priestly mediation of Moses and on his unique relation to God."[9] The problems arose for Israel, and would later arise for the church, when liturgy was separated from the Word of God, separated, that

5. John McLeod Campbell makes this claim, recognizing its roots to lie in the deep sense of human religiosity and of our preciousness before God. See *The Nature of the Atonement* (1856; reprint, Edinburgh: Handsel; Grand Rapids: Eerdmans, 1996), 21.

6. Richard D. Nelson, *Raising Up a Faithful Priest: Community and Priesthood in Biblical Theology* (Louisville, Ky.: Westminster John Knox Press, 1993).

7. Ibid., 46. See also T. F. Torrance, *Royal Priesthood*, 3ff.

8. Nelson, *Raising Up a Faithful Priest*, 85.

9. T. F. Torrance, *Royal Priesthood*, 5.

is, from the way in which through the Word God has chosen to address the people, for the response to God itself rests upon the Word of God. This is a very important point, for otherwise the response to God is set upon a merely human religious foundation. It is surely warranted to suggest that such a move is directly contrary to the whole movement of Scripture, wherein God always provides the means of response to God.

In the New Testament, Christ's priesthood in its wider sense means (1) the Word of God addressing us in the incarnate flesh of Jesus of Nazareth, and (2) the human work of Jesus Christ, wholly God, in response in his dealing with the Father on our behalf, as our representative before God. Like the priests of Israel, Jesus stands between God and humankind as the Word of God made flesh and our perfect human response to that Word. The church has insisted that Jesus in this regard is not a kind of third entity between God and humankind—this was the mistake of Arius that prompted the clarifying rebuttal of the Nicene *homoousios to Patri*. Unlike the priests of Israel, Jesus does not stand at the boundary between God and humankind, at a tangential point of connection, for he is wholly of God and wholly of humankind, interpenetrating both the realm of God and the realm of created nature. Christ is not a mathematical point of connection between God and humankind, but a mediator between them as one in being with both God and humankind. This is a significant point of the doctrines of the *homoousion* and the hypostatic union. What had been a two-person office in Israel, prophet and priest, and often broken in their relationships, is now unified in Jesus Christ, and as unified it is healed because the union is a soteriological and personal union. The twofold office of priesthood in Israel is joined in the hypostatic union of his person which is from God and for us, and for God and from us. This is what Hebrews 3:1 means when it refers to him as the apostle and high priest of our profession. He is in himself God's apostolic saving word toward humankind, and the perfect priestly and human obedience to that word. According to T. F. Torrance,

> As Apostle Christ bears witness for God, that He is holy. As High Priest He acknowledges that witness and says Amen to it. Again as Apostle of God He confesses the mercy and grace of God, His will to pardon and reconcile. As High Priest He intercedes for men, and confesses them before the face of God. . . . From the side of God He acts in the steadfastness of divine truth and love in judgment, from the side of man He acts in unswerving obedience to the Father.[10]

10. Ibid., 12, and throughout chapter 1 for what follows.

This priestly response, of course, is offered in an ontological unity of person and act, and the consequence is the cross, in which he bears in his body the terrible fact of our separation from God, which is an act of self-sacrifice in which priest and victim are identical, united in his person. His *homologia* or confession of our sin as apostle and high priest (Heb. 3:1; 4:14; 10:23), as he enters within the veil of the holiness and judgment of God, is a substitutionary atonement, an offering on our behalf in which he the sinless one (Heb. 4:15) bears the judgment of God and confesses our sin before God. This is utterly an act of God's grace and love, because Christ the Son of God offers himself in unfailing obedience from and to the Father, with whom he is unbreakably linked, and in an unbreakable link with us, with whom he chose to join himself in the incarnation. T. W. Manson sums up Christ's priesthood "as his complete self-dedication in unreserved obedience to God his Father and in unlimited love and compassion toward [humankind]."[11]

The completed and continuing unity of the twofold priesthood of Christ becomes, then, the basis for hope (Heb. 6:19), that which the church confesses, in which we trust. Living continually as the Word of God, and as the one who ever makes intercession for us, he is our high priest, both the apostle of God and our advocate (1 John 2:1), who stands in for us, offering us the new life of sharing in his own life before God.

The priesthood of Jesus is a significant biblical category, especially in Hebrews, 1 John 2:1–2, and Romans 8:34, though the whole New Testament doctrine of reconciliation depends upon it. As T. W. Manson observes:

> Here we have the essential characteristics of a perfect high-priesthood: on the one side an unbreakable link with God the Father in the unfailing obedience of the Son; on the other an unbreakable link with his brother men through an unfailing sympathy and understanding. This solidarity with God and man uniquely fits Christ to be the Mediator, to represent God to men and men to God, to make the Holy One of Israel real to his children and to fit those sinful children to enter into the divine presence.[12]

The ministry of Jesus Christ is the practical center of the gospel, on which everything else in faith, life, and ministry depends, and the reconstruction of pastoral theology begins here. Christ comes as the incarnate

---

11. T. W. Manson, *Ministry and Priesthood: Christ's and Ours* (London: Epworth, 1958), 63.
12. Ibid., 58.

Word of God who makes the response of faith, life, and ministry in our place, not instrumentally in our humanity but as wholly human in a personal and vicarious manner.[13] The gospel is not a religious idea proclaimed, a moral ideal asserted, or even a cosmic drama conducted "above our heads." It is God's personal or hypostatic act in and through Jesus Christ by which God comes as Jesus, God's Word, in an atoning incarnation and to which Word Jesus our brother and advocate responds. Further, the gospel includes us in the benefit of this twofold action through a sharing in his person, not by imputation but through relationship with Christ, in union with Christ, as we will see in the next chapter. This dual movement in and through the hypostatic union of the one person of Jesus Christ forces us to understand our salvation in terms not only of the act of God in Christ that deals with our sins, but also the act of God in Christ that offers to God from the side of our humanity the life of satisfaction through the worship and service that God desires—the life of communion with God. There is no gospel and no atonement that brings us into communion with God and allows us to worship and serve God as God desires, without both the worldward and Godward movements of God in Christ, in which there is both a real and not just an apparent incarnation, and a worthy and acceptable response to God out of the heart and in the flesh of our humanity to which we are joined. In particular, there is no gospel at the point where we are called to worship and serve God without the vicarious humanity of Jesus Christ for us in and through which he gives to the Father the life of worship and service in which we, by the grace of the Holy Spirit, participate. Without the twofold ministry of Jesus Christ in the body of the flesh there is no possibility of the faithful response to God that God desires, and the gospel is cut off from us at just that place where we are required by God to respond with worship and service.

From this discussion we can draw three brief conclusions, which anticipate the later discussion on the ministry of the ascended Christ. First, Christ's substitution is not just an act done for us two thousand years ago. Always standing as our mediator, in his substitutionary priestly office he continues to be the one who stands between God and humankind, setting aside our deeply inadequate and sinful attempts at obedience, worship, and service in a soteriological displacement, offering his own obedience, worship, and ser-

---

13. "In this event atonement is not an act of God done *ab extra* upon man, but an act of God become man, done *ab intra*, in his stead and on his behalf; it is an act of God as man, translated into human actuality and made to issue out of the depths of man's being and life toward God." T. F. Torrance, *The Trinitarian Faith: The Evangelical Theology of the Ancient Catholic Church* (Edinburgh: T. & T. Clark, 1993), 158–59.

vice in our place. Second, he continually prays for us, interceding with the Father on our behalf (Heb. 6:20; 7:25–28; 8:1–6). He takes our prayer, for we do not know how to pray (Rom. 8:26), and perfects it in himself, giving us his prayer in a "wonderful exchange."[14] Third, he sends us the Holy Spirit to join us to his own obedience, worship, and service, making us an apostolic priesthood, obeying, worshiping, and serving God in and through Jesus Christ, to the glory of the Father. His ministry becomes our ministry by grace, and this is the theological basis for ecclesiology in general, and for pastoral care in particular. John McLeod Campbell sums up the consequence: "Therefore Christ, as the Lord of our spirits and our life, *devotes us to God* and *devotes us to men* in the *fellowship of his self-sacrifice*."[15] What this means in specific terms is the subject matter of part two of the book.

Christ's Apostolic and Priestly Ministry in the Theology of the Church

The biblical theology I have outlined has profoundly shaped the theological mind of the church from earliest days to the present. As far as contemporary pastoral theology is concerned, however, this heritage appears to be largely unknown and unappropriated. In order to continue to secure the foundation for the reconstruction of pastoral theology we need now to consider the treatment of the apostolic and priestly ministry of Jesus Christ in the work of Athanasius of Alexandria, John Calvin, and the Scottish Christology tradition of grace, represented by John McLeod Campbell and Thomas Torrance. These four theologians, who span the period from the fourth century to the present, and represent both Eastern and Western approaches, are the principal players in the formation of the theological consensus on which I am reconstructing pastoral theology.

Athanasius

Athanasius is famous for his ferocious defense of Nicene orthodoxy in the immediate decades following the Council of Nicea in 325. Our concern

14. J. Calvin, *Institutes of the Christian Religion*, ed. John T. McNeill; trans. Ford Lewis Battles; 2 vols. (Philadelphia: Westminster, 1960), 4.17.2. See also J. B. Torrance, *Worship*, 35.

15. McLeod Campbell, *Nature of the Atonement*, 255. For a contemporary development see the whole argument of J. B. Torrance, *Worship*. This dual theme of forgiveness and renewal was already expressed in Scottish theology in John Knox's Liturgy: "I confess that Jesus Christ did not only justify us by covering all our faults and iniquities, but also renews us by his Spirit and that these two points can not be separate, to obtain pardon for our sins, and to be reformed into a holy life." Cited in Thomas F. Torrance, *Scottish Theology* (Edinburgh: T. & T. Clark, 1966), 20.

here is not with the theology and politics of the defense of the Nicene *homoousion*, but with the specific presentation of the ministry of Jesus Christ embedded in the heart of that defense, especially as it is given in one treatise, *Contra Arianos*, a long, detailed, and subtle theological statement written between 356 and 360. Highlighting some of the main thrusts of the argument will illustrate and support my broad goal in this chapter.

The connection with the discussion above, and a place to begin, is found in Athanasius's own reflection on Hebrews 3:1: "Now when became He 'Apostle,' but when He put on our flesh? and when became He 'High Priest of our profession,' but when, after offering Himself for us, He raised His Body from the dead, and, as now, Himself brings near and offers to the Father those who in faith approach Him, redeeming all, and for all propitiating God?" (2.7).[16] Athanasius makes this point in the context of his argument that the statement in Hebrews 3:2, that Jesus was faithful to the one who appointed him, is to be interpreted in the light of the Son who in becoming flesh did not become other than himself. Here in a nutshell is the Athanasian argument: Jesus Christ "was Very God in the flesh, and He was true flesh in the Word" (3.41). In order to explicate the theology behind this statement we must conider three points: (1) God saves through and as the man Jesus; that is, Jesus of Nazareth ministers the things of God to us as God; (2) as such, Jesus receives the Word of God on our behalf; (3) as God precisely and singularly as this man, Jesus ministers the things of humankind to God.

1. Athanasius emphasizes that while Christianity must speak of the incarnation of God, there is to be no doubt that it involves both a real becoming of God and at the same time the true humanity of Jesus. The doctrine of the hypostatic union asserts just this. According to Athanasius, Jesus "was not man, and then became God, but He was God, and then became man, and that to deify us" (1.39). The incarnation is a real becoming on the part of God,[17] not a particular man becoming God by some means or other. To emphasize the point, Athanasius suggests that Christ was not promoted from a lower state, but was God, who took the form of a servant. Because of us and for us (1.42) God became a man—not *in* a man, but *as* a man: "He became man, and did not come into man" (3.30). To appreciate what this means we must understand that in the incarnation

---

16. References are to Athanasius, *Four Discourses Against the Arians*, in *The Nicene and Post-Nicene Fathers*, ed. Philip Schaff and Henry Wace, 2d series, vol. 4 (reprint, Edinburgh: T. & T. Clark; Grand Rapids: Eerdmans, 1998).

17. T. F. Torrance, *Trinitarian Faith*, 150.

Jesus' humanity should not be thought of in what Torrance calls an instrumental way, for his humanity then becomes a means to an end, something external to his being, and not then part of the gospel itself. Athanasius's point is that God does not work through the man Jesus, as though the humanity of Jesus was merely the vehicle of grace and in the end disposable; rather, the incarnation means that God comes to us and for us *as* the man Jesus in a particularly personal way as the man for others. God comes as the man Jesus in such a way that God saves as this man. The *egeneto sarx*, the becoming flesh, is real, not apparent, a becoming as the son of Mary in the personal particularity of his actual historicity.

Athanasius's argument means that we have to hold together both the becoming of God and the integrity of Christ's humanity. On the one hand, this implies the anhypostatic movement of the incarnation; Jesus' humanity was not independent of God's becoming human. On the other hand, it implies the enhypostatic movement, for it was a real humanity (thus "born of the Virgin Mary"). Athanasius emphasizes the becoming flesh with Christ's becoming a man (3.30). So when we deal with Jesus in the flesh, we deal with God, not with a representative of God in whom divine principles are at work or with some kind of third thing between humankind and God, as taught by Arius.

What is intended when Athanasius argues that Jesus Christ is the Word of God to humankind, or that he ministers the things of God to us? Although Athanasius uses the word *homoousios* only once in his treatise, at 1.9, the meaning of the Nicene affirmation runs through the argument in no uncertain manner: "He is very God, existing one in essence (*homoousios*) with the very Father. . . . He is the expression of the Father's Person, and Light from Light, and Power, and very Image of the Father's essence."[18] Thus Christ is the Son of God, from the Father (1.27), rightly understood as the Word, Wisdom, and Radiance of God (1.28). According to Athanasius, because the whole being of the Son is proper to the Father's essence (3.3), there is a oneness in being between the Father and the Son. Thus Athanasius understood that God is antecedently and eternally in himself what he is toward us in the Son.[19] He suggests that we see the Father in the Son, and we contemplate the Son in the Father (3.5). In this way Athanasius shows that through Jesus Christ we have access to God, which

18. The alternative leads to theological chaos: "if the Saviour be not God, nor Word, nor Son, you shall have leave to say what you will" (1.10). This is to rob God of his Word (1.14).

19. The concept is Athanasian, but the language is from T. F. Torrance. Torrance uses this kind of language in many places—see, for example, *Trinitarian Faith*, 135; and *The Christian Doctrine of God: One Being, Three Persons* (Edinburgh: T. & T. Clark, 1996), 142.

means not just forgiveness of sins, but also communion with God through our union with the Son (2.55, 59, and 3.21). These insights are critical both for knowledge of God and for confidence in salvation through Jesus Christ.[20]

According to Athanasius, then, in Jesus Christ God has really come among us, indwelling our history in his flesh as the actual Word of God in such a way that he is the "place" where God speaks and acts in saving love for us and for our salvation. "Whereas the Son and the Father are one . . . and in such wise is the Son like the Father Himself and from Him . . . when the Son works, the Father is the Worker, and the Son coming to the Saints, the Father is He who cometh in the Son. . . . For one and the same grace is from the Father in the Son, as the light of the sun and of the radiance is one, and as the sun's illumination is effected through the radiance" (3.11). In Jesus Christ it is with God for us that we have to do, "for though the Father gives it, through the Son is the gift" (3.13). The incarnation, then, falls within both the sphere or reality of God and the sphere or reality of humankind, meaning that Jesus Christ is mediator between God and humankind, bringing God to us, and, as we now turn to consider, us to God.

2. We must take notice of Athanasius's argument that Jesus Christ not only gives God's Word to and for us, but also as a man he hears and receives God's Word on our behalf. With this point, and more fully in the next, we turn to what has become known as the vicarious humanity of Christ, a doctrine that is critical for my argument.

Athanasius illustrates this point, "giving as God's Word, receiving as man. . . . For when he is now said to be anointed in a human respect, we it is who in Him are anointed; since also, when He is baptized, we it is who in Him are baptized" (1.48). Clearly Athanasius regarded us as not having a free mind (2.56) but as a people under sentence of death (2.69). Further, we could not become sons and daughters of God other than by receiving the Spirit of the true Son (2.59; 3.19). The argument presupposes that even were God to speak, outside of the Spirit of the Son hearing on our behalf, we would not hear and receive that Word, for we are not children of God by nature, but only in the Son, and only the Son can hear the Word of the Father. So Christ received the Word of God when he took flesh, not for his own sake but for us (3.39). To make clear what this means, Athanasius insists that in so receiving, Christ as the Word of God received nothing that he did not possess before; it is in the flesh, as the man for us,

---

20. For a valuable discussion of the hermeneutical and evangelical significance of the *homoousion* see T. F. Torrance, *Trinitarian Faith*, chapter 4.

that the one who is the Word of God received that Word in his humanity for us (3.40). Jesus Christ then is both speaking God and a hearing man,
and this for us. "For He who is the Son of God, became Himself the Son
of Man; and, as Word, He gives from the Father, for all things which the
Father does and gives, He does and supplies through Him; and as the Son
of Man, He Himself is said after the manner of men to receive what proceeds from Him, because His Body is none other than His, and a natural
recipient of grace" (1.45).

　　3. We now consider the saving work of Christ in his human agency, in
which he ministers the things of humankind to God as the high priest of
our confession. What Christ offers is himself (2.7), and because he has
taken our flesh, that is, us, upon himself, his offering of himself to the
Father is an offering on our behalf (2.8). This means, says Athanasius, the
sanctification of our flesh (2.10). Thus:

> Since then the Word, being the Image of the Father and immortal,
> took the form of the servant, and as man underwent for us death in
> His flesh, that thereby He might offer Himself for us through death
> to the Father; therefore, as man, He is said because of us and for us
> to be highly exalted, that as by His death we all died in Christ, so
> again in the Christ Himself we might be highly exalted, being raised
> from the dead, and ascending into heaven. (1.41)

Thus the ministry of Christ to the Father takes us into the heart of the
atonement as a work of grace that belongs within the very being of Jesus
Christ: "By His dwelling in the flesh, sin might perfectly be expelled from
the flesh, and we might have a free mind" (2.56). Thus by humbling himself and taking our "body of humiliation" (Phil. 3:21), and putting on the
flesh that was enslaved to sin, becoming a servant, Christ has become
Adam for us, rendering the flesh now capable of the Word, making us walk
no longer according to the flesh, but according to the Spirit (1.43, 51, 60).

　　Athanasius's summary statement is given toward the end of *Contra Arianos*, at 4.6 and 7:

> We must say that our Lord, being Word and Son of God, bore a body,
> and became Son of Man, that, having become Mediator between God
> and men, He might minister the things of God to us, and ours to
> God. . . . He receives (our human affections) from us and offers to the
> Father, interceding for us, that in Him they may be annulled. . . . Nor
> again were men sufficient to minister these things for themselves, but

through the Word they are given to us; therefore, as if given to Him, they are imparted to us. . . . The word then was united to us, and then imparted to us power, and highly exalted us. . . . Wherefore if anything be said to be given to the Lord, or the like, we must consider that it is given, not to Him as needing it, but to man himself through the Word. . . . For as He takes our infirmities, not being infirm, and hungers not hungering, but sends up what is ours that it may be abolished, so the gifts which come from God, instead of our infirmities, doth He too Himself receive, that man, being united to Him, may be able to partake of them. . . . For He prayed for us, taking on Him what is ours, and He was giving what He received. . . . For as He for our sake became man, so we for His sake are exalted . . . referring what is ours to Himself, and saying, "All things whatsoever Thou hast given Me, I give unto them."

The consequence of this dual mediatorial ministry of Jesus Christ is, in the well-known words from Athanasius's *De Incarnatione*, written before Nicea, that the Savior "became human that we might be made divine" (54.3). This refers to the transition of humankind from one state into another, which the theological tradition came to call "the wonderful exchange," as a commentary upon 2 Corinthians 8:9: "You know the generous act [grace] of our Lord Jesus Christ, that though he was rich, yet for your sakes he became poor, so that by his poverty you might become rich." Out of the measureless love of God, Jesus Christ became what we are in order to make us what he is.[21] Our divinization, of course, is "in Christ." "He descended to effect their promotion, therefore He did not receive in reward the name of the Son and God, but rather He Himself has made us sons of the Father, and deified men by becoming Himself man" (1.38). This for Athanasius is the glorious conclusion to Christ's ministry to the Father on our behalf.[22]

John Calvin

Although it is well known that the threefold office of Christ as prophet, priest, and king derives largely from the later editions of Calvin's *Institutes*

---

21. For this paragraph see ibid., 179.

22. This third point was wonderfully expounded by the Scottish Reformer John Knox in his treatise on prayer. *Select Practical Writings of John Knox* (Edinburgh: Johnson and Hunter, 1882), 45.

of the Christian Religion, the case is well made that the change from the twofold office of priest and king to the threefold office is peripheral rather than essential.[23] Much more in line with Calvin's thought, especially as developed in his commentaries, though also in the *Institutes*, is the view that Christ is to be understood as priest and king, so that he is set before us "as in a double mirror" (*Inst.* 2.7.2). Whenever we consider our salvation, says Calvin, we must remember two things: (1) that we cannot be God's sons and daughters unless Christ has freely expiated our sins and thereby reconciled us to God, and then (2) not unless Christ also rules us by his Spirit. Now these two things—Christ as priest and Christ as king— have been joined together by God, and what God has joined together, we ought not to separate.[24] Given the duality-in-unity of the confession that Jesus is Lord, he is both the one whom we worship and the leader of our worship.[25]

Absolutely central to Calvin's doctrine of the priestly ministry of Christ is the idea already noted of the high priest of Israel who represented God to Israel and Israel to God. The high priest of Israel is a type of Christ, anticipating obliquely what only Christ would fulfill. The one stands in for the many in a vicarious priesthood. This is summed up by Calvin in his commentary on Hebrews 6:19, a passage that is a remarkable piece of pastoral theology, holding together the doctrines of the priesthood of Christ and of our union with Christ in a way that recapitulates the biblical and patristic perspective:

> Because Christ has entered heaven our faith must also be directed there. This is the source of our knowledge that faith must not look anywhere else. It is useless for men to look for God in His majesty, because it is too remote and far from them: but Christ stretches out his hand to lead us to heaven, as was indeed foreshadowed earlier in the Law. The high priest used to enter the holy of holies not only in his own name, but *in that of the people, as one who in a way carried all the twelve tribes on his breast and on his shoulders*, because twelve stones were woven into his breastplate and their names were engraved on the two onyx stones on his shoulders to be a reminder to them, *so that*

23. John Frederick Jansen, *Calvin's Doctrine of the Work of Christ* (London: James Clarke, 1956), 75.

24. Commentary on Ezek. 11:19–20, referenced by Jansen, *Calvin's Doctrine*, 75.

25. These images are from James B. Torrance, "The Vicarious Humanity and Priesthood of Christ in the Theology of John Calvin," *Calvinus Ecclesiae Doctor*, ed. W. H. Neuner (Kampen: Kok, 1980), 70. I have been greatly assisted by this article in what follows.

they all went into the sanctuary together in the person of the one man. The apostle is therefore right when he states that our High Priest has entered heaven, because *He has done so not only for Himself, but also for us.* There is therefore no cause to fear that the door of heaven may be shut to our faith, since we are never disjoined from Christ.[26]

James B. Torrance eloquently expresses Calvin's view:

> Calvin interprets Christ's whole life of prayer and obedience and love, His whole life in the Spirit, as His self-consecration for us, in offering Himself in death that he might be the lamb of God to take away the sin of the world, saying Amen in our humanity to the just judgments of God, not to appease an angry God to condition Him into being gracious—that God might as a result begin to love us!— but rather as God Himself in love in the person of His Son offering Himself for a sinful world, that His covenant purposes for mankind might be sealed by His blood.[27]

Clearly Christ is here understood as God acting as a man, though not in an instrumental way in which his humanity is incidental to his work, but in such a way that our salvation is to be understood as in Christ as well as through Christ.

Calvin again admirably sums this up *as pastoral theology* in another passage at the close of his discussion on how Christ has fulfilled his work as our redeemer:

> We see that *our whole salvation and all its parts are comprehended in Christ* (Acts 4:12). We should therefore take care not to derive the least portion of it from anywhere else. If we seek salvation, we are taught by the very name of Jesus that it is "of him" (1 Cor. 1:30). If we seek any other gifts of the Spirit, they will be found in his anointing. If we seek strength, it lies in his dominion; if purity, in his conception; if gentleness, it appears in his birth. For by his birth he was made like us in all respects (Heb. 2:17) that he might learn to feel our pain (cf. Heb. 5:2). If we seek redemption, it lies in his passion; if

---

26. *Calvin's Commentaries: The Epistle of Paul the Apostle to the Hebrews and the First and Second Epistles of St. Peter,* ed. David W. Torrance and Thomas F. Torrance, trans. William B. Johnston (Edinburgh: Oliver and Boyd, 1963), 87, emphasis added.
27. J. B. Torrance, "Vicarious Humanity," 75.

acquittal, in his condemnation; if remission of the curse, in his cross
(Gal. 3:13); if satisfaction, in his sacrifice; if purification, in his blood;
if reconciliation, in his descent into hell; if mortification of the flesh,
in his tomb; if newness of life, in his resurrection; if immortality, in
the same; if inheritance of the Heavenly Kingdom, in his entrance
into heaven; if protection, if security, if abundant supply of all blessings, in his Kingdom; if untroubled expectation of judgment, in the
power given to him to judge. In short, since rich store of every kind
of good abounds in him, let us drink our fill from this fountain, and
from no other. Some men, not content with him alone, are borne
hither and thither from one hope to another; even if they concern
themselves chiefly with him, they nevertheless stray from the right
way in turning some part of their thinking in another direction. Yet
such distrust cannot creep in where men have once for all truly
known the abundance of his blessings. *Inst.* 2.16.19 (emphasis added)

The argument leads to a theologically inevitable conclusion, namely,
that through union with Christ we participate in that which is his, becoming priests in him. Priesthood, of course, belongs to Christ alone—a point
that must be emphasized in any discussion of orders of ministry. From a
biblical or theological perspective there can be no tolerance of a minister
as an *alter Christus*. The point of Christ's priesthood, according to Calvin,
is that in this office he alone is the point or place of access to God, washing away our sins, and taking us, as by the hand, into the presence of God.
As such, he ever prays for us, pleading our favor, from which arises, says
Calvin, both trust in prayer and a good conscience, leaning upon God's
fatherly mercy and knowing that whatever has been consecrated through
Christ is pleasing to God.

Now Calvin develops his argument further: "Christ plays the priestly
role, not only to render the Father favorable and propitious toward us by
an eternal law of reconciliation, *but also to receive us as his companions in this
great office. For we who are defiled in ourselves, yet are priests in him. . . .* This
is the meaning of Christ's statement: 'For their sakes I sanctify myself'
(John 17:19)" (*Inst.* 2.15.6, emphasis added).

Without too much of a stretch of meaning one can argue that this is the
foundation of practical theology, namely, that his priesthood becomes
ours by grace, through union with Christ and in the Holy Spirit to share
in his communion with the Father and in his priestly and apostolic mission from the Father, for the sake of the world, in obedience to John 20:21:
"As the Father has sent me, so I send you." As Calvin has noted, there is

nothing that we can add to Christ's blessings. Likewise, there is nothing we can add to Christ's ministry without implying that he has not done enough either for our salvation or to honor the glory of God. Our task is to receive and rejoice in the salvation that is ours in Christ and to share in his continuing ministry, knowing that by a single offering he has perfected for all time those who are sanctified (Heb. 10:14). The church has a ministry by sharing in a common anointing in the ministry of Christ:

> Let us learn to begin with the Kingdom and the Priesthood when we speak of the state and government of the Church. . . . This then is the only true happiness of the Church, even to be in subjection to Christ, so that he may exercise toward us the two offices here described. Hence also we gather that these are the two marks of a true Church, by which she is to be distinguished from all conventicles who falsely profess the name of God, and boast themselves to be Churches. For where the Kingdom and Priesthood of Christ are found, there, no doubt, is the Church. But where Christ is not owned as a King and a Priest, there is nothing but chaos.[28]

As James B. Torrance comments, "These two offices of King and Priest cannot be separated, not only because Christ as Messiah was anointed to be both, but because Christ reigns from the Cross, and the Word of the Cross is the sceptre by which Christ reigns."[29]

John McLeod Campbell

The priesthood of Christ takes us into the center of the gospel, not only at the point of atonement for sin, but also at the point of our sharing in the fellowship of Christ's self-sacrifice, which is the sum of Christian life and ministry. Christ's priestly ministry enables us to hold salvation and discipleship together *as gospel*. The great danger is always that at the last moment the gospel becomes its opposite, in which everything depends upon us rather than upon God—our faith, our decisions, or our works. In a remarkable way, in the context of his own time yet with significance for ours, John McLeod Campbell, albeit with a cumbersome writing style, redirected the basis of the theology of atonement, the experience of assurance, and the understanding of the Christian life back on to a gospel basis

---

28. Calvin, commentary on Jer. 33:17–18, cited by J. B. Torrance, "Vicarious Humanity," 83.
29. J. B. Torrance, "Vicarious Humanity," 83.

on the ground of the priestly ministry of Christ. Hitherto they had been refracted through the prism of Federal Calvinism. In doing this McLeod Campbell insisted on the difference between a legal and a filial standing before God[30] that led him to define atonement not as the penal reconciliation of God to humankind, but as the restoration of loving relations, which is the more basic or original meaning of the word.[31] His major work, *The Nature of the Atonement*, both illustrates and takes us more deeply into the soteriological implications of the priestly ministry of Christ.

Restoration to communion with God is the center of McLeod Campbell's theological vision. This means in particular a participation in Christ's divine sonship through the fellowship of the mind of the Son toward the Father.[32] The issue atonement must deal with is not broken law as much as a broken relationship with God, which leads to sin. Campbell shows how the atonement has two aspects. First, there is a retrospective aspect, by which Christ reveals God's judgment upon us and confesses our sin before the Father. Second, there is a prospective aspect, by which Christ reveals God to be our Father, while enabling the good to which Christ intends to raise us, namely, our adoption in Christ as children of the Father. This means that we need to place appropriate emphasis upon "adoption as children," as upon redemption "of those who were under the law," echoing Galatians 4:5–6. The atonement included not only dealing retrospectively with our sin, but also dealing prospectively with our becoming children of God. This latter aspect especially has not always been seen to be part of the doctrine of the atonement, yet it is the heart of the nature of the atonement and the basis for living the Christian life.

McLeod Campbell's theology is framed by the assertion that forgiveness precedes atonement: "If God provides atonement, then forgiveness must precede atonement; and the atonement must be the form of the manifestation of the forgiving love of God, not its cause."[33] He follows Augustine and Calvin in insisting that the gospel is to be understood theologically in the movement from the love of God to reconciliation.[34] The "first tone" of the gospel that catches our ear is the loving indicative, "You are forgiven." This echoes Calvin's teaching especially, the reformer's distinction

---

30. McLeod Campbell, *Nature of the Atonement*, 145.

31. See Robert S. Paul, *The Atonement and the Sacraments: The Relation of the Atonement to the Sacraments of Baptism and the Lord's Supper* (New York: Abingdon, 1960), 19.

32. McLeod Campbell, *Nature of the Atonement*, 26.

33. Ibid., 45.

34. Thomas F. Torrance, *Scottish Theology: From John Knox to John McLeod Campbell* (Edinburgh: T. & T. Clark, 1996), 296.

being between "repentance of the law" and "repentance of the gospel,"[35] for, while forgiveness of sins requires repentance as an obligation, repentance is not the cause of forgiveness of sins.[36] God does not need to be conditioned into forgiveness of sins, with the atonement of Christ as the cause and God's love toward us the effect. Rather, McLeod Campbell argued, the inner theological meaning of the gospel represents the love of God as the cause, the atonement as the effect,[37] and repentance as the human response. "God so loved the world *that* . . ." (John 3:16). This means for McLeod Campbell that atonement presupposes incarnation; indeed, incarnation is the necessary condition for atonement,[38] as well as the act of God's love toward us, of which atonement in its retrospective and prospective aspects is the goal.

All of this has a pastoral setting. From the very beginning of his ministry in the parish of Rhu (pronounced "row") in the county of Argyll in Scotland in 1825, McLeod Campbell preached a gospel that was both doctrinal and evangelical. This led to his deposition from the ministry of the Church of Scotland in 1831 on the ground of teaching and preaching that was contrary to the Westminster Confession of Faith. In faithfulness to his calling to be a minister of the love of God in Jesus Christ, McLeod Campbell was forced to think in such a way that he was brought into sharp conflict with Federal or Westminster Calvinism, the prevailing theology of the Church of Scotland in the first half of the nineteenth century.

Federal Calvinism (*foedus* can mean "covenant," but more likely, "contract") was a theology of law and grace governed by contractual notions of covenant. It arose in Europe from the end of the sixteenth century, and came into English-speaking theology through English Puritanism, from which it came to be the framework for the Westminster Confession of Faith. This confession has, since 1647, been the doctrinal standard of the Church of Scotland, shaping the Presbyterian mind ever since. It proposed a hard distinction between a covenant of works and a covenant of grace. This two-covenant theology was unknown to Calvin, and is noted only once by Augustine alone of all the church fathers. The first covenant, law, ostensibly made with Adam, the federal head of humankind, enjoined moral obedience known through natural reason as the condition for divine blessing. When Adam fell, by failing to live up to the demands of obedi-

---

35. Calvin, *Inst.* 3.3.4.
36. Calvin, *Inst.* 3.4.3.
37. McLeod Campbell, *Nature of the Atonement*, 46.
38. Ibid., 49.

ence, salvation was no longer a possibility. Christ, the federal head of believers, established the second covenant, the covenant of grace, by atoning for sin and bringing the elect into salvation through their obedience to an easier way. God was seen as moral lawgiver and judge whose demands have to be met—by us, or in our stead, by Christ. God has to be appeased in order to be gracious toward us, but then only for the benefit of the elect. Atonement, then, affects the attitude of God toward us. Because the issue is broken law, atonement is cast in terms of penal or transactional substitution, in which Christ contracts with God to pay the punishment due to sinners. God inflicts punishment upon him, and the debt is paid.

Federal Calvinism imposed conditions of faith and obedience that signaled a departure from the Reformation view of grace as unilateral and established instead a bilateral view of God's promise and human duty. As Samuel Rutherford, one of six Scots to attend the Westminster Assembly, wrote: God promises us forgiveness and eternal life, "upon condition of beleeving in Christ."[39] When atonement is conditional and contractual, four serious theological problems arise.[40]

1. Covenant becomes confused with contract, which leads to confusing the obligations of grace as conditions for grace, turning the gospel into a legal transaction. For the Reformers, in contrast, there is only one covenant, the covenant of grace that from the very beginning is rooted in love, not law, and that filial relationship with God, not a legal arrangement, is God's purpose. This means that law is properly understood within the framework of grace and love.

2. Federal Calvinism adopted a doctrine of limited atonement: Christ died only for the elect, not for all. In this scheme it matters not that one looks to the mercy of God. If one is not elected by God, one is not saved.

3. A serious issue arises over where one looks for assurance of faith and salvation. However we press into the mystery of election and the economy of salvation in order to understand it more fully, Calvin and Luther stressed that we look to Christ for the assurance of salvation and not to our own, even our best, efforts. As Calvinists have insisted, the Christian must even repent of his or her virtues. Federal Calvinism, in contrast, imposed an anxious, introspective self-examination in search of the fruits of one's sanctification. Federal Calvinism comes to grief on the same issue

---

39. Samuel Rutherford, *The Covenant of Life Opened* (1655), 310, cited by William C. Placher, *The Domestication of Transcendence* (Louisville, Ky.: Westminster John Knox Press, 1996), 158. Placher's book has been helpful in writing this brief account of Federal Calvinism.

40. For a discussion, see James B. Torrance, "Introduction," to McLeod Campbell, *Nature of the Atonement*, 1–16.

that undoes Puritanism: the search for assurance turns inward.[41] The doctrine of limited atonement and the consequent introspective piety left the residue of an intractable pastoral problem that directed attention away from confidence in what Christ has done. The impact is still felt as Puritanism and Federal Calvinism have metamorphosed into the psychologically oriented Christianity of the modern era. This was precisely the point that led McLeod Campbell to examine the nature of the atonement in the first place.

4. Federal Calvinism defined the atonement as effected by punishment through pain and death. Its emphasis was on overcoming the wrath of God through an equivalent suffering in Jesus, rather than on a sufficient repentance. This latter act is what McLeod Campbell was at pains to emphasize. In the popular theological mind, however, the image of atonement that endures is of a punishment that ameliorates the consequence of judgment, suggesting that the word or concept itself must be broadened in its reference and application.

Federal Calvinism is largely unknown by name in mainline Protestantism today, but its legacy remains clearly felt. It involves a fatal blunting of the evangelical dimension of the gospel of the love of God and a loss of confidence in assurance of salvation. Federal Calvinism undercut the heart of the gospel, in which the love of God is revealed in Jesus Christ, to whose life we are joined, by substituting a legal for a filial standing between God and ourselves, and by redirecting us to look to ourselves and our best efforts rather than to Christ.

McLeod Campbell's work on the nature of the atonement has at its center the Christian teaching of the relationship between the Father and the Son, of the Son lying in the bosom of the Father, knowing and doing the will of the Father. Two texts lie close to the heart of his argument. The first is Psalm 40:8: "I delight to do your will, O my God; your law is within my heart." He calls this "the key to the atonement,"[42] for Christ is the revelation of the will and choice of the living God in relation to us; the heart of the Father is seen in the life of the Son. The second text is John 14:6, "no one comes to the Father except through me," which he calls "the great and all-including necessity that is revealed to us by the atonement."[43] Salvation is the sharing in the communion of the Son with the Father, a participation in the fellowship of Christ's own sonship. These

---

41. See Placher, *Domestication of Transcendence*, 159.
42. McLeod Campbell, *Nature of the Atonement*, 225.
43. Ibid., 150.

two themes—Christ comes from and knows the heart of the Father, and only through sharing in Christ's filial life do we share in his communion with the Father—are dominant throughout McLeod Campbell's discussion of the atonement. As such, the atonement cannot be understood outside the framework of the doctrine of the Trinity. In this regard, McLeod Campbell's theological instincts are entirely classical and orthodox.

McLeod Campbell defended the gospel of the love of God precisely at the point where the atonement is actual, that is, in and through the priesthood of Jesus Christ, from which light alone he sought to expound it. He outlined the nature of the atonement specifically in terms of the dual nature of Christ's priestly ministry, which reached both backward to deal with our separation from God, which he called the retrospective aspect, and forward to bring us into communion with God, the prospective aspect. He developed each in view of a dynamic understanding of the dual aspect of classical Christology that we have been considering. Thus in an Athanasian mode: "The active outgoing of the self-sacrificing love in which the Son of God wrought out our redemption presents these two aspects, first, His dealing with men on the part of God; and, secondly, His dealing with God on behalf of men. These together constitute the atonement equally in its retrospective and prospective bearing."[44] God in Christ acts in a twofold way in the flesh of our humanity as our atoning priest, bringing God to us and us to God, to bridge the gulf that separated between what sin had made us and what it was the desire of God's love that we should become.[45] The redemption of us who stand condemned in our sins through a broken communion with God is only truly and fully seen in its relation to the results contemplated, namely, our participation in eternal life through our adoption as children of God.[46]

Retrospectively, Christ bears witness for God, revealing God, and as such suffering in his body the divine judgment against and sorrow over our sin. McLeod Campbell develops this in line with the love of God and not in line with a theology of punishment. Christ's suffering shows that our sins break God's heart and bring God's condemnation upon our heads—Christ, as it were, is in full sympathy with God's condemnation of sin. Insofar as sin involves suffering the judgment of God, Jesus suffers. Christ's suffering is on account of human fault and God's judgment upon it. But this suffering arises from God's love for us. God in Christ has

44. Ibid., 113.
45. Ibid., 127.
46. Ibid., 128.

entered into humanity's sinful separation from God because it is the nature of divine love to suffer with humanity. What Christ suffered on the cross was not a punishment for imputed sin, but the revelation of God in it. This, however, is not yet the atonement.

It is in Jesus Christ as the righteous man dealing with God on our behalf that McLeod Campbell's originality shines through in what has come to be called his doctrine of vicarious penitence (although he does not use the term):[47] as God with us, Jesus Christ sees and knows sin for what it is. He knows the judgment of God upon it. Yet it was in his humanity that Christ, as the priest of all in the body of our flesh, turned to the Father and offered to God what we were unable to do. "That oneness of mind with the Father, which toward man took the form of condemnation of sin, would in the Son's dealing with the Father in relation to our sins, take the form of a perfect confession of our sins. This confession, as to its own nature, must have been *a perfect Amen in humanity to the judgment of God on the sin of man. . . .* He who would intercede for us must begin with confessing our sins."[48]

How does this "Amen" overcome God's judgment?

> He who responds to the divine wrath against sin, saying, "Thou art righteous, O Lord, Who judgest so," is necessarily receiving the full apprehension and realization of that wrath, as well as of that sin against which it comes forth into His soul and spirit, into the bosom of the divine humanity, and, so receiving it He responds to it with a perfect response—a response from the depths of that divine humanity—and *in that perfect response He absorbs it.* For that response has all the elements of a perfect repentance in humanity for all the sin of man—a perfect sorrow—a perfect contrition—all the elements of such a repentance, and that in absolute perfection, all—excepting the personal consciousness of sin—and by that perfect response in Amen to the mind of God in relation to sin is the wrath of God rightly met, and that is accorded to divine justice which is its due, and could alone satisfy it.[49]

This is a dogmatically controlled intuitive insight into the nature of the atonement that illustrates both the task and the risk of theology—the task,

47. Yet see Karl Barth, *Church Dogmatics*, IV.1, ed. G. W. Bromiley and T. F. Torrance, trans. G. W. Bromiley (Edinburgh: T. & T. Clark, 1956), who writes of Christ's "perfect repentance," 172.

48. McLeod Campbell, *Nature of the Atonement*, 118.

49. Ibid.

because he thinks through or beyond the narrative of the scriptural texts, seeking to apprehend the reality of God to which they bear witness; the risk, because he ventures into the mystery of God and our redemption, where there is always the danger of saying too much. According to McLeod Campbell, then, Christ responds to the judgment of God as the true priest with a perfect response, a perfect sorrow, an adequate repentance on behalf of all that alone can satisfy God's judgment. Our sin has been borne away not by an equivalent punishment and pain, as required by the penal theory, but by an equivalent repentance in our stead and on our behalf.[50] In this way similar to the theology of Athanasius, in the interceding life of Jesus itself, by the virtue of his vicarious active obedience in the flesh of our humanity, the atonement is not only rendered possible by the incarnation, but also is itself a development of the incarnation.[51] McLeod Campbell saw that the atonement was not something done "over our heads," as it were, but was an act of God's grace from within Christ's humanity that entailed both God for us and us for God.

The gospel of our atonement, however, not only deals with our sins and the judgment of God upon us, but also with the restoration to a life of communion with God. We who are called to repentance, to say "Amen" to Christ's righteous "Amen" to God's judgment upon us, are not to be abandoned at the last minute to our own devices. In fact, we who are called to respond make our "Amen" to Christ's "Amen" by the grace of our union with Christ through the Holy Spirit. In his move from the retrospective to the prospective aspects of the atonement, McLeod Campbell moves from theistic language, with its reference to God, to filial language, with its reference to the Father, as befits the goal of the gospel.

The atonement is not just a sharing in Christ's benefits, but even more a sharing in his filial love for the Father, a sharing in a relationship that is uniquely his. Jesus reveals God precisely as Father, and only in that revelation do we know who the Father is and the desire of the Father's heart. This knowledge teaches us of our loss through sin and of the Father's will to restore us from our orphan state to communion through adoption. To do this, Christ, who has made the perfect confession, now presents his own righteousness in humanity expressed as perfect love toward and in service of God. Christ has consecrated a way into the holy company of

---

50. This idea of vicarious repentance had already been found in Scottish theology in Samuel Rutherfurd's *Christ's Dying and Drawing Sinners to Himselfe, Or A Survey of our Saviour in his soule suffering, his lovelyness in his death, and the efficacie thereof* (London: 1647), 79, cited in T. F. Torrance, *Scottish Theology*, 100.

51. McLeod Campbell, *Nature of the Atonement*, 122.

God through the purification of his blood, enabling us, in his name, that is, in union with him, not only to worship God in truth and to draw near to God, crying, "Abba, Father," but also to serve God as we are called to do. We come to God only as God's children, or not at all,[52] and that alone in union with the priestly sonship of Jesus Christ, in his revealing of the Father as our Father, and in his offering of us in his own humanity to share in his divine sonship.

Two aspects of Calvin's theology deeply influenced McLeod Campbell at this point: our union with Christ (considered more fully in chapter 4) and the notion of the wonderful exchange that lay at the center of Calvin's understanding of the Eucharist (which we have already seen with respect also to the theology of Athanasius). The two concepts interpret one another. Christ, who has joined himself to us in his incarnation, joins us to himself through the Spirit, and, by his continuing priestly intercession for us, makes us to share in his filial communion with the Father, effecting a wonderful exchange, a glorious substitution, taking to himself our sin, enmity, and death, giving us what is his—his righteousness, love, and eternal life, leading us to say, "Our Father, who art in heaven . . . ," which is salvation. In sum, to cite again the wonderful statement of McLeod Campbell: "Therefore Christ, as the Lord of our spirits and our life, *devotes us to God* and *devotes us to men* in the *fellowship of his self-sacrifice*."[53] This one sentence is the sum of all practical theology. The dogmatic development of practical theology within an ecumenical, catholic, and evangelical perspective is based on a comprehensive doctrine of the atonement.

McLeod Campbell's theology of the atonement, developed precisely in line with the priestly ministry of Jesus Christ, opens up fresh vistas of theological insight. In view of his reflection on the nature of the atonement, the doctrine never looks quite the same again. Yet it suffers from single-mindedness. He has taken one soteriological metaphor—our restoration to communion with the Father—and allowed it to open up the whole of the gospel. Other metaphors, of course, must also be included and developed to open up the soteriological vista in a comprehensive way. His argument is incomplete, therefore, in part because of his unremitting pastoral resistance to penal atonement and its effect upon the spiritual well-being of his people. It may be too that he pushed his reflections into speculations because he took the risk of thinking theologically as far as he thought he could penetrate into the truth of the gospel. Nevertheless,

52. Ibid., 243.
53. Ibid., 255.

because his theology is before us as a corrective to a diminished view of the gospel, we can look again at the biblical metaphors that express the majesty and holiness of God in legal terms and allow them an appropriate, though not a controlling, place. For our purposes, however, the priestly ministry of Christ is both illustrated and deepened in our awareness as an integral aspect of the gospel. Above all, we see how it is only by sharing in Christ's priesthood that we come to a knowledge and service of God that is acceptable to God.

Thomas F. Torrance

Torrance is deeply indebted to Athanasius, John Calvin, and John McLeod Campbell,[54] especially in his development of Christ's twofold ministry[55] to not only the things of God to humankind, but also to the things of humankind to God.[56] We will look especially at how Torrance understands the role of Jesus Christ as the true human in his response to God on our behalf. As developed in relation to the doctrine of union with Christ, Torrance introduces directly his understanding of our specific forms of response that are called forth by the gospel. The theological understanding of these responses serves as an indicator of the direction in which this whole discussion is moving.

Following Athanasius, Torrance asserts that in Christ's vicarious humanity in the incarnation is both a humanward and a Godward direction. In this dual movement Christ mediates both God to us and us to God in the unity of his incarnate personhood. Torrance refers to the

> double fact that in Jesus Christ the Word of God has become man, has assumed a human form, in order as such to be God's language to man, and that in Jesus Christ there is gathered up and embodied, in obedient response to God, man's true word to God and his true speech about God. Jesus Christ is at once the complete revelation of God to man and the correspondence on man's part to that revelation required by it for the fulfilment of its own revealing movement.[57]

---

54. A longer version of this material is published in Andrew Purves, "The Christology of T. F. Torrance," in *The Promise of Trinitarian Theology: Theologians in Dialogue with T. F. Torrance,* ed. E. Colyer (Lanham, Md.: Rowman and Littlefield, 2001), 51–80.

55. See Thomas F. Torrance, *The Mediation of Christ* (Grand Rapids: Eerdmans, 1983), 83.

56. See Thomas F. Torrance, *Theology in Reconciliation* (London: Geoffrey Chapman, 1975), 228.

57. Thomas F. Torrance, *Theology in Reconstruction* (Grand Rapids: Eerdmans, 1965), 129.

Because the Word of God has been addressed to us and, as such, has actually reached us because it has been addressed to us in Jesus Christ, the Word has found a response in our human hearing and understanding. We begin not with God alone or with humankind alone,

> but with God and man as they are posited together in a movement of creative self-communication by the Word of God. . . . A profound reciprocity is created in which God addresses His Word to man by giving it human form without any diminishment of its divine reality as God Himself speaks it, and in which He enables man to hear His Word and respond to it without any cancellation of his human mode of being. . . . Thus the Word of God communicated to man includes within itself meeting between man and God as well as meeting between God and man, for in assuming the form of human speech the Word of God spoken to man becomes at the same time the word of man in answer to God.[58]

Torrance identifies the foundation of the christological development of the incarnate reciprocity between God and humankind in the nature of the covenant partnership between God and Israel established at Mount Sinai.[59] God knew that Israel would not be able to be faithful as God required. Thus God, within the covenant established and maintained unilaterally by God, freely and graciously gave a covenanted way of responding so that the covenant might be fulfilled on their behalf. Israel was given ordinances of worship designed to testify that God alone can expiate guilt, forgive sin, and establish communion. This was not just a formulaic rite to guarantee propitiation between God and Israel, however. By its very nature, the covenanted way of response was to be worked into the flesh and blood of Israel's existence in such a way that Israel was called to pattern their whole life after it. Later, in the prophecies of the Isaiah tradition especially, the notions of guilt bearer and sacrifice for sin were conflated to give the interpretative clue for the vicarious role of the servant of the Lord.

It was the incarnation that brought that to pass, however, for Jesus Christ was recognized and presented in the New Testament both as the servant of the Lord and as the divine Redeemer, now not only of Israel but of all people.

---

58. Thomas F. Torrance, *God and Rationality* (London: Oxford University Press, 1971), 137–38.

59. For the following, see T. F. Torrance, *Mediation of Christ*, 83–86.

As the incarnate Son of the Father Jesus Christ has been sent to fulfil all righteousness both as priest and as victim, who through his one
self-offering in atonement for sin has mediated a new covenant of
universal range in which he presents us to his Father as those whom
he has redeemed, sanctified and perfected for ever in himself. In
other words, Jesus Christ constitutes in his own self-consecrated
humanity the fulfilment of the vicarious way of human response to
God promised under the old covenant, but now on the ground of his
atoning self-sacrifice once for all offered this is a vicarious way of
response which is available for all mankind.[60]

Jesus Christ has fulfilled the covenant from both sides—from God's and
from humankind's. In the incarnate unity of his person he is the divine-
human Word "spoken to man from the highest and heard by him in the
depths, and spoken to God out of the depths and heard by Him in the
highest."[61] "Expressed otherwise, in the hypostatic union between God
and man in Jesus Christ there is included a union between the Word of
God and the word of man."[62] Thus the gospel is not to be understood only
as the Word of God coming to us, inviting our response, but also as
including "the all-significant middle term, the divinely provided response
in the vicarious humanity of Jesus Christ."[63]

It is in terms of the vicarious humanity of God in Christ that the full
meaning of the obedience of Christ and the cross may be understood.
Thomas F. Torrance often cites Hebrews 3:1–6, where reference is made
to Christ as the apostle and high priest of our confession. There is, he says,
a twofold function in Christ's priestly mediation, for Christ is both the
apostle of God and our high priest, made as we are, but without sin.[64] As
high priest, Jesus is contrasted with Moses, who was faithful in all his
house as a servant (Num. 12:7 and Heb. 3:5), while Jesus is Son over his
own house (Heb. 3:6).

In this particular passage the work of Christ as Apostle and High Priest,
both in the sense of "the Son over the House," is described in terms
of confession, *homologia*, a word which occurs in three other passages
(3:1; 4:14; 10:23). In each case it sets forth primarily the confession

60. Ibid., 86.
61. T. F. Torrance, *God and Rationality*, 138.
62. Ibid., 142.
63. Ibid., 145.
64. T. F. Torrance, *Royal Priesthood*, 11.

made by the High Priest as he enters within the veil. It is the confession of our sin before God and the confession of God's righteous judgement upon our sin. As Apostle Christ bears witness for God, that He is Holy. As High Priest He acknowledges that witness and says Amen to it. Again as Apostle of God He confesses the mercy and grace of God, His will to pardon and reconcile. As High Priest He intercedes for men, and confesses them before the face of God.[65]

This confession of Christ as apostle and high priest is not in word only, but includes the judgment of God at the cross and the submission of Christ in full and perfect obedience. But Christ's obedience to God's judgment must not be limited to his passive obedience, in which he was "made under the Law" to bear its condemnation in our name and on our behalf. For he lived also to bend back the will of humankind into a perfect submission to the will of God through a life lived in active filial obedience to his heavenly Father. Torrance understands, therefore, that the humanity of Christ was not external to the atonement. The atonement cannot be limited only to his passive obedience. Rather, Jesus Christ "*is* our human response to God"[66] in such a way that both his passive *and* active obedience are imputed to us,[67] for he not only suffered the judgment of God on the cross for us, but fulfilled the will of God in an obedient life of filial love. In view of this development of the vicarious humanity of Christ it is clear why Torrance insists that incarnation and atonement must be considered together, and why revelation and reconciliation are inseparable. It is also clear why a place must be found for complete consideration of the life of Jesus in the system of Christian theology, and, as already noted, avoid the approach that jumps from Christ's birth to his death in the manner of the Apostles' Creed.

Preparing the way for what lies ahead, yet appropriate here too because of its immediate continuity with the foregoing, we now consider briefly Torrance's doctrine of union with Christ, for it is only through this union that we partake of the blessings of Christ's holy and obedient life.[68] On the doctrine of deification through grace he notes,

> Reformed theology interprets participation in the divine nature as the union and communion we are given to have with Christ in his

---

65. Ibid., 12.

66. T. F. Torrance, *Mediation of Christ*, 90.

67. Reformed theology argues that grace is imputed, not inferred or infused. The righteousness always remains Christ's.

68. T. F. Torrance, *Theology in Reconstruction*, 158.

human nature, as participation in his Incarnate Sonship, and therefore as sharing in him in the divine Life and Love. That is to say, it interprets "deification" precisely in the same way as Athanasius in the *Contra Arianos*. It is only through *real and substantial union* (Calvin's expression) with him in his human nature that we partake of all his benefits, such as justification and sanctification and regeneration, but because in him human nature is hypostatically united to divine nature so that the Godhead dwells in him "bodily," in him we really are made partakers of the eternal Life of God himself.[69]

Torrance has observed that Scottish theology at the Reformation gave a place of centrality to the union of God and humankind in Christ and to the understanding of the Christian life therefore as an offering to God only "by the hand of Christ" (Knox).[70] Thus "it is in and through our union with him, that all that is his becomes ours."[71] And again: "It is only through union with Christ that we partake of the blessings of Christ, that is through union with him in his holy and obedient life. . . . Through union with him we share in his faith, in his obedience, in his trust and his appropriation of the Father's blessing."[72] In this way through union with Christ, Torrance's Christology moves seamlessly to his exposition of the Christian life. Union with Christ is given to us through the gift of the Holy Spirit, and as such is the ground of the church. "The Christian Church is what it is because of its indissoluble union with Christ through the Spirit, for in him is concentrated the Church and all ministry. . . . [Thus], there is only one ministry, that of Christ in his Body."[73] This is a theme with which we are by now already familiar. The Holy Spirit constitutes the church in union with its head, joining us to Christ to share in his communion with the Father, and to bear faithful witness to him in the life of the world.

Torrance makes the point with reference to Galatians 2:20, and especially to the words, "I yet not I but Christ."[74] The message of the vicarious humanity of Christ is the gospel on which we rely. The whole of the Christian life in all regards is included in the "I yet not I but Christ," for in Jesus Christ all human responses

69. Ibid., 184.
70. See T. F. Torrance, *Scottish Theology*, 42; and idem, *Theology in Reconstruction*, 151.
71. T. F. Torrance, *Theology in Reconstruction*, 151.
72. Ibid., 158–59.
73. Ibid., 208.
74. T. F. Torrance, *Mediation of Christ*, 107. See also idem, *Preaching Christ Today: The Gospel and Scientific Thinking* (Grand Rapids: Eerdmans, 1994), 31.

are laid hold of, sanctified and informed by his vicarious life of obedience and response to the Father. They are in fact so indissolubly united to the life of Jesus Christ which he lived out among us and which he has offered to the Father, as arising out of our human being and nature, that they are *our responses* toward the love of the Father poured out upon us through the mediation of the Son and in the unity of his Holy Spirit.[75]

Before we refer to our own faith, faith must be understood first of all in terms of Jesus "as stepping into the relation between the faithfulness of God and the actual unfaithfulness of human beings, actualising the faithfulness of God and restoring the faithfulness of human beings by grounding it in the incarnate medium of his own faithfulness so that it answers perfectly to the divine faithfulness."[76] Jesus acts in our place from within our unfaithfulness, giving us a faithfulness in which we may share. He is both (1) the truth of God and human being keeping faith and truth with God in the unity of God revealing himself, and (2) human being hearing, believing, obeying, and speaking his Word.[77] In this way our faith is grounded objectively yet personally in the one who believes for us; our faith depends upon the faithfulness of God in Christ for us. "Thus the very faith which we confess is the faith of Jesus Christ who loved us and gave himself for us in a life and death of utter trust and belief in God the Father. Our faith is altogether grounded in him who is 'author and finisher,' on whom faith depends from start to finish."[78] We are summoned to believe, but in a way "in which our faith is laid hold of, enveloped, and upheld by his unswerving faithfulness."[79] We do not rely upon our own believing, "but wholly upon [Christ's] vicarious response of faithfulness toward God."[80]

Likewise with regard to worship, Torrance insists that Jesus Christ embodies our response to God in such a way that henceforth all worship and prayer is grounded in him. "Jesus Christ in his own self-oblation to the Father *is* our worship and prayer in an acutely personalised form, so that it is only through him and with him and in him that we may draw near to God with the hands of our faith filled with no other offering but that

75. T. F. Torrance, *Mediation of Christ*, 108.
76. Ibid., 92.
77. T. F. Torrance, *God and Rationality*, 154.
78. T. F. Torrance, *Mediation of Christ*, 94.
79. T. F. Torrance, *Preaching Christ Today*, 31.
80. T. F. Torrance, *God and Rationality*, 154.

which he has made on our behalf and in our place once and for all."[81] Any approach to God is in the name and significance of Jesus Christ, "for worship and prayer are not ways in which we express ourselves but ways in which we hold up before the Father his beloved Son, take refuge in his atoning sacrifice, and make that our only plea."[82] Christ has united himself to us in such a way that he gathers up our faltering worship into himself, so that in presenting himself to the Father he presents also the worship of all creation to share in his own communion with the Father. Christ takes our place, and we trust solely in his vicarious self-offering to the Father.

The essential nature of the church, as of individual Christians, is participation in the humanity of Jesus Christ. That is, "the Church is Church as it participates in the active operation of the divine love."[83] As the Son is sent from the Father, so the church, sent by the Son, shares in the mission of Jesus Christ. In this way, ministry is grounded upon a christological and missional pattern (*hypodeigma*). Thus "the Body of which he is the Head the Church participates in His ministry by serving Him in history where it is sent by Him in fulfilment of His ministry of reconciliation."[84] The ministry of the church is not another ministry, different from the ministry of Christ or separate from it, but takes its essential form and content from Jesus' existence as servant and his mission. The church's mission is not an extension or an imitation of Jesus' mission, but a sharing in it. Ministry has a participative and not a mimetic ground. "Thus Jesus Christ constitutes in Himself, in His own vicarious human life and service, the creative source and norm and pattern of all true Christian service."[85]

Having in chapters 2 and 3 developed the christological basis for pastoral theology in the ministry of God, it is now necessary to turn to the doctrine of union with Christ wherein we participate in his human knowledge and service of the Father.

---

81. T. F. Torrance, *Mediation of Christ*, 97. See also idem, *God and Rationality*, 158.
82. T. F. Torrance, *Mediation of Christ*, 97–98.
83. T. F. Torrance, *Royal Priesthood*, 30.
84. Ibid., 35.
85. T. F. Torrance, *God and Rationality*, 162.

Chapter 4

Union with Christ

Following the only true and steadfast Teacher, the Word of God, our Lord Jesus Christ, who did, through His transcendent love, become what we are, that He might bring us to be even what He is Himself.

Irenaeus, *Against Heresies*, book 5, Preface

For He was made man that we might be made God.

Athanasius, *On the Incarnation* 54

He Himself has made us sons of the Father, and deified men by becoming Himself man.

Athanasius, *Four Discourses Against the Arians* 1.38

This is the wonderful exchange which, out of his measureless benevolence, he has made with us; that becoming Son of man with us, he has made us sons of God with him; that, by his descent to earth, he has prepared an ascent to heaven for us; that, by taking our mortality, he has conferred his immortality upon us; that, accepting our weakness, he has strengthened us by his power; that receiving our poverty unto himself, he has transferred his wealth to us; that, taking the weight of our iniquity upon himself (which oppresses us), he has clothed us with his righteousness.

John Calvin, *Institutes of the Christian Religion*, 4.17.2

Introduction

United to Jesus Christ by the Holy Spirit, and thus in relationship with him, we share in his continuing life of adoration, obedience, and love.[1] In union with Christ, that which is his becomes ours. His Father becomes our Father: his knowledge and love and service of the Father become, in union with him, our knowledge and love and service of our Father. In other words, Jesus Christ and our union with him through the Holy Spirit determine Christian faith to such an extent that union with Christ is the proper framework within which to understand the meaning of Christian faith in all regards. This is the meaning of Paul's teaching: "In him we live and move and have our being" (Acts 17:28); and "For you have died, and your life is hidden with Christ in God" (Col. 3:3).

But before we discuss union with Christ it is important to ground this basic Christian reality itself *in* Jesus Christ as himself the union of God and humankind. That is, in union with Christ we participate in his hypostatic union, the union of his two natures in his one personhood; and this union is prior to and is the basis for our union with Christ. The *homoousion* and the hypostatic union together are the two fundamental doctrines for understanding the church's faith in Jesus Christ. In the hypostatic union Jesus Christ and his incarnation are understood soteriologically as the personal bridge between God and humankind that is grounded in the being of God and anchored in the being of humankind. Thus, according to T. F. Torrance, the *homoousion* is to "be taken along with a cognate conception about the indissoluble union of God and man in the one Person of Christ."[2] Reconciliation is not something that is added to the hypostatic union but is itself the hypostatic union at work in expiation and atonement. In this way the incarnation and the atonement constitute both the ontological and the epistemological center of knowledge of God. Jesus Christ is of God and humankind, being in the union of his person both (1) the Word of God addressed to humankind and (2) humankind hearing and responding obediently to the Word of God in union with whom through the Holy Spirit we have communion with and knowledge of God. Just as God is antecedently and eternally who he is in and through Jesus Christ, so also in the personal union of his two natures Christ assumes the whole of our humanity, not only our corrupted physical nature but also our spiritual nature in which we have become alienated from God in our minds. It is a real union of one who was truly God and fully human.

---

1. For what follows see also Andrew Purves and Charles Partee, *Encountering God: Christian Faith in Turbulent Times* (Louisville, Ky.: Westminster John Knox Press, 2000), 19–20.
2. Thomas F. Torrance, *The Christian Doctrine of God: One Being, Three Persons* (Edinburgh: T. & T. Clark, 1996), 94. See also idem, *The Ground and Grammar of Theology* (Charlottesville: University of Virginia Press, 1980), 165; and idem, *Preaching Christ Today: The Gospel and Scientific Thinking* (Grand Rapids: Eerdmans, 1994), 57.

The hypostatic union is the personal union that takes place when the one person of the Son assumes human nature into himself and thus into his divine nature. The union of divine and human natures is entirely the act of God in becoming a man, and the result is that the Son of God exists as the man Jesus, son of Mary, in the integrity of his human agency. Because apart from this act of God in becoming human, however, Jesus would not have existed, his fully human life must be regarded as grounded in the act of the Word of God becoming flesh. Nevertheless, Christ's human nature was a real and specific existence in which Jesus had a fully human mind, will, and body. This is why we must think of the incarnation in terms not of God in humankind, but in terms of God as a man yet without ceasing to be God. And everything that we must say concerning Jesus Christ must have as its subject the one action of the "God-man," maintaining the unity of his person, in which personhood grace is understood in terms of Christ's human as well as his divine nature.[3] This means that the hypostatic union is to be understood not just in terms of incarnation but also soteriologically in terms of the reconciliation between God and humankind, while reconciliation is to be understood not just in terms of the cross but also in terms of the incarnation.

My point here is that in the hypostatic union, God has set forth in the person of Jesus Christ the union of God and humankind, and we may be united to God by sharing in that union through the action of the Holy Spirit and by faith. On this ground, now, the doctrine of union with Christ is the central, organizing feature of all Christian faith and life, a basic belief in the act of God that influences every other belief and every act of believing faith. In all things we do not stand before God on the strength of our own piety, faith, good works, and knowledge. Rather, because the Holy Spirit joins us to Jesus Christ we share in everything that is his, including in his union and communion with the Father. In and through him we are children of the heavenly Father and share in his own life in, before, and from God. Joined to Jesus Christ we share in the communion and mission of the Holy Trinity—Christian faith and life mean no less than this! We stand before God in Christ's name alone, and we serve in Christ's name alone. The real meaning of the Christian's faith is the trust that "for Christ's sake" we are enfolded into the inner life of the Holy Trinity, to share in Christ's communion with the Father and in his mission from the Father.[4]

3. Thomas F. Torrance, *Theology in Reconstruction* (Grand Rapids: Eerdmans, 1965), 183.
4. For this formulation see James B. Torrance, *Worship, Community and the Triune God of Grace* (Carlisle: Paternoster, 1996), ix, and throughout the book.

This is also the meaning of baptism. We are baptized *into* the name of the Father, the Son, and the Holy Spirit. Thus it is *in* God that we live, move, and have our being. The Christian life is not just lived through Christ, but also in Christ. Christ is not only the agent through whose works and merit we have access to the Father but also, by way of sharing in his person through union with him, the one in whom we come to the Father.[5] Because we are united with Christ, for example, he takes our sin as his own and bestows his obedience upon us. As Calvin writes, "For this reason, he is called 'our Head' [Eph. 4:15] and 'the first-born among many brethren' [Rom. 8:29]. We also, in turn, are said to be 'engrafted into him' [Rom. 11:17], and to 'put on Christ' [Gal. 3:27]; for as I have said, all that he possesses is nothing to us until we grow into one body with him" (*Inst.* 3.1.1).

If Christ remains outside us we do not receive the benefits of his work. We must, therefore, be joined to him, and in such a way that he defines our life in every respect: "For to me, living is Christ," Paul writes (Phil. 1:21). Union with Christ applies both to the objective work of salvation, our being forgiven, and to our personal transformation from sinners into saints, our regeneration and sanctification, the expression of which is Christian life and vocation. God not only justifies but sanctifies (1 Cor. 1:30). Necessarily, then, there is a double grace, for, as Calvin observed, there are two dimensions to Christ's work in this regard: "by partaking of him, we principally receive a double grace: namely, that being reconciled to God through Christ's blamelessness, we may have in heaven instead of a judge a gracious Father; and secondly, that sanctified by Christ's Spirit we may cultivate blamelessness and purity of life" (*Inst.* 3.11.1).

At the beginning of his discussion of faith and the Christian life in book 3 of the *Institutes*, Calvin asks how Christ's accomplishments come to have relevance for us. "First, we must understand that as long as Christ remains outside of us, and we are separated from him, all that he has suffered and done for the salvation of the human race remains useless and of no value for us. Therefore, to share with us what he has received from the Father, he had to become ours and dwell within us" (*Inst.* 3.1.1). In other words, for Christ's work to benefit us we must be united with him and he with us. Thus, according to Calvin,

> That joining together of Head and members, that indwelling of
> Christ in our hearts—in short, that mystical union—are accorded by

---

5. Thus James B. Torrance, "The Vicarious Humanity and Priesthood of Christ in the Theology of John Calvin," *Calvinus Ecclesiae Doctor*, ed. W. H. Neuner (Kampen: Kok, 1980), 72.

us the highest degree of importance, so that Christ, having been made ours, makes us sharers with him in the gifts with which he has been endowed. We do not, therefore, contemplate him outside ourselves from afar in order that his righteousness may be imputed to us but because we put on Christ and are engrafted into his body—in short because he deigns to make us one with him. (*Inst.* 3.11.10)

This union of the believer with Christ and of Christ with us is the principal work of the Holy Spirit, a topic I address later in this chapter.

In his commentary on 1 Corinthians Calvin notes "that it is only after we possess Christ himself that we share in the benefits of Christ. And I further maintain that he is possessed not only when we believe that he was sacrificed for us, but when he dwells in us, when he is one with us, when we are members of his flesh, in short, when we become united in one life and substance, in a manner of speaking, with him."[6] This is the great evangelical doctrine of our union with Christ on which the whole of the Christian faith and life depend in their practical aspect. Bound to Christ through the bond of the Holy Spirit, we receive his benefits, and receiving his benefits, his righteousness and holiness become our righteousness and holiness. It is this work of God that makes both salvation and the Christian life possible. Says Calvin: "When we hear mention of our union with God, let us remember that holiness must be its bond; not because we come into communion with him by virtue of our holiness! Rather, we ought to cleave unto him so that, infused with his holiness, we may follow whither he calls" (*Inst.* 3.6.2).

Here, in this doctrine of Christ's union with us and our union with Christ in the power of the Spirit, is the theological thread that ties together confession of Christ with an understanding of faith, discipleship, authority, mission, and Christian unity in and as the church. As the Holy Spirit unites believers with Jesus Christ, faith and discipleship become an expression and an outgrowth of his life within us: "It is no longer I who live, but it is Christ who lives in me" (Gal. 2:20). Our approach to Scripture finds its anchor in Christ's own knowledge of the Father: "For who has known the mind of the Lord so as to instruct him? But we have the mind of Christ" (1 Cor. 2:16). Our mission becomes a participation in and extension of his mission from the Father for the sake of the world: "As the Father has sent me, so I send you" (John 20:21). Our unity with one another emerges as

---

6. Cited by Charles Partee, "Calvin's Central Dogma Again," *The Sixteenth Century Journal* 18, no. 2 (summer 1987): 197.

the product of union with him: "So we, though many, are one body in Christ, and individually members of one another" (Rom. 12:5).

A touching, winsome, and poignant sentence from Calvin makes the point: "Take courage, my friends. Even if we are nothing in our own hearts, perchance something of us is safely hidden in the heart of God" (*Inst.* 3.2.25). Calvin is reflecting Colossians 3:3, which affirms that "our life is hid with Christ in God." Paraphrasing Karl Barth, this verse is the center of the gospel.[7]

The Holy Spirit is the bond of union between the Father and Son and the bond between Christ and us. Faith is the confidence that because we are united with Jesus Christ, all that is his has become ours, and all that is ours, broken and feeble as it most likely is, is now also his, and in him is healed and made holy before God. This is the fruit of the "wonderful exchange" (*Inst.* 4.17.2) on which everything turns and that gives Christian faith and the Christian's faith their identifying marks.

The Christian life is through and through the work in us of the Father, and the Son, and the Holy Spirit. In and through Christ men and women enter into his knowledge of and communion with the Father ("Whoever has seen me has seen the Father," John 14:9). In and through Christ men and women share in his mission from the Father for the sake of the world. In the shorthand formulation of classical Trinitarian theology, the whole of the Christian life is a process of our coming to the Father, in and through union with the Son, in the Holy Spirit, and of our sharing through the same Spirit in the life and ministry of the Son given from the Father.

In what follows I consider five aspects of union with Christ that lay the ground for the continuing reconstruction of pastoral theology:

1. Union with Christ is the principal work of the Holy Spirit.
2. God bestows the gift of union with Christ through what are called the "ordinary means of grace," namely, Word and sacraments.
3. United with Christ we share in his righteousness and his knowledge of and love for the Father.
4. The work of the Holy Spirit in joining us to Jesus Christ creates the church and orders Christian ministry accordingly.
5. In union with Christ we participate in his mission from the Father.[8]

---

7. Karl Barth, *Church Dogmatics*, II.1, ed. G. W. Bromiley and T. F. Torrance (Edinburgh: T. & T. Clark, 1957), 149.

8. For an earlier treatment of some of these themes in a systematic manner see Andrew Purves and Mark Achtemeier, *Union in Christ* (Louisville, Ky.: Witherspoon, 1999); and Purves and Partee, *Encountering God.*

Union with Christ: The Principal Work of the Holy Spirit

The communion of the Holy Spirit means, first of all, union through the Holy Spirit with Jesus Christ himself. To be clear: union with Christ does not lead to an imitation of Christ, a life spent following Jesus' example in the hope that we will become better people. The Christian life is not to be understood as obedience to either an ethical imperative or a spiritual ideal. Rather, the Christian life is the radical and converting participation in Jesus Christ's own being and life, and thus a sharing in his righteousness, holiness, and mission through the bond of the Holy Spirit.

Note, too, the emphasis I place on the work of the Holy Spirit. Union with Christ is entirely a work of God. Our human acts, beliefs, and decisions are powerless to effect a relationship with God. John Calvin understood that our deepest self had to become reconfigured and reconstituted or, to use his words, "regenerated" or "vivified," through relatedness to Jesus Christ. He likened this to a second birth: God must reorder us by turning us in a new direction by uniting us to Jesus. So our being and becoming Christian is a divine initiative and not something that can be worked out through heightened religiosity, morality, activity, will, or spirituality. We are conjoined to Christ by the unilateral work of God through the Holy Spirit—to effect what Calvin called a "mystical union" (*Inst.* 3.11.10). By the bond of the Holy Spirit we become one with him and thereby partake of his benefits.[9] Calvin's term "mystical union" parallels Paul's phrase "in Christ," meaning that God through the Holy Spirit saves us by engrafting us into Christ.

Central to this argument is the understanding of the Christian life as a union with Christ that entails the Spirit-created participation in his righteousness and holiness. The Holy Spirit is the bond—Calvin's word, ambiguous as it is—by which Christ unites us effectually to himself and enables us to share in that which is his. Being bonded to Jesus Christ is a miracle wrought by the Spirit of God. Says Calvin:

> Perfect salvation is found in the person of Christ. Accordingly, that we may become partakers of it he baptizes us in the Holy Spirit and fire [Luke 3:16], bringing us into the light of faith in his gospel and so regenerating us that we become new creatures [cf. 2 Cor. 5:17]; and he consecrates us, purged of worldly uncleanliness, as temples holy to God [cf. 1 Cor. 3:16–17; 6:19; 2 Cor. 6:16; Eph. 2:21]. (*Inst.* 3.1.4)

9. For discussions see Partee, "Calvin's Central Dogma Again," 191–92; and Dennis E. Tamburello, *Union with Christ: John Calvin and the Mysticism of St. Bernard* (Louisville, Ky.: Westminster John Knox Press, 1994).

Note also Calvin's striking series of images to describe the work of the Holy Spirit. The Spirit is a bond (*Inst.* 3.1.1) that unites us to Christ; the Spirit does this work "by his secret watering," which brings forth the "buds of righteousness" (*Inst.* 3.1.3). The Spirit is the "inner teacher by whose efforts the promise of salvation penetrates into our minds, a promise that would otherwise only strike the air or beat upon our ears" (*Inst.* 3.1.4). The Spirit is "the key that unlocks for us the treasures of the Kingdom of Heaven" (*Inst.* 3.1.4). Calvin greatly emphasized the work of the Holy Spirit in whom we share in Christ's glorious life as Son of the Father, becoming thereby in him the holy people of God.

As the only Son of the Father, with the Father from before all ages, of whom there never was a time when he was not, Jesus Christ, with the Father, in the unity of the Holy Spirit, is God. The consequence of union with Christ through the Holy Spirit is a sharing in his communion with the Father. By this sharing, that which is his as Son of the Father becomes ours through grace by adoption. This is the heart of Christian worship and prayer, whereby through union with Christ we share in the filial life of love between the Father and the Son in the unity of the Holy Spirit. This is summed up in the words of 1 John 1:3, "we declare to you what we have seen and heard so that you also may have fellowship with us; and truly our fellowship is with the Father and with his Son Jesus Christ."

Union with Christ through the Ordinary Means of Grace

God bestows this gift of union with Christ through the Holy Spirit by means of the ordinary means of grace—the church's ministry of Word and sacraments. Through this ministry God brings people to faith and nurtures and sustains them in union with Christ, although God, of course, may bring a person to Christ through extraordinary means—there are apparently no atheists in foxholes. The point is that faith is God's work before it is a human response.

The Word of God is different from human words because it is the transcendent, creating, and redeeming Word, yet also a Word that has come among us bearing the flesh of our humanity: "The Word became flesh and lived among us" (John 1:14). The Word of God is God; it is not a word about God. With all its life-transforming power it is active in, through, and as Jesus Christ, who is given in the preaching and sacramental ministry of the church. Athanasius makes the argument concerning the divinity of the Word, who is Jesus Christ, and of our union with him throughout *Contra Arianos,* and sums up his main point: "For since the Word is in the

Father, and the Spirit is given from the Word, he wills that we should receive the Spirit, that, when we receive It, thus having the Spirit of the Word which is in the Father, we too may be found on account of the Spirit to become One in the Word, and through Him in the Father" (3.25).

According to the Second Helvetic Confession, "the preaching of the Word of God is the Word of God" (chapter 1). In the sermon God really addresses people directly in such a way that it is Jesus Christ who is before the people. It is through the power of this Word that the Holy Spirit strengthens and renews our life in Christ, sustaining our union with him. (I will return to the place of the Word of God in pastoral theology and pastoral care when considering the ministry of the Word of God in chapter 7.)

In baptism the Spirit engrafts us into Christ, establishing the church's unity and binding us to one another in him. Baptism has been described in the Reformed tradition as a "sign and seal" of our union with Christ. For Calvin and the Reformed tradition, sacraments are signs that genuinely make present what they signify. This view receives an especially forthright statement in the Scots Confession, chapter 21.

> These sacraments . . . were instituted by God not only to make a visible distinction between his people and those who were without the Covenant [i.e., by admitting them to church membership], but also to exercise the faith of his children and, by participation of these sacraments, to seal in their hearts the assurance of his promise, and of that most blessed conjunction, union, and society, which the chosen have with their Head, Christ Jesus. And so we utterly condemn the vanity of those who affirm the sacraments to be nothing else than naked and bare signs. No, we assuredly believe that by Baptism we are engrafted into Christ Jesus, to be made partakers of his righteousness, by which our sins are covered and remitted, and also that in the Supper rightly used, Christ Jesus is so joined with us that he becomes the very nourishment and food of our souls.

The Scots Confession here reflects New Testament affirmations that we are baptized "into" Christ (Rom. 6:3); that all who are baptized are clothed with Christ (Gal. 3:27); and that by one Spirit we have all been baptized into one body of Christ (1 Cor. 12:12–13). In other words, baptism is most fully understood in the light of union with Christ.

If the sacrament of baptism unites all of us to Christ, it also unites us *with one another* in him. We who have been baptized are all one body, with Christ as the head (Rom. 12:4–5; Eph. 4:4–6). The foundation of the church's unity therefore comes to us as a gift from Christ, as the Spirit engrafts us together into him.

The Lord's Supper is the sign and seal of the Spirit's nourishing us in union with Christ through our spiritual feeding upon the body and blood of Christ. According to the Scots Confession, "Thus we confess and believe without doubt that the faithful, in the right use of the Lord's Table, do so eat the body and drink the blood of the Lord Jesus that he remains in them and they in him" (chapter 21). Calvin called union with Christ the "special fruit" of the Lord's Supper, which results in the assurance both of salvation and of forgiveness of sins:

> Godly souls can gather great assurance and delight from this Sacrament; in it they have a witness of our growth into one body with Christ, such that whatever is his may be called ours. As a consequence, we may dare assure ourselves that eternal life, of which he is the heir, is ours; and that the Kingdom of Heaven, into which he has already entered, can no more be cut off from us than from him; again, that we cannot be condemned for our sins, from whose guilt he has absolved us, since he willed to take them upon himself as if they were his own. (*Inst.* 4.17.2)

In a similar vein, Martin Luther compared union with Christ to a marriage between Christ and the soul of the believer, which is his bride. Though the comparison reflects sixteenth-century marriage customs, the analogy is effective. The bride brings to this marriage a dowry, says Luther, consisting of all the soul's sins. These sins become the property of Christ the bridegroom and no longer belong to the believer. In exchange, the bride comes to share in all her husband's property, that is, in all of Christ's righteousness. So our union with Christ, nourished and nurtured in the Lord's Supper, is essential to a proper understanding and appropriation of the forgiveness of sins, and lies therefore close to the heart of an evangelical expression of Christian faith.

Union with Christ: Sharing in Christ's Righteousness before God, and in His Knowledge and Love of the Father

It is clear by now that the theology of Hebrews 3:1—that Jesus Christ is the apostle and high priest of our confession—runs through my argument. He is the only mediator between God and creation. As the Son of the Father, bearing always the flesh of our humanity, he brings God to us and us to God in a salvific union of God's own making. Bringing God to us, he is the true apostle, the true Word of God. He comes not just revealing something about God, but as God himself in saving atonement in the humanity of his personhood as the bearer of our sin. Bringing us to God, he is our high priest, leading us to share both in his own (human) relationship with the Father and in his mission from the Father for the sake of the world. By our union with Christ he gives us to share in what is his: (1) his righteousness before God, (2) his knowledge of the Father, and (3) his love of the Father. By this sharing the things that are his become ours by grace through adoption.

Before we consider these three themes, we must first address briefly the relationship between the Father and the Son, because the center of the New Testament is the relationship between Jesus Christ and the one he addressed as Father. The communion between Jesus and the Father is a unique relationship, of which we can know nothing apart from the Apostles' own testimony. God is Father not by comparison to human fathers, but *only* in the Trinitarian relation, as Father of the Son in the Holy Spirit. Whenever the word "Father" is used of God it means "the one whom Jesus called Father." John 1:18, for example, instructs us that Jesus makes the Father known, *exegesato*—Jesus "exegetes" or "interprets" the Father. The Fatherhood of God has no meaning outside the Father-Son relationship, but by the gift of grace Jesus unites us with himself in the power of the Holy Spirit so that in union with him we share in his sonship. By ourselves we have no right or ground to address God as "Father." It is only as we are united with Christ, partaking of his "sonly" communion with the Father, that we can truthfully address God in this way. We come to the Father *through the sonship of Jesus Christ, becoming sons in him*. In Paul's words, "For all who are led by the Spirit of God are sons (*huioi*) of God. For you did not receive the spirit of slavery to fall back into fear, but you have received the spirit of sonship (*huiothesias*). When we cry, 'Abba! Father!' it is the Spirit himself bearing witness with our spirit that we are children (*tekna*) of God, and if children, then heirs, heirs of God and fellow heirs with Christ" (Rom. 8:14–17, RSV; the NRSV I think misses the theological point by translating *huioi* as "children of God." We become children of God because through union with Christ we share in his sonship). We come into communion with the Father through a union with Christ *in his sonship*. We know God only in and through Christ's relationship of sonship to the Father, in which we share through the Holy Spirit. This means that salvation is understood as our communion *with* the

Father *in* and *through* the Son *in the power of* the Holy Spirit. Knowledge of God and our hope for salvation are directly Trinitarian in their scope.

Thus we come now to consider the implications of our union with Christ: our sharing in (1) his righteousness before God, (2) his knowledge of the Father, and (3) his love of the Father.

Sharing in Christ's Righteousness before God

Righteousness means "standing in a right relationship." Used of God as in Romans 3:5, it means God's faithfulness or truthfulness. God keeps promises. It is also used of God in Romans 3:25–26 to show the quality of holiness that not only condemns sin but also, on the cross, decisively conquers sin. God is true to who God is. The Heidelberg Catechism states that "God is indeed merciful and gracious, but he is also righteous. It is his righteousness which requires that sin committed against the supreme majesty of God be punished" (Q. 11). The Catechism goes on to speak of our redemption in and through Jesus Christ "who is freely given to us for complete redemption and righteousness" (Q. 17).

Second Corinthians 5:21 is a guiding scriptural verse: "For our sake [God] made him to be sin who knew no sin, so that in him we might become the righteousness of God." We cannot attain a right relationship with God by ourselves; we cannot stand before God in the strength of our own faith, piety, or good works. This is what the doctrine of human depravity intends to communicate. Only he who was not a sinner yet was wholly human, God for us in and as Christ Jesus, could do for us what we could not do for ourselves. In Christ we become all that we can never be in the eyes of God if we are left to ourselves. Our sins are dealt with. The gulf that separates us from God on account of sin has been bridged. Christ has borne our sins and thus they are borne away. We are not now suddenly functionally perfected saints, of course. We still limp along straining between sin and mercy, going on to perfection but very slowly indeed. Nevertheless, united with Christ we share in *his* right relationship with God. This is surely the center of the Christian gospel and the summary of all preaching.

Given the very nature of the gospel that Christ died for our sins, the corollary is obviously true: we cannot stand before God *apart* from the saving life and death of Jesus Christ. Let us be clear what this means. There is no way to God—no salvation, in other words—outside the person and work of Jesus. Jesus is singularly the one through whom God "was pleased to reconcile to himself all things, whether on earth or in heaven, by making peace through the blood of his cross" (Col. 1:20). All the other claims to divinity and strategies pursued with a mind to union with God are rejected not just as worthless religious striving, but also as sinful assertions of human disobedience in the face of the sole righteous obedience of Jesus Christ. Jesus Christ is God's sovereign choice, God's singular mediating and saving agent. The gospel then insists that Jesus Christ alone is Savior, in and through whom there is sure access to the Father. This can be read off virtually every paragraph of the New Testament. It is the core assertion of the kerygma of the church.

Sharing in Christ's Knowledge of the Father

The Son knows the Father; the Father knows the Son—this theme is fundamental to the gospel. Knowledge of God, therefore, is by the will of the Father and, through union with Christ, a sharing in Jesus Christ's (human) relationship with the Father. We share not in his divinity, but in his humanity as the one Son of God. By union with Christ we share in the intimate knowledge of the Father that is Christ's alone *in his humanity*. True faith *is* a sharing in Christ's own human knowledge of the Father, as we are united with him in the bond of the Spirit. As Paul put it,

> The Spirit searches everything, even the depths of God. For what human being knows what is truly human except the human spirit that is within? So also no one comprehends what is truly God's except the Spirit of God. Now we have received not the spirit of the world, but the Spirit that is from God, so that we may understand the gifts bestowed on us by God. . . . "For who has known the mind of the Lord so as to instruct him?" But we have the mind of Christ. (1 Cor. 2:10–12, 16)

This is knowledge of God that, because it is through our union with Christ, is knowledge of the Father through the Father-Son relationship that Jesus has in his humanity. It is therefore a saving knowledge, knowledge of God by grace in and through Jesus Christ.

Jesus reveals God—not just something about God—because he is God. By the fourth century the church encapsulated this belief in the doctrine of the consubstantiality of the Son and the Father, which is the theological assumption behind the whole of the New Testament: Jesus, son of Mary, speaks for God, as God. John McLeod Campbell refers to this in his treatment of the retrospective aspect of the atonement, calling it Christ's witness-bearing for God, reflecting Revelation 1:5.[10] Christ shows us the Father (John 14:9), he vindicates the Father's name in the condemnation of our sin, he witnesses to the goodness of the will and heart of God, he affirms the love of God.

But we must go further. In his priestly ministry Jesus does not just reveal God; he also utters the appropriate human speech about God. Jesus speaks of God and, in his praying, to God; this is a priestly ministry that continues eternally. His speech names God in a way appropriate to and acceptable to God. His priesthood is not distant from us, as if he spoke and prayed removed from us. Because he speaks and prays in the flesh of our humanity he, by his Spirit, has joined himself to us and us to himself in such a way that he joins us to his own naming of and praying to God. As Calvin once said that we pray by the mouth of Christ, we can go on to say also that we speak of God by the mouth of Christ. There is no truthful human speech of God and to God otherwise. In Christ our feeble attempts to speak of and to God are set aside, and his speech becomes our speech. This is the soteriological aspect of theological speaking that all nonchristological theological speech fails to recognize. Because God is God, there is no way our human speech to God honors the holiness of God or refers accurately to God. It is not we who name God; God names himself, revealing his name to us. In his priestly love, Christ takes what is ours, our stumbling speech and mumbled prayers, and transforms them in himself, forgiving us our blasphemies, giving us in return his own speech of God in a wonderful exchange that makes our theology and praying possible in the first place. Aside from this, all theological speech is merely metaphorical referencing that has more to do with human religious pride than with theology properly conceived. At the center of all of this is Jesus' speech that he puts into the voice of the church: "When you pray say, 'Our Father, who art in heaven. . . .'" The rejection of this speech—and especially here one thinks of the rejection of the fatherhood of God in manifest attempts at inclusive language theology—is a rejection of Christ's priesthood and the sinful assertion of our own speech in place of his speech, and a rejection of the filial relationship of love between the Father and the Son in the unity of the Spirit that is the heart of the Trinity. It is in this sense that pride as the claim to autonomy is the basic sin.

---

10. John McLeod Campbell, *The Nature of the Atonement* (1856; reprint, Edinburgh: Handsel; Grand Rapids: Eerdmans, 1996), 114.

This has been powerfully expressed by John Knox, the Edinburgh reformer. Exiled in France in 1554, he wrote a brief *Treatise on Prayer*. It is a bit rambling, but at its heart is a magisterial understanding of the mediation of Christ. The title of the relevant section is: "Of necessity we must have a Mediator," and Knox's point is this: no one is worthy to appear in God's presence by reason of sin, which offends the majesty of God:

> to exeme us from this horrible confusion, our most merciful Father, knowing that our frail minds should hereby have been continually dejected, hath given unto us his only beloved Son, to be unto us right-eousness, wisdom, sanctification, and holiness. If in him we faithfully believe, we are so clad that we may with boldness compeer and appear before the throne of God's mercy, doubting nothing, but that whatso-ever we ask through our Mediator, that same we shall obtain most assuredly. Here, is most diligently to be observed, that without our Mediator, *forespeaker* [emphasis added], and peace-maker, we enter not into prayer; for the incallings of such as pray without Jesus Christ are not only vain, but also, are odious and abominable before God. . . . For as within the *sanctum sanctorum*, that is, the most holy place, entered no man but the High Priest alone, and as all sacrifices offered by any other than by priests only, provoked the wrath of God upon the sacrifice-maker; so, whoever doth intend to enter into God's presence, or to make prayers without Jesus Christ, shall find nothing but fearful judgment and horrible damnation. . . . For he who honoureth not the Son, honoureth not the Father. . . . So we are commanded only to call through Jesus Christ, by whom alone our petitions we obtain; for in him alone are all the promises of God confirmed and compleat. . . . He is our leader, whom, unless we follow, we shall walk in darkness.[11]

Needless to say, neither saints nor angels can be mediators between us and God. Only Jesus Christ, God and human being, is mediator. The force of the "only" here, or the "alones" above, should be noted and appre-ciated. Here the whole theology and practice of prayer—and not just Christian prayer, but all and every approach to God—stands or falls based on whether it is through the mediatorial personhood and life of Jesus Christ. And he is not just mediator in the past when on earth. For the mediator, says Knox, has not resigned his office to his servants but con-tinues forever, our perpetual high priest.

11. *Select Practical Writings of John Knox* (Edinburgh: Johnson and Hunter, 1882), 44–45.

In practice, this means that all theology in union with Christ must be done in the mode of worship and prayer, in which repentance and gratitude are at the forefront. To speak and pray by the mouth of Christ, in and through the efficacy of his priestly ministry, compels us to an obedience of thought and speech in union with Christ that is directed by the intention to follow Jesus to the point at which we are profoundly transformed in our very patterns of thinking, living, and speaking. Therefore our words about God must be offered humbly, insofar as we offer them, and hopefully, insofar as we offer them in the name and through the priesthood of Jesus. They are never for our own advancement or for the glory of a school of theology, but for the glory of God, the sake of the church, and our own growth in grace.

Sharing in Christ's Love of the Father

"Whoever does not love does not know God, for God is love" (1 John 4:8). The great theological themes of righteousness and the knowledge of God through our union with Christ must finally give way to our sharing in Christ's love of the Father. While believing in Jesus as Lord means a new standing before God and a new knowledge of God, it also means a new relationship with God. Love becomes the criterion of Christian faith and life in union with Christ. If we do not share in Christ's love of the Father, we do not really know the Father or stand in a right relationship with the Father.

As noted, the great dangers in speaking of the love of God are trivialization and sentimentalization. Nevertheless, love is a reality that we must struggle to reclaim because it takes us to the heart of the gospel: love is the nature of Christ's relationship with the Father, and through union with Christ we share in this love. To explore the meaning and depth of this extraordinary love of God, the fourth-century Greek fathers coined a word to describe the mystery of the interior relations within the Holy Trinity: *perichoresis* (*chora*, "space" or "room").[12] It refers to a way of coinherence by which the Persons of the Trinity dwell in one another in a mutual way, while remaining distinct from one another. Thus the church could speak of God as one being, three persons, and the Holy Trinity could be understood as the loving movement of communion among the three persons in the sublime, ineffable holiness of the unity that is God's true nature. This is a love that also goes out to reach us in Christ and that, through our union with Christ by the Holy Spirit, joins us back to itself,

---

12. For a discussion, see T. F. Torrance, *Christian Doctrine of God*, 102.

as it were, so that we share in this divine movement of love. Thus the center of Christian faith and life is sharing through union with Christ in the love within the Holy Trinity, as the Son adores the Father in the unity of the Holy Spirit.

This love is manifest in Christ's obedience even unto death on the cross (Phil. 2:8). Of course, Jesus himself laid down the principle that "no one has greater love than this, to lay down one's life for one's friends. You are my friends . . ." (John 15:13–14). Theologically, this is expressed by Paul: "God proves his love for us in that while we still were sinners Christ died for us" (Rom. 5:8). It is important to affirm the basic logic of divine love: God did not send Jesus to die for our sins so that God would love us. Rather, God so loved the world—us—that God sent Jesus to atone for our sins. The cross is the action *of* the love of God, not the condition *for* the love of God, and it is a love that went all the way into the hell of our separation from God in order to restore us to union and communion with God.

To share in that love by our union with Christ is to share in the fellowship of his suffering. To share in his love of the Father is also to share in his mission from the Father, which is the outpouring of his love for the sake of the world. Thus we share in his obedience, for there is no sharing in Christ's love of and for the Father without also a sharing in his obedience to the will of the Father. This is an integral aspect of practical theology. Love and will are not two things, but one thing seen from different perspectives. Thus sharing in Christ's love of the Father means sharing in what that love led him to do and taking up our cross daily and following him.

United with Christ: Church and Ministry

Here I now shift the focus from God's mission to our sharing in Christ's mission. In Christ, united with Christ, we are awakened from the sloth of self-interest to a life that longs for a deeper conversion to God and a more faithful service of God. Union with Christ means also union *in* Christ. Thus this shift in focus requires reflection on the nature of the church and its ministry. Two areas require comment. The first is the nature of the church in union with Christ. The second is the relation between the priesthood of Christ and the ministry of the church.

The Church in Union with Christ

As the body of Christ, the church has its life in Christ and is, therefore, decisively shaped by union with one another in him (e.g., Rom. 12:4–5;

1 Cor. 12:27). As the Second Helvetic Confession puts it, "Since there is always but one God, and there is one mediator between God and men, Jesus the Messiah, and one Shepherd of the whole flock, one Head of this body, and, to conclude, one Spirit, one salvation, one faith, one Testament or covenant, it necessarily follows that there is only one Church" (chapter 17). The unity confessed is with *believers* in every time and place. Union with one another, because it takes place in Christ, is grounded in the fact that all are joined to Christ in faith by the power of the Spirit. The church has a powerful witness to make here, both to society and to the world at large, as the Spirit helps us live into the oneness that is ours in Christ. Union with him and in him transcends and overrules every lesser loyalty that threatens to separate people one from another.

Union with Christ also calls the church into particular communities of worship and mission. The oneness in Christ takes on flesh and blood, confronting the church in the form of a real and tangible connection with this particular sister or brother in the life of this particular church. That union is given concrete form by our life together with the sisters and brothers of our own worshiping and serving congregations. "We know that we have passed from death to life because we love one another. Whoever does not love abides in death" (1 John 3:14). Because union with Christ is responsible for calling the church into particular communities of worship and mission, individual congregations are more than just voluntary associations of like-minded individuals gathered together for a common religious purpose. The church is divinely called and empowered, as well as being a human institution; the power of the risen Christ in our midst gives rise to these particular communities of faith, mission, and worship. While the church is catholic, or universal, each congregation represents, in however splendid or modest a way, the local presence of the universal church. "For where two or three are gathered in my name, I am there among them" (Matt. 18:20).

Union with Christ leads to union *in* Christ, uniting Christians of all races and cultures across denominations, determinations, and times. Jesus' high-priestly prayer provokes the church toward a coming future de facto that captures well the reality de jure: "that they may all be one. As you, Father, are in me and I am in you, may they also be in us, so that the world may believe that you have sent me" (John 17:21).

Thus by union with Christ the church participates in Christ's resurrected life and awaits in hope the future that God has prepared for us. In this way the church confesses the way things *are:* the true nature of the church is in union with Jesus Christ. The future that awaits the church is not the result of our own work, however, but the redemption of all things in Christ. The present is not characterized by laborious righteousness weighted down by the oppressive awareness that everything rests on our shoulders. Rather, the church's present pilgrimage is properly embarked upon in joyous anticipation of the promise that God is at work to make all things new in Christ, and in thankful recognition that God has gifted us to participate in that work of redemption by union with Christ in the power of the Holy Spirit.

As the grace and mercy of God reach out to us *from* the Father, *through* and *in* the Son, *in* the power of the Holy Spirit, so our joyous response to the divine goodness rises *to* the Father, *with* and *through* the Son, *by* the acting of that same Spirit. By union with Christ the church joins—as a pure gift of God's grace—with the perfect praise that the Son eternally renders to the Father on our behalf. It thus assumes its place, however modest, in the unending chorus of praise that rises to the throne of God from the lips of the faithful, on behalf of all creation.

The Priesthood of Christ and the Ministry of the Church

The great danger in modern functional ecclesiology is the assumption that the church's identity is institutional. When we speak of church growth, congregational renewal, and denominational survival, we may reveal a way of thinking that leads to pragmatic responses to situational demands so that function follows need rather than the gospel of Jesus Christ. We make the serious mistake of replacing the christological constitution of the church with contingent considerations that redefine the church according to worldly rather than christological patterns. This is ostensibly a way forward but in fact denies the gospel. The increasing sense today of the loss of christological and soteriological clarity regarding the person and work of Christ has brought with it correspondingly great confusion with respect to the identity and purpose of the church. This confusion is evident in pastoral care, where auxiliary concerns, such as counseling methods, theories of human development, and family systems perspectives, good in themselves but at best only construed and constrained remotely by christological considerations, now control the practice. In particular, it is the failure to think of pastoral theology out of a center in the priesthood of Christ that has cast pastoral ministry back upon programs of its own devising. The effect has been to replace the vicarious humanity of Christ with the ministry of the pastor and his or her skills. Pastoral theology and pastoral care, I am insisting, must be first of all a theology for and a work of the church, and as such, an expression of the one gospel of Jesus Christ.

The starting point in ecclesiology is the ontological connection between Christ and the church. The church exists as church only insofar as it is Christ's body, in union with him, meaning also our union in him, both of which are a matter of his free and gracious choice. The church has no other ground of being than Jesus Christ. This means in a primary way that the church is not the church as institution, or as a voluntary collection of free, religiously and ethically motivated individuals, or, with its episcopate, as an historically ordered hierarchy that determines what it is and what it must do. It is Christ alone who determines the "that" and the "what" of the church, who loves the church and calls and forms it according to his own purpose. The church is what he is in that he is Lord of the church in whom and from whom alone it has life. As such, the church belongs to Christ, not to itself. The church is not self-referenced. In a primary sense, its being is iconic, not institutional, as it points away from itself to Christ. As Christ is in heaven the Son of the Father, so the church is, in an appropriate way, his body on earth, the body of the Son, formed in union with him. While the church is one with Christ, however, it is not synonymous with Christ and is not to be confused with him. He is always Lord over the church, having his being apart from the church. His identity is given in that as he is one in being with the Father through the Spirit in the communion of love within the Holy Trinity, he is sent from the Father through the Spirit for the sake of the world to take upon himself the body of our flesh. Likewise, the church has identity, and therefore purpose, as sent from Christ to go into the world as the means of his continuing salvation. It is in the Spirit that the church has this life and identity only from and in union with Christ. Its task, its only task, then, is to bear witness to Christ in a manner rooted in his own being for us as savior and Lord.

Nevertheless, the church exists as the body of Christ only insofar as the church is also apostolic. The inseparable biblical relations between *ruaḥ* and *dabar, pneuma* and *logos,* means that the Word of Christ, empowered by the Spirit of Christ, is given through the historical apostolic revelation. Were we to insist otherwise, the church would remain an abstract or ideal entity. According to T. F. Torrance,

> in the Apostolic Revelation Jesus Christ returns clothed in His Spirit, the Spirit of Truth, and gives Himself to be known and appropriated by the Apostles in His own Spirit, in His own Truth, in His own

Light. . . . In this way the Apostles formed the *hinges* of the divine mission, where, so to speak, the vertical mission in the sending of the Son by the Father, is folded out horizontally into history at Pentecost.[13]

We cannot separate the being of the church in union with Christ from the mission given in and through the apostolic kerygma.[14] It is because the church is apostolic and, as such, kerygmatic, that it is inherently a missional church, shaped in all regards by its call to share in the *missio Dei*, given in and as incarnation and atonement. As the apostolic witness refers to the ministry of Christ in his person as Son of the Father in the flesh of our humanity, its purpose in and for the church is the purpose of that ministry. The church has neither being nor life apart from this. Consequently, the mission and ministry of the church is constituted according to a christological and soteriological pattern, correlative to the person and ministry of Christ, through a participation in his ministry.[15]

Just as Christ is prophet, priest, and king, with his priesthood as the aspect of his being the anointed One through which he exercises his prophetic and royal ministries, so the church is called to prophetic, priestly, and royal ministries in union with Christ, and its sharing in Christ's priesthood is the means of sharing in his prophetic and royal ministries. Just as the heart of Christ's saving ministry is found in his perpetual priesthood, by which he proclaims the Word of God to and for us and offers us in himself to God, so the church's primary identity is the exercise of a priestly ministry that proclaims the Word of God, celebrates the sacraments of baptism and the Lord's Supper, and serves others in ministries that share in Christ's mission from the Father for the sake of the world. He who is priest in heaven calls his body to a priestly work on earth in which through the church Christ offers up his worshiping and serving people to the Father. In this way the church is a holy and royal priesthood (1 Pet. 2:5, 9), participating in Christ's atoning priesthood in the ministries of worship and service with which it is charged. This is no new thing, no other ministry, but the ministry of the same Christ to the Father in the Holy Spirit for the world, now, however, undertaken through the corporate priesthood of the whole church contained in all of its members. In this way, "the Church participates in Christ's ministry by *serving* Him who is Prophet, Priest and King."[16]

13. Thomas F. Torrance, *Royal Priesthood*, 2d ed. (Edinburgh: T. & T. Clark, 1993), 27.
14. Ibid., 28 and 30.
15. Ibid., 35.
16. Ibid., 37.

The concept of the priesthood of the church gives rise to two problems. First, there is the general problem of what such a difficult theological concept means in practice. Are we saying anything at all when we use the phrase "priesthood of all believers"? What more is intended than an honorary status without defined function?[17] Second, there is the question of ministry as priesthood, an issue that still remains close to the center of ecumenical concerns over ministerial orders, authority, and Eucharist. If, as we have done throughout, we emphasize the singularity of Christ's priesthood in and through which he presents us to the Father, does that leave a role for ministerial priesthood at all?

Insofar as the church has a priesthood, it is a corporate priesthood of the body rather than a priesthood belonging to certain individuals within the church. But even to say that the church has a corporate priesthood is problematic, for it suggests that the church has a mediatorial or sacerdotal capacity. It is Christ through his priesthood and by his Spirit who establishes the church's union with himself and who offers God's creation back to God as the acceptable offering, not the work of any priest, even the corporate priesthood of the church, on earth. Because of the emphasis on the singular priesthood of Christ, there is a sense then in which we have to speak of the nonpriesthood of all believers! The primary calling is to be the *laos* or people of God in which all share in some way in Christ's whole ministry. Thus we should speak of the laity of all believers, and especially perhaps of the laity of the clergy! This is one primary meaning of baptism. It is only when the vicarious atoning and mediating priesthood of Christ in the flesh of our humanity slips away from the mind of the church that some form of mediation between a glorified Christ and sinful humanity is needed. It was as a result of just this theological vacuum that the mediatorial role of Mary, the saints, and a sacerdotal order of priests properly emerged in the Roman Church, with its counterpart in Protestantism, arguably, in its form as the religion of the book, where the Bible functionally replaces Christ as the mediator, confusing the Word with the witness to the Word.[18]

We move toward a practical answer to our questions when we consider what it is that the Spirit of the risen Christ actually affects in and through the church at the point of the exercise of his priesthood. Christ's own

17. See T. W. Manson, *Ministry and Priesthood: Christ's and Ours* (London: Epworth, 1958), 37 n. 5.

18. See Josef A. Jungmann, *The Place of Christ in Liturgical Prayer* (Collegeville, Minn.: Liturgical Press, 1965).

priesthood was given in the form of his sacrificial servanthood: "The Son of Man came not to be served but to serve, and to give his life a ransom for many" (Mark 10:45). After washing the disciples' feet, Jesus said: "So if I, your Lord and Teacher, have washed your feet, you also ought to wash one another's feet. For I have set you an example, that you also should do as I have done to you" (John 13:14–15). This is the christological *hypo-deigma* or pattern that must frame the church's life in Christ. The lived expression of sharing in Christ's priesthood—which holds together the sacrifice of service, for which we are ordained by our baptism, and the sacrifice of praise, celebrated especially in the Eucharist—takes two forms. First, in obedience to God through the church's sacrificial suffering servant ministry of love and service, Christ is diaconally present to the world, and he offers this service as his own body in the name of his own priesthood to the Father. According to T. W. Manson, "we may conclude, then, that the priesthood of all believers lies in the fact that each believer offers himself as a sacrifice according to the pattern laid down by Christ; and—what is equally essential—that all these individual offerings are taken up into the one perpetual offering made by the one eternal high-priest of the New Covenant."[19] Insofar as the church shares in Christ's eternal priesthood, this is a ministry of personal sacrificial sharing in Christ's self-sacrifice and self-offering to God for the sake of the world.

The second lived expression of sharing in Christ's priesthood is the celebration of the Lord's Supper. Here Christ comes in word and elements, bringing God to the people; here Christ takes the sacrifice of praise and in his own name offers it as a rational worship (Rom. 12:2) to God. In the Eucharist Christ is truly present with his people and by the Spirit binds them to himself in bread and wine and to his priestly self-offering to the Father. Again Manson puts it helpfully: "The focus of the high-priestly work, in which Christ and his people share, is the sacrament of the Eucharist. Here Christ-in-his-Church renews the gifts of God's love to his people. Here Christ-in-his-Church, which is his body, offers to God his-Church-in-himself on the altar of self-sacrifice with the ritual of obedience and love."[20]

It is by sharing in Christ's priesthood that the church holds together the seemingly separate ministries of *diakonia* and *eucharistia*, loving care for and service of God's people and thankful worship to God. They are, in fact, the one work of Christ and express the truth of McLeod Camp-

---

19. Manson, *Ministry and Priesthood*, 64.
20. Ibid., 70.

bell's contention that "Christ, as the Lord of our spirits and our life, *devotes us to God* and *devotes us to men* in the *fellowship of His self-sacrifice.*"[21]

The matter of the Eucharist raises finally the issues of ministerial orders and priesthood as ministry. It is significant that Jesus Christ never called anyone to be a priest and was not himself a priest in the Hebrew sense, because Joseph was not a priest; further, priesthood is missing from the Pauline lists at 1 Corinthians 12:28–30 and Ephesians 4:11–12. (On a semantic note, the word "priest" was originally used in the church as an administrative rather than a sacerdotal term. It is a long stretch from *presbyteros* to *sacerdos*, from leader of the worshiping congregation to sacrificing priest.) The issue, finally, comes down to the theology of who celebrates the Eucharist, and what we understand their status and function to be. If all are priests, is the eucharistic minister a different kind of priest? On the one hand, that person is called out by charismatic endowment and is set apart for a decent ordering of the Lord's Table. That person serves as a steward (*oikonomos*) of the mysteries, presiding as *episkopos* over the fellowship by exercising the ministry of Word and sacraments so that the order of the presbyterate is itself ordered by the celebration of the Lord's Supper.[22] On the other hand, the authority in the Eucharist lies not in the person appointed (as in the phrase "my priesthood"), but in Christ's priesthood alone, who builds the body through the Spirit, and who calls some to minister to the body in a ministry of eucharistic superintendency, homiletical service, intercessory discipline, and pastoral oversight. As the superintendent of the Eucharist (to use a neutral term), the minister recalls for the congregation the institution, and speaking for the congregation leads the prayer of thanksgiving. To cite T. F. Torrance, "in the last analysis it is Christ Himself who is the one Priest, and men are ordained only in the sense that He gives them to share in His Priesthood, but to share in it *alius rationis*, in a mode appropriate to those who are but stewards and servants."[23]

Whether such persons should be called priests is a moot point, because they are not priests in any usual sense of the term. In fact, it may be dangerous to call people priests in that it suggests that Christ's priesthood is not wholly efficacious. What they are called to is a vital task in the earthly life of the church, of that there is no doubt. While certain functions are designated for persons appropriately called and suitably trained, at a far

21. McLeod Campbell, *Nature of the Atonement*, 255.
22. Thus T. F. Torrance, *Royal Priesthood*, 77.
23. Ibid., 81.

deeper level all Christians are called and equipped by the Spirit for Christ's service, and the exercise of eucharistic superintendency must be understood in that context. And because Christ's priestly ministry belongs to him in the flesh of his vicarious humanity, by which he has assumed all flesh, no one by virtue of gender or race can be excluded from sharing in Christ's ministry, eucharistic or diaconal. The limiting of eucharistic ministries to men only is a deep and sinful violation of Christ's encompassing and inclusive priesthood given for all in incarnation and atonement. There is neither a privileged class nor a privileged service in Christ's body. Only Christ is Lord over the church, and all leadership within the church must be the leadership of service in Christ that glorifies God, but no office or person. The issue finally comes down to the thoroughgoing radicalism of the church's Christology.

Union with Christ: Sharing in Christ's Mission from the Father

By union with Christ we participate in God's mission to the world. Here we emphasize the *missional character of the church*. If Christ is indeed God's gracious mission to the world, and if the church is united with him, then it follows that the church shares in every aspect of Christ's mission. In Christ God has come to redeem every aspect of human existence. To claim that the church's mission embodies only the spiritual aspect of God's compassion or only the social or economic aspects would be to deny the church's union with the whole Christ.

Every human being, whether within or without the walls of the church, is a person for whom Christ died. God's gracious yes to humankind uttered in Jesus Christ is intended for every single human being: rich and poor, powerless and powerful, born and unborn, old and young, healthy and sick, criminal and law-abiding, able and disabled. There are no limits to the compassion God has shown toward the human race in Jesus Christ; there can be no limits upon the scope of the church's mission in union with Christ to the whole of the human family. This is not to say, of course, that any particular congregation or Christian individual is obligated to reach out in all these ways. God distributes different gifts and vocations to different parts of the body, for the good of the whole (1 Corinthians 12ff.). But considered as a whole, the scope of the church's mission to the human race is unlimited, just as the love God has shown to us in Jesus Christ has no limit.

The love, forgiveness, and new life that God extends to humankind in Jesus Christ are intended for everyone. "As I live, says the Lord God, I have no pleasure in the death of the wicked, but that the wicked turn from their ways and live" (Ezek. 33:11). If Jesus Christ *is* in his own person this love, forgiveness, and new life, that is, God's missional turn outward toward the wicked, nothing could be more inhuman and unloving than to withhold the proclamation of Christ from any of the world's peoples. To be clear: union with Christ in his apostolic and priestly ministry rules out the view that posits the existence of "many paths to God" apart from Jesus Christ, the sole mediator between God and creation. Evangelism in union with Christ must be a universal commitment for the church, for everything in life and death, the present and the future, depends on Jesus Christ and our union with him.

Further, in union with Christ the church is called to establish Christ's justice and peace in all creation. In Jesus' resurrection from the dead we witness the firstfruits of the *new creation* that God has inaugurated in him.

> They shall not labor in vain, or bear children for calamity; for they shall be the offspring of the blessed of the LORD, and their children with them. Before they call I will answer, while they are yet speaking I will hear. The wolf and the lamb shall feed together, the lion shall eat straw like the ox; and dust shall be the serpent's food. They shall not hurt or destroy in all my holy mountain, says the LORD. (Isa. 65:23–25 RSV).

The kingdom of God that dawns among us in Jesus Christ is a kingdom of *shalom*—a kingdom of benevolent order and peace and goodness in every sphere of relation among human beings, God, and the created world. *Shalom* is the order of the world as God intended it from the beginning.

Christ comes to us as the bearer of this *shalom* and as the firstfruits of God's promised restoration of all things. The church that lives in union with him prays and hopes and works toward this *shalom* in every aspect of its earthly existence. The promotion of social righteousness and the exhibition of the kingdom of God to the world are rightly considered among the great ends of the church.

We must reject nonmissional understandings of the church. The link between God's mission to the world in and as the person of Jesus Christ and the calling of the church are inseparable. Neither can or should be understood apart from the other. We understand God's mission to the world only as we understand what God has done in and through Jesus Christ and continues to do in and through the church's work in the power of the Holy Spirit in union with Christ. We understand Jesus aright only as we come to understand him as God's gracious mission to the world and for the world, which mission continues even now in and as the mission of the church, which is his body. And we understand what the church is about only as we come to recognize its union with Christ in the power of the Spirit and its consequent participation in God's mission to the world in Christ.

Chapter 5

The Heavenly Priesthood of Christ

He therefore sits on high transfusing us by his power, that he may quicken us to spiritual life, sanctify us by his Spirit, adorn the church with divers gifts of his grace, keep it safe from all harm by his protection, restrain the raging enemies of his cross and of our salvation by the strength of his hand, and finally hold all power in heaven and on earth.

Calvin, *Institutes* 2.16.16

From that moment [the ascension] He could rule His people, not by the exercise of outward authority alone, but by inwardly assimilating them to Himself. From that moment he was in a position to present His "many brethren" along with Him, amidst the sanctities of a new creation and in eternal submission to the Father, to Him who, alike in the natural and in the spiritual world, must be "all in all."

William Milligan,
The Ascension and Heavenly Priesthood of Our Lord[1]

Introduction: The Gracing of the Church for Ministry

I have argued throughout that the basic practice or ministry of God is the man Jesus of Nazareth in the power of the Spirit. I must emphasize two points. First is the stubborn historicity entailed in this ministry of God. Second, it is God who makes us practical, not we who make God practical. The

---

1. William Milligan, *The Ascension and Heavenly Priesthood of Our Lord* (1892; reprint, Greenwood, S.C.: Attic, 1977).

historicity and priority of the divine reality and act are the basis for all practical theology; all churchly practice depends on the God who acts in history.

Ministry always remains God's ministry before it is the church's or the pastor's ministry. This hierarchy must in no way now be undercut as we consider the nature of the ministry of the church. Rather, our goal must be to build on what has gone before, to develop in some detail specific forms of ministry as participation in the actual ministry of Jesus Christ, forms of ministry that Christ calls forth and empowers as a sharing in his vicarious life through union with him. My goal is to be concrete, but in such a way that the practice of ministry is seen to be inherently theological in the sense of inhering in God and by means of sharing in the vicarious obedience of the Son to the will of the Father. Now I will show in what manner Christ becomes concrete in a new way in the actual gracing of the church for ministry.

Sometimes, as we shall see, Christ slips away from the mind of the church precisely at the point where ministry becomes actual. We may, in error, presume a spiritualized Christ dwelling in heaven, his present and continuing work subsumed somehow into the work of the Holy Spirit; or, equally in error, the church may turn him into abstract nouns that function as ethical norms or wisdom maxims—such as diversity, justice, love, and peace—to guide ministerial practice. Against these approaches, I argue in this chapter that Christ's heavenly priesthood is the basis for understanding the divine mediation, advocacy, and empowerment for the response of faith to the work of Christ. Christ's heavenly priesthood points toward the church's action and makes it an essential component in the construction of pastoral theology that is avowedly Christian. Douglas Farrow observes that "Calvin's attention to Christ's heavenly priesthood, which was furthered by Knox and by the divines of various traditions influenced by Calvin, was in many respects salutary. Indeed there is little of real significance in the Reformation that can be sustained in a wholesome way without reference to that concept."[2] We are clearly forced to deal with a major Christian doctrine that expresses in no small way the dynamic center of pastoral theology within a framework faithful to the Reformation.

That I discuss the issues in this chapter under the head of the heavenly priesthood of Christ may seem odd and somewhat arcane, perhaps even an antiquated designation, to some. Yet it is critical to my argument and is both correct and profoundly practical for two reasons. First, the work

---

2. Douglas Farrow, *Ascension and Ecclesia* (Edinburgh: T. & T. Clark, 1999), 179.

of Christ the heavenly priest connects the priesthood of Christ completed "for all time" (Heb. 10:12) and ministry today, keeping in mind the language and argument I have already developed. Second, and perhaps more importantly at this stage, the work of Christ the heavenly priest suggests the nature of the continuing ministry of Christ—often a rather enigmatic and elusive issue[3]—while also locating within the argument a place for gathering together the material basis for ministry. This basis for ministry is found in Christ's bringing us to communion with the Father, his intercession as our advocate, and his benediction and blessing in the gift of the Holy Spirit. This threefold work of the heavenly priesthood of Christ is surely the meaning of the reference to God's power that is put to work when God raised Christ from the dead and seated him at his right hand in the heavenly places (Eph. 1:20). Or as Douglas Farrow put it, "He who appears before God on man's behalf will also reappear before man on God's behalf, to bestow the fullness of his high-priestly blessing."[4]

In what light are we to understand Christ in his work as the heavenly priest? In this chapter I consider what it means that Christ is priest in heaven for the life and ministry of the church.[5]

The Ascension: An Essential Part of Salvation History

We can hardly speak of the heavenly priesthood of Christ without dealing with the ascension as an event in the history of Jesus, and as such, as a public rather than a metaphorical event. Yet the doctrine today languishes unnoticed on the liturgical fringes of mainstream Protestantism, and its profound significance to a proper understanding of the gospel is lost to the church. This is all the more remarkable when we notice that the ascension (and exaltation) of Christ is undoubtedly within the

---

3. See in part the argument of Farrow, ibid.

4. Ibid., 35.

5. A note about the provenance of this chapter: while the ascension has received some scholarly attention in recent years, from Thomas F. Torrance and Douglas Farrow especially, the heavenly ministry of Christ for us seems to have remained largely unexamined, most notably in twentieth-century pastoral and practical theology. Calvin's brief treatment is very important, and we shall return to it, but of especial interest is Milligan, *Ascension and Heavenly Priesthood of Our Lord.* This remarkable though largely unknown book opens up a seriously neglected area, and in a beautiful and rigorously biblical and dogmatic way points to a chapter sadly missing in pastoral theological reflection today. My reliance upon Milligan's work will demonstrate further my indebtedness to the magisterial christocentric theology of grace in Scottish Reformed reflection, and found already in this study in John McLeod Campbell and Thomas F. Torrance.

mainstream of the New Testament. As a fact of Christ's and the world's history, it is the hinge on which the understanding of the church turns, at least for Luke-Acts and Paul. It is the presupposition for Pentecost.

My concern here is not with the exegetical and historical arguments for the ascension, however; neither do I deal with the differential and relational understanding of time-space that a proper account demands.[6] My concern is strictly with the dogmatics of the ascension as the framework within which to set the discussion of the heavenly priesthood of Christ. The point is this: in and through the ascension the incarnation continues. Without it the ministry of Jesus remains in the past tense,[7] and the risen Lord slips quietly to his eternal rest, slumbering, presumably, at the right hand of the Father, and a spectator to the dramas of the church's life. Indeed, every hope for the reality of and empowerment for the ministry of the church depends on the truth and reality of the ascension and on the continuing ministry of our Lord in heaven.

Who ascended? This question is more theologically compelling than the perhaps more obvious questions concerning whether and how the ascension actually happened. Confusion in the answers given has had serious effects on the church. The correct answer is that Jesus of Nazareth ascended, and he, in his humanity ("the self-same body," according to John Knox in the Scots Confession, chapter 11), sits with the Father in the communion of the Holy Spirit in the unity of God. Many New Testament texts certainly teach a doctrine of an exalted and ascended Christ as a man—in Luke-Acts, Paul and his tradition, and Hebrews, among others.[8]

Two problems have arisen in the church's doctrinal history concerning the nature of the ascension. On the one hand, at times the church has tended to place Christ so far above us in his ascension that his humanity slips away, swallowed, as it were, into his divinity. Lose his humanity in the ascension, however, and the mediator then needs a mediator, for one is confronted with negotiating a way to approach the sheer dread majesty of God (*horribilis Dei maiestas*, Calvin, *Inst.* 3.20.17).[9] The church itself,

---

6. On this latter point see especially Thomas F. Torrance, *Space, Time and Resurrection* (Grand Rapids: Eerdmans, 1976), 123–24.

7. This wonderful point was made by Gerrit Scott Dawson, "Recovering the Ascension for the Transformation of the Church," *Theology Matters* 7, no 2 (March/April 2001): 1.

8. Luke 24:50–53; Acts 1:9–11; 2:32–33; 5:30–31; Rom. 8:34; Phil. 2:6–9; 3:20; Eph. 4:8–10; Col. 3:1; 1 Tim. 3:16; 1 Pet. 1:21; 3:22; Heb. 2:9; 10:12; 12:2.

9. The whole sentence is worthy of note: "For as soon as God's dread majesty comes to mind, we cannot but tremble and be driven far away by the recognition of our own unworthiness, until Christ comes forward as intermediary, to change the throne of dreadful glory into the throne of grace."

Mary *theotokos*, a sacerdotal priesthood, and the saints have all done duty in this regard at various times in the theological journey of the church. Ironically, as Josef A. Jungmann has shown,[10] this exaltation of Christ above or beyond his vicarious humanity happened in the fourth and fifth centuries and in defense of orthodoxy against Arianism, when Christ in his divinity become so elevated in the mind of the church that it increasingly hesitated to pray "through Christ," choosing instead to pray "for Christ's sake." Medieval theology is characterized in part by the consequential loss of the role of the vicarious humanity of Christ. Yet in contrast, consider Athanasius:

> Since then the Word, being the image of the Father and immortal, took the form of the servant, and *as man* underwent for us death in His flesh, that thereby He might offer Himself for us through death to the Father; therefore also, *as man*, he is said because of us and for us to be highly exalted, that as by His death we all died in Christ, so again in the Christ Himself we might all be highly exalted, being raised from the dead, and ascending into heaven.[11]

It is important to note Athanasius's double use of "as man." As a man Christ underwent death; as a man he was highly exalted. In this way Athanasius indicates that the union between God and humankind, entered into at the incarnation, continues through and beyond the ascension. This unbreakable personal union is critical to properly understand Christology, Christian hope, and the ministry of the church.

On the other hand, lose Christ's divinity and the ascension becomes a moral metaphor of perfectibility, Jesus assumes the role of exemplar, and the church emerges as an ethics-driven community. This has been the route chosen by liberal theology for over two hundred years as Christianity came increasingly to be interpreted through the prism of ethical imperatives. In this case, while the church is understood to be quickened by the Holy Spirit to follow the example of Jesus, Jesus himself is mortally stuck in the past, and the church's hope is the living memory of a dead Lord.

In neither case is Christian faith understood in terms of participation in the life of God through the humanity of Christ in and by which he both

---

10. Josef A. Jungmann, *The Place of Christ in Liturgical Prayer* (Collegeville, Minn.: Liturgical Press, 1965), 172–73.

11. Athanasius, *Four Discourses Against the Arians* 1.41, in *The Nicene and Post-Nicene Fathers*, ed. Philip Schaff and Henry Wace, 2d ser., vol. 4 (reprint, Edinburgh: T. & T. Clark; Grand Rapids: Eerdmans, 1998), emphasis added.

brings us to union with the Father *and* imparts the plenitude of his high-priestly blessing upon us. Both approaches fail because of a defective Christology.

Two important points concerning the nature of the ascension deserve attention, the first already alluded to, the second a new point. First, as Athanasius insisted, in his ascension Jesus Christ retained his humanity. Just as Christ came in the incarnation in union with us in the flesh of our humanity, likewise he continues to be in hypostatic union with us in his ascension. This means quite basically (though hardly simply!) that we, through Christ's union with us and our union with Christ, continue to be included in the life of God.[12] Thus Christ returns to the Father as he came to us, in the flesh and bearing our humanity with him. In no case have we to do with a *logos asarkos*, a discarnate word. What the incarnation united the ascension did not divide. It was the same "I" who spoke to the disciples of his going away who would afterward remember them and dwell with them, and, at the end, come for them again. John 14, for example, could be interpreted in the light of this unity of being between the historical and ascended Jesus Christ. In any case, it is the same Lord who is high priest in heaven who has been tested as we are, yet is without sin (Heb. 4:14–15). In sum, "if our Lord is now in the heavenly world at all, He is there not as God only, but as man."[13] This is surely the meaning of John 3:13, "No one has ascended into heaven except the one who descended from heaven, the Son of Man."

The incarnation and the ascension must be held together in such a way that the ascent (*anabasis*) corresponds to the descent (*katabasis*) in the hypostatic unity of Christ's undivided and indivisible priestly personhood. Thus while in his incarnation Christ became human, he did so without ceasing to be what he was and is eternally in himself as the Creator-Word of God.[14] The ascension is the reverse of the incarnation in that the ascended Lord ever lives as the man, Jesus from Nazareth, Son of the Father and son of Mary. Torrance has put it succinctly:

> As in the incarnation we have to think of God the Son becoming man without ceasing to be transcendent God, so in his ascension we have to think of Christ as ascending above all space and time without ceasing to be man or without any diminishment of his physical historical

---

12. Thus Dawson, "Recovering the Ascension," 2.
13. Milligan, *Ascension*, 28.
14. Torrance, *Space, Time and Resurrection*, 124.

existence.... In the incarnation we have the meeting of man and God in man's place, but in the ascension we have the meeting of man and God in God's place, but through the Spirit these are not separated from one another.[15]

The incarnation, then, is not the summary, keystone, or organizing principle of the gospel. A higher end is contemplated than that given in the life, death, and resurrection of Jesus Christ in which God through Christ will bring us into union with the Father *and* bestow upon us the graced giftedness to become children of God (John 1:12). The incarnation and atonement could not together accomplish what the incarnation and the ascension could do together, namely, unite us in communion with the Father through the mediation of Christ's self-oblation and intercession and give us the gift of the Spirit of the risen Christ, our advocate. Thus, for example, Philippians 2:7–9 refers not only to the one who assumed our humanity, but also to the one in whom humanity has been glorified. As Milligan notes, "Christ is not merely the Incarnate Son: He is in his human nature exalted and glorified.... The Ascension must thus be combined with the Incarnation if we would understand the process by which the Almighty designs to realise His final purpose with regard to humanity."[16] To make the same point in a liturgical vein, it is right and necessary that the ascension receive the same emphasis as that commonly given to the celebration of "Incarnation Day," that is, Christmas.

Second, as Milligan observes, the ascension is the Lord's entry into his reward. This is at first look a rather odd notion, yet it carries profound significance for the evangelical hope of the gospel. Thus Christ spoke of his peace and his joy (Heb. 12:2), of his coming into his kingdom (Matt. 16:28), often of the eschatological banquet (Matt. 26:29), and so on. But it is especially under three categories that the biblical message is to be understood: in relation to himself, his body, and his enemies.[17] With regard to himself, people of faith see and acknowledge Christ's glory. Before his incarnation, as eternal Son of the Father, he was "the reflection of God's glory" (Heb. 1:3). In his incarnation his glory was hidden in servant form, especially as he bore the cross in weakness unto death. With his resurrection and ascension, however, his glory that he had eternally with the Father was now seen to have tabernacled among us during his

---

15. Ibid., 129.
16. Milligan, *Ascension*, 33–34.
17. See ibid., 35ff.

life on earth (John 1:14). Thus his prayer to be glorified, as in John 17, corresponds to the Son's glorification of the Father, that all people may see the ways of God in the glorification of the Son. The glory that he prayed for and anticipated is communion with God now precisely as a man, a glory made visible in his humanity as the redeemer.

With regard to the members of the body, the New Testament teaches that the exalted Christ is not far removed, but as the head of the body (Col. 1:18) is the one in and through whom the *pleroma* or fullness of God's blessing is given (Col. 2:10; see also Eph. 1:3). He is now the center of the redeemed creation into whose hands all things have been placed. Thus the church as his body has only one source of illumination, quickening, and guidance, namely, the ascended Christ.

With regard to his enemies, the powers of evil and death, Christ's ascension is the assurance of his victory (see 1 Cor. 15:23–28). He tells his disciples that although he goes away (ascension), he will send the Advocate, who will convince the world about sin, righteousness, and judgment (John 16:7–11). This will be the vindication of God. Thus, in sum, Christ's own glory is acknowledged; he is the fullness of God's blessing for his people; and he conquers and judges all evil.[18]

The glory of Christ then is the ever-perfect union between God and humankind in and as Jesus Christ (*totus Christus*), once upon earth in history, now eternally with the Father in the communion of the Holy Spirit. He will come again to gather all things to give to the Father, but meanwhile he pours out his benefits upon us. What this means for us in its practical import has been beautifully stated by Calvin in his fourth sermon on the ascension, which illustrates the way in which a properly dogmatic theology—theology in accordance with the nature of God[19]—becomes inevitably pastoral theology.

> Thus, since He has gone up there, and is in heaven for us, let us note
> that we need not fear to be in this world. It is true that we are subject
> to so much misery that our condition is pitiable, but at that we need
> neither be astonished not confine our attention to ourselves. Thus,
> we look to our Head Who is already in heaven, and say, "Although I
> am weak, there is Jesus Christ Who is powerful enough to make me

---

18. Ibid., 55.

19. See Thomas F. Torrance, *Theology in Reconciliation* (London: Geoffrey Chapman, 1975), 248, where also the references to Athanasius, *Four Discourses Against the Arians*, are found.

stand upright. Although I am feeble, there is Jesus Christ who is my strength. Although I am full of miseries, Jesus Christ is in immortal glory and what he has will some time be given to me and I shall partake of all His benefits. Yes, the devil is called the prince of this world. But what of it? Jesus Christ holds him in check; for He is King of heaven and earth. There are devils above us in the air who make war against us. But what of it? Jesus Christ rules above, having entire control of the battle. Thus, we need not doubt that he gives us the victory. I am here subject to many changes, which may cause me to lose courage. But what of it? The Son of God is my Head, Who is exempt from all change. I must, then, take confidence in Him." This is how we must look at His Ascension, applying the benefit to ourselves.[20]

The Nature of Christ's Heavenly Priesthood

Before we discuss the actual ministry of the ascended Christ, it will be helpful to make three observations concerning the general character of his heavenly priesthood.[21]

1. Christ's heavenly priesthood is not an office given to him as an addendum to his personhood. It is as the Son of the Father, the reflection of God's glory, and the exact imprint of God's very being that he makes purification for sins, after which he sits down at the right hand of the Majesty on high (Heb. 1:3). He is high priest in his eternal sonship, first on earth, "faithful over God's house as a son" (Heb. 3:6), then fully as glorified Lord over all things. As Son he is priest, and they—sonship and priesthood—cannot be separated, for he is as God with and for us the one mediator between God and humankind, fulfilling his eternal priesthood. Thus Milligan: "Whatever our Lord effects for his people in His heavenly Priesthood He effects by reason of the very constitution of His nature as the ascended and glorified Lord. His Priesthood is not merely an office conveyed to Him by the gift of God. . . . In Himself he fulfils the mediation in which priesthood aims. He is *the* mediator, the bond in which the mediation is actually accomplished and realised."[22] Thus in reflecting upon the heavenly priesthood of Christ, we have to deal with Jesus Christ himself, in the actuality of his being as Son of the Father, in such a way

---

20. Cited by Dawson, "Recovering the Ascension," 8, from John Calvin, *The Deity of Christ and Other Sermons* (Audubon, N.J.: Old Paths Publications, 1997), 238–39.
21. For the following see Milligan, *Ascension*, 97ff.
22. Ibid., 100.

that he is not separated from his acts that constitute his priesthood, whether on earth or in heaven. His priesthood is exercised not in an instrumental way but in a personal way so that in his priestly ministry he acts as he is; and who he is, is entirely one with his acts.

2. Christ is priest in heaven as the Word who became flesh and dwelt among us. There seems to be a difference of emphasis between Milligan and Torrance at this point. Milligan moves toward the idea of Christ's heavenly priesthood as the real work of redemption, beginning certainly with the cross, but omitting the life and ministry of Jesus, indicating thereby a certain spiritualizing, perhaps even docetic, tendency with regard to Christ's priesthood. In fairness to Milligan he continues to see the human Christ as the ascended Lord, but he appears to leave the earthly ministry of Jesus behind when he turns to the ministry of the ascended Christ, seeing the former only as "preparation for His priestly work."[23] Torrance, on the other hand, rigorously maintains the humanity of Christ, so much so that he insists that the ascended Christ sends us back, as it were, to the historical Jesus as the covenanted place on earth that God has appointed for meeting between God and humankind.[24] Jesus remains the locus within history where God and humankind are hypostatically united. That is, while Milligan seems to slide away from the vicarious humanity of Christ at the critical point, turning away from the fact that the ascended Christ meets us in and as the historical Jesus who is given to us through the witness of the gospel, Torrance pushes the hypostatic union vigorously, and correctly, I suggest, insisting that we encounter the ascended Christ still in and as the historical Jesus. This insistence, as we shall see, is very important for understanding the church's ministry.

The incarnate Jesus Christ finds his reward in the ascension, as we saw above; the ascended Christ, however, pushes us back to his incarnation, to his history in time and space as the place where we can know him. This means that Christ's work in heaven does not lead us behind the back of Jesus Christ in some kind of *theologia gloriae;* rather, we remain tied to the crucified One, for in him we meet the risen and ascended Lord. Thus Torrance argues that it is in the Spirit that we are now able to hold together in our minds the linkage between the historical Jesus and the risen and ascended Lord, apprehending the ascension first as an historical event in which Christ left our human place, and second as a transcendent event in which he went to God's place. Christ is at once historically absent and

23. Ibid., 82.
24. Torrance, *Space, Time and Resurrection*, 133.

in the Spirit actually present, remaining nearer to us than we are to ourselves.[25] The hypostatic union then means not only that in his divine and human natures Christ is one person, but also that the historical and ascended Christ is one person, knowledge of whom and relationship with whom have their locus, through the Holy Spirit, within space and time on the ground provided by God himself in the incarnation and mediated to us through Word and sacrament.

In worship, the Word spoken and the sacraments celebrated share in the life of the ascended Christ. By the Spirit and in union with Christ, that which is disjoined by nature and history becomes united by grace. In the present, through Scripture studied and preached, and sacraments celebrated, the historical reference and institution is joined to a heavenly empowerment for the sake of the continuing life of the believer and the church. That is, the ascended Christ becomes actual for us in and through common worship so that worship is a real sharing in his life. To share thusly in his ascended life, however, involves also sharing in his continuing ministry for the sake of the world. For as in worship Christ joins us to his heavenly communion with the Father, in sending the same Spirit he joins us also to his commission from the Father.

3. The ascended Christ exercises his kingdom through his priesthood.[26] Until the Parousia the church shares in Christ's exalted reign only in a priestly way as the suffering servant. According to Torrance, "It is as suffering servant that the Church in history is the covenant-partner of the Royal Priest above, and reigns with Him as it carries the Cross, proclaiming the Word of the Gospel and dispensing the mysteries of God."[27] Milligan also notes that Christians are Christians by being drawn close to God through the priestly work of Christ. What he accomplishes as priest has priority over his other offices.[28] The meaning of this for practical theology is given through the historical ministry of Jesus Christ, though not as an example to be imitated but in which Christ really has no personal stake. Rather, through union with Christ "the ministry of the Church is thus the function of the Body appropriate to it as the Body of which He is the Head and Saviour (Ephesians 5:23). Or to put it the other way round, as the Body of which He is the Head the Church participates in His ministry by serving Him in history where it is sent by him in fulfilment of His ministry of

25. Ibid., 134–35.
26. Thomas F. Torrance, *Royal Priesthood: A Theology of Ordained Ministry*, 2d ed. (Edinburgh: T. & T. Clark, 1993), 61.
27. Ibid.
28. Milligan, *Ascension*, 62–63.

reconciliation."[29] The form of the church's ministry derives from participation in the form of Christ's ministry as God's suffering servant insofar as he has given this to us through his ministry on earth.

The Work of the Heavenly Priesthood of Christ—in Heaven

Calvin identified three benefits imparted to our faith by Christ's ascension: our access to heaven, Christ's appearance before the Father's face as our advocate and intercessor, and his gracing of his people with his divine gifts (*Inst.* 2.16.16). According to Milligan, on the other hand, the work of the heavenly priesthood of Christ in heaven has four aspects: his self-offering, his intercession, his benediction, and his gift of the Holy Spirit, although the last two are really two parts of one gift. In that Calvin's notion of access to heaven is much the same in intention as Milligan's notion of self-offering, it is under three heads that we grasp the gracing of the church by Christ and the relations, therefore, between the human priesthood of Christ in heaven and the royal priesthood of the church (1 Pet. 2:9): (1) Christ's self-offering in heaven, (2) Christ our advocate and intercessor, and (3) the gift of the Holy Spirit.

1. Christ's self-offering in heaven. While on earth Jesus Christ lived in obedience to and in communion with the Father, and during his sacrificial ministry and in the shedding of his blood on the cross he offered himself up to God for the sake of the whole world. In this way he exercised his priesthood once and for all. This much is clear. Does Christ, however, continue to make offering at the right hand of the Father? Does he have a continuing ministry of self-oblation, and if so, what does it mean? Hebrews 12:2 states that as the pioneer of our faith Christ not only endured the cross but also has taken his seat at the right hand of God. As the one who goes ahead of us into communion with the Father, he completes the work of the ministry and cross on earth. Hebrews 8:3 suggests that when Christ as high priest in his exaltation entered heaven, he had "something to offer." Is this "something" more than presenting his earthly self-sacrifice to the Father? If it is, what is it?

Milligan takes the view that the self-offering of Christ is not limited to his ministry on earth. Christ's work, he suggests, has two great stages: his dying upon the cross, and his presenting himself to the Father.[30] In his exaltation we must certainly leave aside any thought of Christ offering to

29. Torrance, *Royal Priesthood*, 35.
30. Milligan, *Ascension*, 133.

the Father the humiliation, dereliction, pain, and dying of the cross in some kind of continuous way. (Likewise, we must entertain no notion of the church through the Eucharist offering again and again the self-same sacrifice.) That work is finished (John 19:30). The heart of the atonement is not in these terrible things themselves as external acts interpreted instrumentally in a forensic way, but in Christ's self-giving. The emphasis is on the person who gives, not on a mechanistic or causal consequence of the self-sacrifice as such. Thus, while Christ's death cannot be repeated, and there is a sense therefore in which the atonement is completed, it must also be the case that he continues to offer himself to the Father, because he is the same Christ. This offering in death and in heaven is the heart of the atonement, but now considered as both a past event and a continuing act. I may put it this way: what Christ did in his sacrificial ministry and on his cross on earth was a self-oblation offered once for all (Rom. 6:10; Heb. 10:12) under the conditions of historical existence. Yet, because Christ remains one person, as on earth so also in heaven at the right hand of the Father, what he did on earth he continues to do in heaven, offering himself to the Father in love and obedience, although not now under the human regime unto death. Thus we hold together in our minds his singular death upon the cross for our salvation as his self-giving for the sins of the world with his continual offering of himself as the risen and ascended redeemer who died once for all.

To clarify this two-stage presentation of Christ's work, Milligan develops an argument that is helpful, probably influenced by a similar emphasis of John McLeod Campbell. In summary form: what Christ gave to God on the cross, and what he continually offers to God in heaven, is his *life*. It is the self-offering of Christ's life that saves us, not his death! "The thought of 'offering' on the part of our Lord is not to be confined to His sacrificial death: it is so to be extended as to include in it a present and eternal offering to God of Himself in heaven. What He offered on the cross, what He offers now, is His life, a life unchangeable not only in general character as life, but in the particular character given it by the experience through which it passed."[31]

Thus this irresistible conclusion takes us into the evangelical heart of the gospel: because the life he carried with him into the heavenly sanctuary was not only of God but also of humankind, because it was the life of the Lamb that was slain paying once for all the cost of sin, we now in union with him are offered to the Father "holy and blameless before him in love"

31. Ibid.

(Eph. 1:4). In other words, following McLeod Campbell, it is not salvation that our sins have been forgiven; we must still be brought into communion with the Father, and it is this latter need that the self-offering of the heavenly session of Christ fulfills.

Obviously the argument leads away from a penal concept of the atonement, that is, of a penalty paid for violated law, to one grounded in the life or being of Christ that has both a once-for-all and a continuing aspect. Once for all Christ passed through death, but he continues eternally to give a self-offering of his life on our behalf in heaven. In so doing, Christ continually offers himself *as a man for us*. Thus in him, in union with him, he presents us to the Father in the strength of his own continuing self-offering. For whatever is to be ours must first be his. Here the very center of Christian hope, namely, communion with the Father, has its source not only in the cross but also in Christ's offering of himself in heaven, for we, in union with him, share what is his. The point is: communion with the Father is not a static entity or something to be understood in contractual or legal terms following the Latin or Western *ordo salutis*.[32] Rather, it is a communion of such mutual self-giving between the Father and the Son that, with the Holy Spirit, it constitutes the unity and being of God in a thoroughly relational way. Communion with God means sharing in that self-offering and in that Trinitarian relationship within God that is given us through the priestly ministry of Christ for us in heaven. Whatever then is fulfilled in us must first exist in Christ. We do not live simply in the power of something that he bestows on us as a gift, apart from what he is. Therefore, says Milligan, when we present ourselves as an offering to the Father, he in whom we do so must himself be an offering to the Father.[33] In sum: the life "of Christ was liberated on the cross in order that our life in His might be united to the Father in the closest communion and fellowship."[34]

Just as the self-offering of Christ is not adequately expressed as a penal concept, neither is the continual self-oblation of Christ a symbolic or metaphoric representation. The doctrine of salvation depends on this endless self-offering as a reality in which Christ receives us through union with himself, offering us in and through himself to the Father in love. This is how we draw near to God in love and praise, and it is the center of a

---

32. See Alan J. Torrance, *Persons in Communion: An Essay on Trinitarian Description and Human Participation* (Edinburgh: T. & T. Clark, 1996), 58ff.

33. Milligan, *Ascension*, 137.

34. Ibid., 139.

Christian theology of worship. This is the glory of his vicarious humanity in heaven: to present us in himself to the Father through his continuing self-offering. The life given to the Father by Christ is a life of love and praise. Love and praise characterized his life on earth and his ascended life as well. Retaining his humanity eternally, Christ ever lives to love and praise the Father, so that in union with him, we too "in the midst of the congregation" (Heb. 2:12) will love and praise God. In this way Christ as the *ton hagion leitourgos*, a minister in the sanctuary (Heb. 8:2), is the leader of our worship, for we live to present ourselves to God in love and praise. Thus the first answer of the Shorter Westminster Catechism—the chief end of being human is to glorify God—recognizes that there is no way in which we can give God this glory other than in him who is the life of the Christian, sharing in his self-offering. If Christ does not lead our worship, and we seek to worship in our own name and piety, we fail to worship as the Father desires and as has been given to us to do.

This point of Christian doctrine—the self-offering of Christ in heaven for us—is not well known. (One can understand why, for too easily the theologian's words may carry the weight of speculation rather than reality.) The arcane nature of this doctrinal issue, however, should not delude us into thinking that the issue is on the edges of Christian faith. Its pastoral power is that in the central issue of faith and hope, namely, our restoration to communion with the Father, we depend upon the ministry of the continuing priesthood of Christ, not upon the efficacy of a past forensic act or on a vague present spiritual "somehow," or even less on our own spiritual experience and prowess. The first is too mechanical; the second has no content; the third casts us back upon ourselves. The source of pastoral power lies in *both* the completed work of Christ on the cross and in his present ministry before the Father on our behalf by which he continually presents himself to God in and through his own self-offering. Thus not only is he the ground of forgiveness of sins, but he also presents us to share in his communion with the Father, and it is here especially that we have the basis for a correct understanding of Christian worship. It is as such that we depend on the *living* Christ, one with us, for he ever bears our humanity, who makes us one with himself through union with him. In this way he is historically, existentially, and eternally the one on whom we depend in life and death. Thus in union with Christ God has "seated us with him in the heavenly places" (Eph. 2:6). The result, according to Calvin, is "that we do not await heaven with a bare hope, but in our Head already possess it" (*Inst.* 2.16.16). In this way Christ ever lives as the mediator between God and humankind (1 Tim. 2:5), and Christians in union with Christ eternally offer the sacrifice of love and praise that is well pleasing to the Father.

2. Christ is our advocate and intercessor. Christ's work pleading our cause before God in heaven is better known. The biblical bases for Christ praying for us are given in Romans 8:34 and Hebrews 7:25. According to Calvin, commenting upon Hebrews 7:25:

> What is the nature and extent of the pledge of His love towards us?
> The fact that Christ lives for us and not for Himself, and that He was
> received into eternal bliss to reign in heaven—this happened, says the
> apostle, for our sakes. Thus the life and the kingdom and the glory
> of Christ aim at our salvation as their target, and Christ has nothing
> that is not to be put to our benefit, because he was given to us by the
> Father on this condition, that everything that was His should be ours.
> At the same time he shows us by what he does that Christ performs
> the office of Priest, it belongs to a priest to intercede, in order that
> the people may find favor with God. Christ is continually doing this
> because he rose from the dead for this purpose. He justifies His right-
> ful Name of priest by His continual task of intercession.[35]

The Greek verb used of Christ's intercessions is *entynchano*, which is used also of the Spirit's intercessions. It does not mean simply to pray for someone, but carries the meaning of pleading with someone or dealing/transacting with one person in reference to another. It involves asking something for or against another. It stands therefore for a series of transactions in which one person may engage with another on behalf of a third person.[36] References to Christ in heaven praying for us mean not that he is merely "saying" prayers, but that he is interceding as an advocate (1 John 2:1) in the sense that Christ takes his own people "into the Father's presence, in order that whatever he Himself enjoys in the communications of His Father's love may become also theirs."[37]

Calvin notes that Christ enjoins his disciples to rest confidently in his intercessions after he has ascended into heaven (John 16:26). Building on the notion that apart from priestly mediation we are barred from God's

---

35. *Calvin's Commentaries: The Epistle of Paul the Apostle to the Hebrews and the First and Second Epistles of St. Peter,* ed. David W. Torrance and Thomas F. Torrance; trans. William B. Johnston (Edinburgh: Oliver and Boyd, 1963), 101.

36. See Milligan, *Ascension,* 151.

37. Ibid., 152.

presence, and consequently we need a mediator to act in our name and on our behalf, Calvin argues that Christ, by his ascension, is a sure advocate, for he is the new way consecrated by his flesh (*Inst.* 3.20.18). In fact, says Calvin, no one can be helped by prayer unless Christ himself intercedes. Christ's advocacy is not limited to his earthly ministry, but in the power of his cross he lives as one who makes everlasting intercession for us, alone bearing to God the petitions of his people, who remain far off, at it were, in the outer courts of the holy of holies (*Inst.* 3.20.20). It would be wrong, then, to draw a straight comparison between our own prayers to God and Christ's advocacy and intercessions with the Father. He approaches the Father not as one asking from without, but as one who stands within the Trinitarian communion of mutual love. It is as the Son of God wearing still the flesh of our humanity and the marks of his atonement that he pleads for us before the throne of grace so that our humanity in its terrible neediness is in him brought acceptably before the Father in love.

According to Calvin, Christ's advocacy and intercession have three related consequences (*Inst.* 2.16.16). First, he turns the Father's eyes to Christ's own righteousness to stop him looking at our sin. "With his worthiness he intercedes that your unworthiness may not come before God's sight" (*Inst.* 3.2.24). There is the sense, then, that while sin is forgiven once for all on the cross, Christ continues to cover our sin with his own righteousness so that in him we, sinners as we are, have communion with the Father. Second, he reconciles the Father's heart to us, thereby preparing a way to the Father's throne. We might say that for Christ's sake the Father has a change of heart, looking on us now with complete acceptance and love. Third, he fills with grace and kindness the throne of God, which apart from Christ would be filled with dread and judgment.

Milligan sums up the argument thus far with words that draw out the pastoral significance of the intercession and advocacy of Christ in his heavenly session:

> Rightly conceived, the work of Intercession on the part of our heavenly High-priest seems to be that, having restored the broken covenant and brought His Israel into the most intimate union and communion with God, He would now, amidst all their remaining weaknesses, and the innumerable temptations that surround them, preserve them in it. And He would do this by keeping them in Himself; so that in Him they shall stand in such unity of love to the Father that the Father will love them as His own Sons, will need no one to remind Him that they are so, and will directly pour out upon them,

as very members of the Body of the Eternal Son, every blessing first poured out upon the Head.[38]

One final point: one can distinguish between the intercession of Christ and the intercession of the Holy Spirit. First John 2:1 states that "we have an advocate with the Father, Jesus Christ the righteous." John 14:16–17 has Jesus say, "I will ask the Father, and he will give you another Advocate. . . . This is the Spirit of truth" (see also John 14:25–26). According to Milligan, this is to be understood thusly: Jesus glorified represents us before the Father's throne; the Holy Spirit dwelling with us represents in us Jesus gone to the Father. In the first case, our Advocate is external; in the second case, the Advocate is internal. The first takes all our needs to the Father, while the second brings the Redeemer, as it were, home to our hearts.[39] Thus there is an utter congruence between the work of the heavenly session of Christ and the Spirit that he will ask to be sent from the Father.

3. Christ gives the gift of the Holy Spirit. Before he considers the gift of the Holy Spirit, Milligan interjects Christ's benediction. Most New Testament epistles and all Christian services of worship end with a benediction. More foundationally, Christ's ministry on earth ends with a benediction: "Then he led them out as far as Bethany, and, lifting up his hands, he blessed them. While he was blessing them, he withdrew from them and was carried up into heaven" (Luke 24:50–51). Jesus blessed his disciples during his ministry when the end was near, giving them his legacy: "Peace I leave with you; my peace I give to you" (John 14:27). Similarly, after his resurrection his first word of greeting to his disciples was a blessing, "Peace be with you" (John 20:21). Even these benedictions, however, are but the anticipation of the full outpouring of blessing, for in Christ every spiritual blessing in the heavenly places (Eph. 1:3) must yet be given in the gift of the Holy Spirit. Thus in the ascension Jesus Christ blesses his people and fulfills that blessing in the sending of the Holy Spirit.[40]

This is not the place to develop a comprehensive theology of the Holy Spirit. It is enough to say that the gift of the Holy Spirit is, as Milligan notes, the leading and characteristic gift of the present dispensation.[41] Calvin put it plainly: "Christ does not otherwise dwell in us than through his Spirit, nor in any other way communicates himself to us than through

38. Ibid., 158.
39. Milligan, *Ascension*, 159.
40. T. F. Torrance, *Space, Time and Resurrection*, 117.
41. Milligan, *Ascension*, 170.

the same Spirit."[42] Thus Torrance notes that it is through the Spirit that the saving work of Christ is actualized in the church, which means that the doctrine of the Spirit has Christology for its content[43]—to a certain end, namely, our union with Christ. Because it is by the Spirit that the church inheres in Christ, the church is not to be thought of first of all as a holy society founded to preserve Christ's memory, observe his teachings, or even proclaim his message. Rather, it is in the Spirit that the church, through union with Christ, grows out of sharing in his being as the incarnate Son,[44] from which all the rest comes. This ordering is critical, else the church is understood according to a form of obligation in which we by our efforts are deemed responsible for its being and ministry. The giving of the Spirit testifies to and maintains an organic and primordial connection between Christ and the church and ensures that there is no kingdom of the church, no kingdom of the Spirit, but only a kingdom of Christ through participation in and by the Spirit in his life and ministry.[45]

Thus the gift of the Holy Spirit is the gift of Jesus Christ, both in the sense that the Spirit is sent from the Father through the Son, and in the sense that it is Christ himself that we receive in and by the Spirit. The chief work of the Spirit, then, is to bind us to Christ and thereby to form the living Christ within us so that we share in his actual life. The intent here is organic, and the result is that in the New Testament Christians are spoken of as those persons who are at once "in" Christ (e.g., 2 Cor. 5:17) and as those whom Christ is "in" (e.g., Rom. 8:10). Thus, says Milligan,

> union with Christ is the fundamental and regulating conception of our state as Christians. We are "in" Christ Jesus. . . . Again, Christ is "in" us. . . . The two modes of expression, when taken together, bring out the closest and most intimate idea of union which is possible to form. . . . And all this is effected by the Spirit. . . . "To be in Christ" and "to have the Spirit of Christ" alternate with each other as equivalent in meaning, showing that if Christ be in us it is only by the Spirit.[46]

Milligan's conclusion is very similar to Torrance's: the Christian life is not construed as *imitatio Christi*. Rather, Christ must dwell within us,

---

42. John Calvin, "Summary of Doctrine Concerning the Ministry of the Word and Sacraments," in *Calvin: Theological Treatises*, ed. J. K. S. Reid (Philadelphia: Westminster, 1964), 172.
43. T. F. Torrance, *Royal Priesthood*, 25.
44. Thomas F. Torrance, *Theology in Reconstruction* (Grand Rapids: Eerdmans, 1965), 201.
45. Ibid., 204.
46. Milligan, *Ascension*, 197–98.

be one with us and us with him, though not directly, but through the Holy Spirit.

According to Karl Barth, the Holy Spirit is the power in which Jesus Christ is alive among people and makes them his witnesses.[47] That is, Christian doctrine teaches that the work of the Holy Spirit is a Christ-related event, and as such, it becomes a God-glorifying, person-empowering, and church/mission-creating event. Because the Holy Spirit binds us to Jesus Christ, we are bound by the same Spirit to share in Christ's communion with and mission from the Father.[48] The Spirit calls the church into existence to be a community of worship and ministry through union with Christ. Thus when we speak of the communion of the Holy Spirit we mean the communion-creating work of the Holy Spirit—communion with the Father through our Spirit-led union with Christ and, consequently, communion with one another as we are formed into the missionary body of Christ, the church. For this reason we do not speak of communion *in* the Holy Spirit, but the communion *of* the Holy Spirit, meaning by this, communion *in Christ*.[49]

What of the form of Christ's ministry in and through the church? While the Holy Spirit given to the church is the Spirit of the ascended Christ by which he joins us to himself to be one with and in him, and he in us, (1) it is the ministry of the historical Jesus to which we are joined, and (2) there is a difference between the ministry of the historical Jesus and the ministry of the church.

1. It is clear by now that the ministry of the church is directly related to Jesus Christ *in a particular way*. Through union with Christ, which is the principal work of the Holy Spirit, the church is joined to Christ's life and ministry, but as lived in history, not in his heavenly session. The empowerment is from the latter, the content from the former. In Christ, we might say, the Lord's Prayer is fulfilled, for God's will is done on earth as it is done in heaven. The ministry of Jesus on earth is the "place" where God's ministry in, through, and as Jesus Christ intersects with the church to form the church's ministry. Therefore the development of a theology of ministry looks to the Gospel accounts for its content, and Christ's ministry on earth, in which we participate, is given as the christological pattern in such a way that the ministry of the church is correlative to the ministry of

---

47. Karl Barth, *Church Dogmatics*, IV.2, ed. G. W. Bromiley and T. F. Torrance, trans. G. W. Bromiley (Edinburgh: T. & T. Clark, 1956), 522.

48. This language is taken from James B. Torrance, *Worship, Community and the Triune God of Grace* (Carlisle: Paternoster, 1996), and is used throughout the book.

49. For a fuller discussion see Andrew Purves and Charles Partee, *Encountering God: Christian Faith in Turbulent Times* (Louisville, Ky.: Westminster John Knox Press, 2000), chapter 5.

Christ.[50] According to Torrance, the basic pattern (*hypodeigma*) is given in the account of the foot washing in John 13:1–20.[51] Thus verse 15: "For I have set you an example (*hypodeigma*), that you also should do as I have done to you." To repeat, this is to be understood not according to a principle of *imitatio Christi* but rather that the church is related to Christ as a student to the Teacher, a disciple to the Lord, and as a servant to the Master through the Spirit's work of union with Christ. Thus the form of the church's ministry is set according to *participatio Christi*, according to a firm anchoring to the Gospel accounts of the life and ministry of Jesus.

More generally, the christological *hypodeigma* that is to characterize the church's ministry in union with Christ is according to the form of the Suffering Servant: "As an example of suffering and patience, beloved, take the prophets who spoke in the name of the Lord" (Jas. 5:10). As Suffering Servant Christ "came not to be served but to serve, and to give his life a ransom for many" (Matt. 20:28; Mark 10:45). By its baptism the church is baptized into Christ's own baptism and as such is engrafted into this ministry of Jesus Christ,[52] to share in his life and to be the present form of his ministry on earth.

2. Concerning the difference between the ministry of the historical Jesus and that of the church, while the church's ministry is properly understood to be in and by the Spirit a sharing in Christ's ministry, it is both like and unlike the ministry of Christ.[53] Because the church is engrafted into Christ, its ministry has a christological pattern, as we have seen. A distinction must be maintained, however, for the church's ministry is related to Jesus Christ as his ministry is related to the Father. Thus the ministry of the church has to be thought through missionally *from* Jesus Christ: "As the Father has sent me, so I send you" (John 20:21), just as the ministry of Jesus Christ has to be thought missionally as *from* the Father. Accordingly, the church's ministry is a ministry of redeemed sinners, whereas his ministry is that of the Redeemer. This essential and fundamental translation in the form of the ministry was carried out by the apostles, so that all true Christian ministry is ever after determined at its root by the special function of the apostles in their immediate relation to Jesus' ministry on the one hand and to the historical church of forgiven sinners and its mission in the world on the other hand.[54]

---

50. T. F. Torrance, *Royal Priesthood*, 35.
51. Ibid., 21, 35, and 85.
52. Ibid., xiv.
53. For the following see T. F. Torrance, *Theology in Reconstruction*, 207.
54. Ibid.

Again we are driven back to the apostolic witness as the hinge of the divine mission where the vertical mission of Christ from the Father is unfolded horizontally into the mission of the church from Christ.[55] And since both the mission of Christ and the mission of the church are in and by the Holy Spirit, as this section has tried to make clear, all ministry is therefore properly understood according to a Trinitarian reality, from the Father, through the Son, and in the Holy Spirit, and to the Father, through the Son, and in the Holy Spirit.

55. T. F. Torrance, *Royal Priesthood*, 27.

Chapter 6

Eschatology and Ministry

Holy, holy, holy, the Lord God the Almighty, who was and is and is to come.

Revelation 4:8

Then I saw a new heaven and a new earth.

Revelation 21:1

What does the promise of God mean? It means that the being of man acquires a direction, because it acquires a destiny and a perspective.

Karl Barth[1]

I t is the burden of all Christian theology to speak of God with us and for us in, through, and as Jesus Christ. As we have seen, this is also the responsibility of pastoral theology. Thus far we have considered the past and present ministry of Jesus Christ. We turn now to consider his ministry as the promised coming One, and to reflect on the meaning of this for pastoral theology. Eschatology must be a chapter in pastoral theology, although it has been absent from the dominant literature since the 1920s. That absence has meant a severe constricting of the vision for pastoral work, a limiting of its remit and a reduction of its role in gospel ministry. This has led to a form of pastoral work that has little connection with the calling of humankind to live in expectation of what God has promised but

---

1. Karl Barth, *Church Dogmatics*, IV.1, ed. G. W. Bromiley and T. F. Torrance, trans. G. W. Bromiley (Edinburgh: T. & T. Clark, 1956), 111. The section from which this citation is taken is a brief (for Barth) overview of the Christian doctrine of hope.

is yet to do, and specifically of the Christian's calling to live in active anticipation of the new heaven and the new earth that is to come and to bear witness to this expectation in social and political life. Thus arising are (1) the mistaken notion that pastoral work and work for social righteousness are distinctly different, even mutually exclusive, and (2) the notion that Christian hope in the kingdom of God is above and beyond history. As Karl Barth has noted: "That kingdom is not merely a kingdom which He possesses in the cosmos created by Him. It is the kingdom which He sets up in the course of a historical movement which has a beginning, a middle and an end. It is the kingdom which comes from heaven to earth."[2]

The ministry of Jesus Christ in his announcement and living of the kingdom of God, at his coming again, and the significance for the life of the church in anticipation of that second coming and kingdom, are basic building blocks for the construction of pastoral theology that is faithful to the full ministry of Jesus Christ as that is attested by the New Testament. Pastoral theology cannot direct attention away from eschatology for fear perhaps of supernaturalism or apocalypticism, for no complete account of Jesus' ministry is given without including his generally accepted teaching concerning the kingdom of God and a reflection on his resurrection and his coming again. Further, as already noted, to speak of the kingdom of God is to speak of a future with God that does not exclude a future for history. Thus here we must develop that part of pastoral theological reflection on the ministry of Jesus Christ that arises out of teaching on the kingdom of God and his promised coming again. Having examined the ministry of Jesus Christ in history and in his ascension, we turn to complete the task of understanding the ministry of the church through union with Christ now in the light of his future.

The last third of the twentieth century saw the rediscovery of eschatology in systematic theology. Through the works of the German theologians Jürgen Moltmann and Wolfhart Pannenberg, for example, eschatology was put center stage in a creative and rigorous way. These theologians argued that eschatology must penetrate all theological thinking, for God is a God with the future as the primary mode of his being. In his landmark systematic development of eschatology, *Theology of Hope*, Moltmann puts the matter in absolute terms: "The eschatological is not one element of Christianity but it is the medium of Christian faith as such, the key in which everything in it is set. . . . The eschatological outlook is characteristic of all Christian proclamation, of every Christian existence, and of the

2. Ibid., 112.

whole Church."[3] He does not intend this to be taken as either rhetoric or hyperbole. Rather, Christian faith is necessarily turned toward the coming Lord Jesus Christ because of the intrinsic nature of the gospel itself. Again according to Moltmann, "All predicates of Christ not only say who he was and is, but imply statements of who he will be and what is to be expected of him."[4] The central theological issue for Christian eschatology, then, is not the future as such as a general category, but the future in the light of the one who was, who is, and who will come again. That is, the issue is the future perceived in terms of Christology:

> If we analyse the direction of the inquiry more carefully [in the New Testament], we find that it begins with the special, contingent history of Jesus Christ, the resurrection of the crucified and his Easter appearances, and aims at the universal deity of God. It inquires after the kingdom of God who raises the dead, on the basis of the appearance of the risen Christ. It inquires after the future of God and proclaims his coming, in proclaiming Christ. Christian theology begins with the eschatological problem.[5]

For Moltmann especially, then, Christianity eschatology is neither an apocalyptic explanation of history nor the basis for a private illumination of existence. It is the horizon of expectation for a world-transforming divine initiative. Eschatological faith directs its attention to the promised new future that God will bring about, and places its hope in that. This future is an historical future—history has a future that is other than the closed causality of the past, for it is a new future that God will bring about. In the light of the coming act of God, history is opened out into an otherwise unhoped-for future. In the light of this, Christian theology is "historico-eschatological thinking about God between cross and parousia."[6] Thus the recovery of eschatology for theology that emerged in the 1960s was not a reminder to find a place at the end of the theological program for "last things." It was a recasting of the whole theological program itself in the light of the meaning of the coming again of Jesus Christ, crucified and risen.

3. Jürgen Moltmann, *Theology of Hope*, trans. James W. Leitch (London: SCM, 1967), 12.
4. Ibid., 17.
5. Jürgen Moltmann, "Theology as Eschatology," in *The Future of Hope: Theology of Eschatology*, ed. Frederick Herzog (New York: Herder and Herder, 1970), 7.
6. Jürgen Moltmann, *Religion, Revolution, and the Future*, trans. M. Douglas Meeks (New York: Charles Scribner's Sons, 1969), 207.

My goal here is to explain the meaning of eschatology for pastoral theology, not as the cast in which all theology is set, but as part of the theological understanding of the whole ministry of Jesus Christ. So developed it has both a positive and a critical role to play. First, I lay out the systematic theological ground for eschatology by way of a discussion of Moltmann's eschatology of the cross. His is not the only treatment that could be used at this point, but it is arguably the most systematically developed and the most useful for our purpose. Next, I discuss the eschatology of the cross and how that results in what Moltmann calls "political theology," meaning by this a view of Christian faith and life in which, while the present experience of history is not yet the kingdom of God, it is both announced and dialectically present in the cross of the resurrected Christ. Anticipation in hope therefore begins to characterize both the Christian mind and Christian action. An existential political and ethical imperative is opened up for faith now in history on the ground of the eschatological indicative of Christ's promised coming again. Third, I discuss the significance of the eschatology of the cross for pastoral theology, seeking to show how the basic framework of pastoral ministry must take on both a sociocritical and a communal-constructive role. For christological and eschatological reasons, therefore, pastoral care must not be limited to psychotherapeutic categories and practices.[7]

Moltmann's Eschatology of the Cross

Promise, the Resurrection, and Eschatology

The theological understanding of Jesus in the New Testament is, for Moltmann, developed in the light of Israel's promissory history. The revelation of God came in the form of promise and in the history marked by promise. In such a framework, revelation is constitutively eschatological. A promise announces a coming reality, one that does not yet exist. If God, then, reveals himself in his promise, eschatology is a necessary correlate of the doctrine of God. Eschatology, however, is not mere speech about the future. Because knowledge of God begins from a definite reality in history through which God announces his promises, a future is called into being that is the future of that promise and the future of that history. History and the future are theologically bound up together with the act of revelation.

---

7. An attempt at a contextual basis for pastoral work that is open to social and political elements is found already in John Patton, *Pastoral Care in Context* (Louisville, Ky.: Westminster John Knox Press, 1993).

Revelation, then, creates its own categories. In announcing a coming, new reality, promise stands in contradiction to present reality. It creates what Moltmann calls an "interval of tension" between utterance and its redemption.[8] The promises of God were not fulfilled within Israel's history. Indeed, Israel's experience of history gave God's promises an ever-wider interpretation. Especially in the prophetic period, the conviction grew that God was creating a new time and future for Israel. The categories of the new and the future became determinative for Israel's self-understanding. The prophets eschatologized Israel's hope by shifting expectation from the safety of the old saving action to an understanding of the basis of salvation on the ground of God's future action.[9] Thus Israel's past history came to be interpreted in the light of a future and expected action of God.

The New Testament understands the God who reveals himself in Jesus Christ to be the same God as the one who is the hope of Israel, for Jesus is the Lord. But a new dimension enters with Jesus Christ, for he is not just the Messiah who is in continuity with Israel; he is also the one who points to himself as the new basis for hope in the future. The Old Testament history is not negated. It is, rather, taken up and given a wholly new breadth and depth, for in the gospel the Old Testament history of promise is not so much fulfilled as given its future.

According to Moltmann, New Testament faith starts with the resurrection of Jesus Christ. "Christianity stands or falls with the reality of the raising of Jesus from the dead by God. In the New Testament there is no faith that does not start *a priori* with the resurrection of Jesus."[10] But the risen Jesus is also the crucified Jesus. Thus the identity of Jesus between his cross and resurrection reveals God's faithfulness and his solidarity with and affirmative judgment on the life and death of Jesus. Jesus' identity is a dialectical identity, incorporating his life on earth and his resurrected being. When Moltmann writes of the resurrection of Jesus he means the resurrection of the crucified Jesus, whose identity is given in terms of the apparent contradiction between the cross and the resurrection. We are thus forced to see in the resurrection the future for history and, especially, the future for the history of suffering, abandonment, and death. "If, as the Easter vision implies, God has identified himself, his judgment and his Kingdom with the crucified Jesus, his cross and his helplessness, then conversely the resurrection of

8. Moltmann, *Theology of Hope*, 103.
9. Ibid., 128.
10. Ibid., 165.

the crucified Jesus into the coming glory of God contains within itself the process of the incarnation of the coming God and his glory in the crucified Jesus."[11] A new future for history is thereby announced in the resurrection, but in the "language of promise."[12] It is an announcement of divine judgment and mercy that is particularized in the history of Jesus.

Moltmann regards the resurrection of Jesus as an history-creating event. It demands a future in which what happened to Jesus will happen to us. This conclusion arises out of the nature of the resurrection itself. If examined on the basis of a prior understanding of what is possible, however, its meaning can never be grasped: "The resurrection of Christ does not mean a possibility within the world and its history, but a new possibility altogether for the world, for existence and for history. . . . By the raising of Christ we do not mean a possible process in world history, but the eschatological process to which world history is subjected."[13] Because the resurrection has no corresponding analogy with other events within history, Christian theology is required to construct its own understanding of history, with the resurrection of the crucified Jesus as the definitive element. The resurrection of Jesus is historical because it makes history and discloses an eschatological future, and not because it fits into prior experiences of history that in some way define or prescribe what history is.

By redefining history according to the resurrection of Jesus Christ, Moltmann has, in effect, opted for a special pleading. As ordinarily understood and perceived since the Enlightenment, history is not capable of providing a framework for the resurrection; modern history is perceived positivistically in such a way that ostensible events that appear to arise outside the empirical causal nexus are denied historical status. History, we might say, is in such a view a closed continuum. Thus an alternative view of history is required in which the resurrection not only can be accepted as an historical event but also be seen to be the history-creating event by which all other events are comprehended. It is not necessary here to flounder under a criticism of Moltmann's view of history for his point to be helpful irrespective of his special pleading. That is, however history is construed so that it allows for a cogent apprehension of the resurrection, the theological point remains valid, namely, that the resurrection of Jesus Christ is an event within history and it opens up a new future for history

---

11. Jürgen Moltmann, *The Crucified God*, trans. R. A. Wilson and John Bowden (New York: Harper & Row, 1974), 169.

12. Ibid., 173; and idem, *Theology of Hope*, 190.

13. Moltmann, *Theology of Hope*, 179–80.

that otherwise is not disclosed. If it happened, as the New Testament insists it did, then it involves a cosmological change in our thinking and living, for the future can never be the same again for those who live with the shadow of death. This is surely a significant part of the burden of Paul's argument in 1 Corinthians 15, his major treatment of the resurrection of Christ and the resurrection of the body.

Unlike the eschatology of Israel, Christian eschatology tells of Jesus Christ and his future. It is necessary, then, to emphasize that Christian eschatology is Christology with an eschatological perspective.[14] Like the eschatology of Israel, Christian eschatology speaks in the language of promise, but now in terms also of an event that creates the promise and understands history in the light of the future that the promise demands. Thus for both Israel and the church, God's promise creates mission, the outward thrust of the promise, because the present reality still stands in contradiction to the as yet unrealized but coming future. For as long as the experience of history is not yet the experience of the presence of God and his kingdom, hope remains unreconciled to the present experience and presses forward in active expectation for its coming fulfillment. Thus Moltmann insists that "those who hope in Christ can no longer put up with reality as it is, but begin to suffer under it, to contradict it. Peace with God means conflict with the world, for the goad of the promised future stabs inexorably into the flesh of every unfulfilled present."[15] I explore later in chapter 10 the implications of this for the practice of ministry.

The Cross of Christ

Programmatically, Moltmann insists that "there is no true *theology of hope* which is not first of all a *theology of the cross*."[16] This dialectical method-ological move is very important for a proper understanding of Christian eschatology. Thus we move from consideration of the meaning of Jesus Christ in the light of the future of the crucified Christ as that is deter-mined by his resurrection to consider now Moltmann's view of the pres-ence of the risen Lord by way of the invocation of the memory of the cross. A full understanding and presentation of eschatology demands that we are driven back to understand who it was who died on the cross and was raised on the third day, and what this means for the doctrine of God.

14. Ibid., 192.
15. Ibid., 21; see also 118, 206, 215, and 224.
16. Jürgen Moltmann, *The Experiment Hope*, trans. and ed. M. Douglas Meeks (London: SCM, 1975), 72. See also Moltmann, *Crucified God*, 5.

The cross of Christ is the foundation and criticism of Christian theology. As such, it is not fully understood in a linear way as a stage on the way to the resurrection but rather as part of the intrinsic dialectical identity of Jesus Christ himself. The scandal of Christian faith, at least in part, has to do with the fact that the one who was raised from the dead was the condemned, forsaken, and executed man called Jesus. Without the cross of Christ, who is Lord and God, theology tends to become either timeless moral teaching or a speculative and gnostic theology of glory.

For Moltmann, Christology stands insofar as it originates in Jesus and his history. This is a theological method that I have followed throughout the argument of this book. Theology does not begin with a speculative or axiomatic concept of God, or of the world and its history. The starting point is what it means that the Christ, the Son of God, lived and was crucified: "It is he, the crucified Jesus himself, who is the driving force, the joy and the suffering of all theology that is Christian. . . . The cross of Christ is the source of a permanent iconoclasm of the christological icons of the church and the portraits of Jesus in Christianity."[17]

In view of the resurrection, the disciples proclaimed the future of the crucified Jesus Christ. The nature of the life and death of this man who was raised from the dead are determinative for all Christian theology. The offense of Christianity lies with the claim that the deity of God is revealed in Jesus' death and the life that necessitated it. The Christian doctrine of God is therefore christologically constituted. Thus Moltmann, following Luther, replaces a natural knowledge of God from his works with the apostolic knowledge of God in the cross of Christ. The dialectic of the cross and the resurrection does not make us forget the cross; rather, it forces us to see in the cross, and the life that preceded it, the very activity of God himself.

Moltmann approaches the understanding of the cross from two directions: from the direction of history and from the direction of the resurrection and eschatological faith. These two directions obviously must be held together so that the life and death of Jesus can be understood within historical and eschatological dimensions.

The history of Jesus that led to his death was a theological history. This means that his life and death cannot be understood apart from the God for whom he lived. Jesus must be seen in terms of his proclamation of God as his Father and of God's will for humankind. Jesus' resurrection from the dead is a commentary by God, as it were, on the legitimacy of his min-

---

17. Moltmann, *Crucified God*, 87.

istry, which was carried out within the public spheres of Judaism, Roman imperial occupation, and the common human lot of suffering unto death. What distinguishes Jesus' cross from all the other crosses in history is that this cross was uniquely also a "God event."[18] It is the task of theology to take up this cross understood as a "God event" and think it through in a foundational way into all other aspects of theology, for it is here that theology becomes specifically Christian theology.

We turn now, also briefly, to look at how Moltmann understands Jesus' life and death in the context of his resurrection and eschatological faith. Easter faith does not merely stand in a chronological order to the history of Jesus; rather, it is from the cross that the resurrection and the doctrine of hope find their real meaning. As a consequence of his resurrection, Jesus' life and death are now perceived as the incarnation of the living and coming God. The resurrection forces us back to the cross and interprets it. Thus Jesus' life within first-century Palestine and Judaism, under Roman imperial occupation, and within the common lot of humankind, is seen in the light of the resurrection to be part of the life and future of God. In this way Moltmann tries to show how a resurrection-based faith, and thus also an eschatological faith, must refer directly to the life and death of Jesus. I stressed this point earlier when considering the meaning of the ministry of the ascended Christ. It is Jesus' ministry on earth that provides the content to the meaning of both the resurrection and the ascension, for it is the same Jesus Christ who lived, died, was raised and ascended, and who will come again. In his resurrection he is not someone other than whom he was in his incarnation. Easter, however, deepens the mystery of the cross and the life that led to it, for they cease now to be merely another contingent event and life within history; they become an eschatological event and life. The resurrection qualifies the cross and the life that led to it because it reveals who lived, suffered, and died upon it. Thus driven back to the cross, we must find our hope there, says Moltmann. In historical terms, the resurrection follows the cross; in eschatological terms, the cross is seen to be the cross of the risen Christ. Eschatologically considered, therefore, the cross becomes the present form of the resurrection. "The cross is the form of the coming, redeeming kingdom, and the crucified Jesus is the incarnation of the risen Christ."[19]

18. Jürgen Moltmann, "The Trinitarian History of God," *Theology* 78, no. 666 (December 1975): 643–44; and Jürgen Moltmann, *The Church in the Power of the Spirit*, trans. Margaret Kohl (London: SCM, 1977), 62–63.

19. Moltmann, *Crucified God*, 185.

The consequence for pastoral theology can be easily drawn out. It is Jesus' death that makes the meaning of his resurrection manifest for those who suffer under their own unrighteousness and who live in the shadow of death. For those who are closed to the future, whose lives are, as classical theology classified it, *homo incurvatus in se*—curved in on themselves—the future of the cross is true hope indeed. In Christ's death we find the significance of his resurrection, for there Christ is in solidarity with the human plight, and from this atonement means that the coming God is one in Christ with all humankind in life unto death, giving all a future that humankind would not have otherwise. "For as all die in Adam, so all will be made alive in Christ" (1 Cor. 15:22).

Political Theology

Political theology does not mean politicized theology. It is, rather, the meaning for life today of the theological consequence of the eschatology of the cross, in which the future of Christ is present in the cross. The eschatology of the cross forces theology to see that the present experience of history does not yet correspond to the kingdom of God. We will look at the development of political theology in three sections: (1) history as the mediating agency of Christian faith, (2) theo-political hermeneutics, and (3) the tasks of liberation.

History as the Mediating Agency for Christian Faith: From Cosmology and Anthropology to History

The history of theology bears witness to the union of the biblical tradition with cosmological metaphysics.[20] The rise of natural science, however, brought this synthesis to a breaking point as nature came to be seen independently of a divine orderer. Transcendence consequently was no longer to be found at the periphery of the cosmos, but was perceived and experienced in one's experience, in oneself. In view of the demise of the cosmological conceptions of God, the world, and humankind, alternative worldviews emerged: psychological (Descartes), moral (Kant), and existential (Kierkegaard) perspectives began to dominate theology. Transcendence came to be experienced in subjectivity. The world was objectified and the human subjectified, which meant for theology the move from a theistic metaphysics of the world to a theological illumination of existence.

---

20. Moltmann, *Religion, Revolution, and the Future*, 204ff., for the argument here described.

The revelation of God was, then, seen as a matter of one coming to one-self,[21] and the question of God considered in terms of questions about humankind, one's identity, autonomy, and authenticity. The problem with this perspective may be the assumption that we can come to personal identity and fullness of life apart from the concern for a just and humane society. The human is pushed into the realm of the private and the personal. It is here that pastoral care in the twentieth century found a home.

This development in theology, Moltmann suggests, misunderstands the nature of the cross. The righteousness of God is properly associated with a specific historical event: the dereliction, abandonment, and dishonor of the crucified Jesus. The eschatology of the cross is the ground for associating the righteousness of God with the future of the world's pain, evil, and death. In this way, we hold together the world (history) and the future (Christ). It is from the history of the risen Christ that Christianity finds itself identified with the temporal, spatial, and historical realms. Christianity becomes public as well as personal.

> The question of man's identity becomes more and more pressing the more man becomes a historical being. But he becomes a historical being only in connection with the social changes of world history. Therefore, this agonizing and impelling question is, in fact, the reverse side of the theodicy question which seeks the meaning of history. Practically speaking, this means that persons and groups of men are to find their identity in history—not apart from it. Their identity is to be found only in concrete historical identification with projects directed to overcoming human misery and enslavement.[22]

Theo-Political Hermeneutics

Moltmann develops his perspective in opposition to Bultmann's existentialist hermeneutics, which liberates the believer from history by placing him or her in an ahistorical "now." He also draws from Marx's revolutionary historical hermeneutics, which promotes action in history, though with a critique of religion as its consequence. Moltmann argues that Christian faith is not merely a consolation for the exploited, but must itself become radical by promoting action in history in the face of suffering.

---

21. See Moltmann, *Theology of Hope*, 65–66, for criticism of the theological program of Rudolf Bultmann.

22. Moltmann, *Religion, Revolution, and the Future*, 101.

Jesus' resurrection is, ultimately, the true protest against suffering and death, and it leads the believer, by the way of the cross, back to earth to protest against all conditions that make for suffering and death. The task of hermeneutics, therefore, is to ask how the biblical horizon of freedom can be mediated to the oppression that characterizes the present experience in history.

According to Moltmann, "Theological hermeneutic is abstract as long as it does not become the theory of practice and sterile when it does not make 'the entrance to future truth' possible."[23] The task of hermeneutics is to interpret the Bible's written promises of freedom. The danger is that this seems to be on the face of it too narrow a perspective on hermeneutics because it imposes an ideological superstructure upon texts. The strength, however, is that as biblical hermeneutics can all too easily appear to lead to interpretation that is etiological rather than theological, it misses thereby the imperatives of the gospel for Christian faith and life. In view of these caveats we turn to Moltmann's development of theo-political hermeneutics.

For Moltmann, hermeneutics must not be concerned solely with proclamation and language. They too stand within a political matrix, and so cannot be the act of understanding written expressions of life. As far as Christian faith is concerned, the constant factor in hermeneutics is Jesus Christ. Thus Christian hermeneutics must move between the poles of the cross and the future of Jesus. It must become a hermeneutics of the eschatology of the cross in which the truth of the gospel is irresolvably bound up with suffering in history and its future. This cannot be done by adjusting human being to private meaning; rather, human being and society must be adjusted to the rectifying future of God.[24] Only if this future is the future of the crucified Christ can the future of our present suffering belong with the future of Jesus.

Lying behind this element of Moltmann's political theology is the view that the kingdom of God does not lie in readiness in the future, so that we must only await it. Instead, Christians have to seek the kingdom in order to find it: "Christian hope anticipates the future in the spirit of Christ and realizes it under the conditions of history. In that this future is anticipated in hope and obedience, it is itself conceived as in the process of coming. . . . This means that Christian hope is a creative and militant hope in history."[25]

---

23. Ibid., 98.
24. Moltmann, *Theology of Hope*, 220–21.
25. Moltmann, *Religion, Revolution, and the Future*, 271.

In order words, good works do not build the kingdom of God, but hope in the kingdom of God assumes ethical forms within history.[26]

The Synoptic writers present Jesus as the one who brings good news of the expected last time. He preached the kingdom of God to the poor and called captives into the liberty of this coming kingdom. His work was with the broken, the captives, and the blind, as in Luke, and with the blind, the lame, the lepers, the deaf, and the dead, as in Matthew; and he understands enslavement and dehumanization in both a spiritual and a sociopolitical sense. Salvation is both communion with God as a restored relationship and a new heaven and a new earth—this is surely the meaning of our sharing in the *life* of Jesus. Jesus binds the "least of them" into a new fellowship with himself, and thus to his future. This ministry provoked conflict between the powers of the past and the power of the future because he bound the concrete release of people to himself and his future. Thus for the least of them Jesus and the future in him challenge the powers of the past that are reified in religion and the state. The ordinances of religious law and political oppression are replaced by a regime of grace. Yet Jesus' punishment was a political event. The cross prevents any purely private interpretation of the atonement and any ultimate separation of faith and public practice. And the Trinitarian history of God, which includes the death and resurrection of Jesus, life in history, and the future as a new creation, means that death is given a future. In this way Jesus' ministry proclaims the range of the kingdom of God: "Behold, I make all things new" (Rev. 21:5 RSV).

> It is not a "purely religious kingdom" which could be realized through the power of a new religion. Nor does it merely hold sway over man's personal relationship with God, which could be represented in the private religion of the heart. It is not a moral authority, confined to a changed way of life on the part of men. It is not even kingship only over the living, from which the dead would be excluded. . . . It embraces the religious life as well as the political one, the private as well as the social, the living as well as the dead.[27]

In this view, therefore, the Christian life cannot be split up into vertical (before God) and horizontal (in this world) dimensions. The way of

---

26. Jürgen Moltmann, "Understanding of History in Christian Social Ethics," *Hope and Planning*, trans. Margaret Clarkson (London: SCM, 1971), 129.

27. Moltmann, *Church in the Power of the Spirit*, 100.

Christ means that both are held together as we share in Christ's communion with the Father and in his mission from the Father. The task of hermeneutics is to work out concretely what the way of Jesus Christ means for Christian theology and life today. No less so is this the task of pastoral theology.

The Tasks of Liberation

The core of Moltmann's argument, as we have seen, is that within the dialectic of the eschatology of the cross, the cross is the present form of the risen Christ. Political theology seeks to join theology to the crucified rule of Christ on earth on behalf of the promised coming kingdom that God has announced.

For Moltmann, this involves a threefold liberation: (1) the liberation of the idea of God from speculative, political metaphors, and thus the liberation of politics from a ratifying quasi-divine authority; (2) the liberation of the church from political and civil religion; (3) the liberating work of Christians to relieve suffering and to humanize society. The first and second tasks are theo-critical in nature, though they include positive statements on the nature of God and politics and on the church. The third task addresses in part the Christian's vocation in the world. As we will see in the final part of the chapter, these critical themes speak directly to the practice of pastoral ministry today insofar as much of what passes for pastoral care falls within their orbit.

1. Concepts of liberation. We consider first the liberation of the concept of God from the hold of speculative metaphors by thinking of God in the light of the crucified Christ.[28] Moltmann insists that thinking rightly concerning God means Trinitarian thinking; there is no place in Christian theology for speculative, moral, or metaphysical speech concerning God. Instead of "a pure theory of God," theology has to develop "a critical theory of God,"[29] in which God is known in the cross of Christ. Otherwise, God cannot be found in the cross and the cross is evacuated of deity. Such a "god" cannot suffer. The Trinitarian notion of God, in which the cross is a God event, separates the Christian doctrine of God from speculative theism and non-Christian speech concerning God. Indeed, Moltmann contends, the apathetic "god" is the "god" who ratifies religious withdrawal from society. Thus the Christian doctrine of God becomes the basis for the

28. Moltmann, *The Experiment Hope*, 69–70.
29. Moltmann, *Crucified God*, 69 and 208.

criticism of and liberation from philosophical monotheism, bringing liberation also from the divinized authority figures that sustain oppression.

It is in Trinitarian thinking about God, that is, God conceived in the unity of the dialectical history of Father, Son, and Holy Spirit in the cross, that Moltmann introduces the important notion of the pathos of God. The "pathetic" theology of the cross stands over against the apathetic theology of Greek antiquity, and in it God suffers with us in Christ, entering into our plight to heal it from the inside out, as it were. Moltmann calls this a revolution in the concept of God.[30] God and suffering do not contradict one another. It is this notion of the Trinitarian and crucified God that becomes the cutting edge of Moltmann's attack on the false divinities in religious and political life.

Consequently Moltmann deals with the need to liberate political language and life from divinized authority figures.

> If the one profaned with crucifixion by the authority of the state is the Christ of God, then what is lowest in the political imagination is changed into what is highest. What the state had considered the deepest humiliation, namely the cross, bears the highest dignity. . . . If this crucified one becomes divine authority for believers, the political-religious faith in authority ceases to hold sway over them. For them, the political forces are deprived of direct religious justification from above.[31]

The cross of the risen Lord deprives political authority of its religious ratification by way of a twofold argument. First, the second commandment forbids all images of God, thus initiating a worldview and a political life freed from religious idolatry. Second, the theology of the cross radicalizes the prohibition on images. Every claim to divinity is relativized and secularized by the cross. Faith in the crucified God forces the believer into a permanent iconoclasm against political personality cults, natural religion, and the fetishism for money and commodities.[32] Thus Christian theology must criticize any attempt by the state to claim either divinity or divine ratification. The state and its ideology are secularized. As such, they are affirmed in their worldly character.

2. Liberation and the church. With reference to Europe and North America, Moltmann inquires into roles the church plays. Modern industrial

30. Ibid., 4.
31. Moltmann, *The Experiment Hope*, 111.
32. Ibid., 115.

society acquired its nature precisely through its emancipation from a religious center. Society became a system of needs, and people came increasingly to organize themselves for the social necessities of production and consumption. Other social intercourse—religion, personal ethics, culture, family, and friendships—was removed from the sphere of necessity to the sphere of voluntary association, the sphere of personal freedom and decision. Dialectically, the age of industrial and commercial organization is the age of individuality and free association. Religion became, then, unnecessary to the administration of the public realms.

In a critical spirit Moltmann identifies three roles for the church in such a society—personal, communal, and institutional. The first role concerns faith as the religion of the personal; the church is assigned the task of providing personal, individual, and private meaning for humanity. Religion and the life of the church are considered private matters of inwardness and feeling. If society is inhumane and objective, faith is the guardian of the uniquely human and subjective. Faith is localized in the sphere of personal and free decisions rather than in the sphere of social behavior, political responsibility, and economic action. Faith becomes a "place" of inner unburdening and spiritual readjustment. In such a context, theological questions cannot be asked of social reality.

> A cultural saving of humanity by means of the cultivating and deepening of our subjectivity in constant metaphysical reflection, in art and religion, is romanticist escapism as long as social conditions are not changed. Where conditions are left as they are, this cultural saving of humanity automatically acquires the function of stabilizing these social conditions in their non-humanity, by providing the inner life of the heart with the things which it has to do without in the outside world.[33]

The second role for the church in modern society is as the mediator of fellowship. Christianity provides the transcendental dimension of humanity as cohumanity. Over and against artificial and arbitrary organization in society, community as cohumanity is personal. There the loneliness and isolation are deterred. People find a way to be human. In this analysis, the congregation has the function of creating the community that is lacking in society, providing warmth and authenticity. Again Moltmann is firm in his criticism.

---

33. Moltmann, *Theology of Hope*, 315.

The subliminal existence of free communities of this kind is for modern society a most salutary thing, because in the domestic economy of the human soul it can provide a certain compensation for the economic and technical forces of destruction. This, however, does nothing to alter the stern reality of the loss of the human in "society." It provides only a dialectical compensation and a disburdening of the soul, so that in the alternating rhythm of the private and the public, of community and society, man can endure his official existence today.[34]

In community as cohumanity over and against society, the church becomes a nonworldly phenomenon. The church gives up its remit to anticipate the coming new society of the kingdom of God, and becomes instead a dialectical counterbalance to society.

The third role of the church in modern society is as an institution. Institutionalization provides balance and order amid rapid change. Questions of meaning need hold no terror if people have confidence in the authority of the institutional church. By abrogating responsibility to the institution, people are not accountable for their own decisions. One is no longer required to understand; one need only accept.

By means of these three roles, Moltmann argues, the church has accommodated itself to the social reality. Christianity meets the needs that society leaves unattended. But Christianity in such a constellation of roles has little to say to the society other than what the society wants to hear.[35] Christianity, says Moltmann, finds itself in a new Babylonian captivity.[36] Christianity has tried to find relevance in the life of the world, but has done so at the expense of shedding the identity given it by the cross of the risen and coming Christ.

Over and against such a position, Moltmann argues for a church living within the horizon of expectation of the coming of the kingdom of God. Christianity is constitutively eschatological, and the Christian community lives from the standpoint of the sovereignty of the risen Christ and his coming future. Because we have balanced this statement with a consideration of the past and present ministries of Jesus Christ in history and in his ascended rule, it can stand as a legitimate perspective of Christian identity. Thus, "The Christian life no longer consists in fleeing the world and in spiritual resignation from it, but is engaged in an attack upon the

34. Ibid., 320.
35. Moltmann, *Religion, Revolution, and the Future*, 117.
36. Ibid., 117; and idem, *Theology of Hope*, 324.

world and a calling in the world."[37] In this sense one might well say that the church exists as a revolutionary force within history.

For as long as Christianity remains the cult of the private, the community, or the institution, it sanctions the public civil religion and consequently ratifies the religious sanctification of society as it is. While eschatology forces Christianity to refuse to identify the present structures of society with the kingdom of God, the cross of Christ forces Christians to become involved in the concrete struggle for public freedom. Thus the cross is the point at which we distinguish between Christianity and civil religion, which has the effect of demythologizing civil religion.

We begin to see that the eschatology of the cross remains abstract until it creates within the church a restless ferment for the critical and reconstructive tasks of vocation. In line, then, with this thesis, Moltmann states, "The true church is to be found where Christ is present. . . . We cannot start from the concept of the church in order to discover the happening of Christ's presence; we have to start from the event of Christ's presence in order to find the church. In this sense we start from the proposition: *ubi Christus—ibi ecclesia.*"[38] The question for ministry and for Christian discipleship is: Where is Christ present? It is this question that I have tried to answer in chapters 1–6, leaving the systematic drawing out of the implications for ministry to chapters 7–10.

3. Liberation and the world. Thus far we have been developing the theocritical aspects of Moltmann's eschatology of the cross. We turn now to the initiatives that mark discipleship when it is framed in this way. If Christian theology is at least in part the theology of the eschatology of the cross, how are Christians to anticipate practically or participate faithfully in the coming future of Christ amid the history of the cross under which they stand?

The initiatives Moltmann suggests are many, and sound at times like a Social Democratic political party platform. They may be none the worse for that. More generally, he proposes that the initiatives of discipleship must confront five vicious circles of death that deny people liveliness in life: poverty, force, racial and cultural alienation, life against nature, and the senselessness and godforsakenness of much human experience, all of which lead to dehumanization and death. By this, he forces faith into the economic, political, and social arenas of life. Correspondingly, Moltmann sees five ways of liberation: meeting material needs, the establishment of

---

37. Moltmann, *Theology of Hope,* 331.
38. Moltmann, *Church in the Power of the Spirit,* 122.

democracy, the advocacy of human dignity, a changed relationship between humankind and nature, and the giving of meaning in life. In sum:

> A messianic stream of renewal runs through history from the Christ of God who died in this world and was raised into the coming new world of God's righteousness. In him there are, and always were found, not only the inner repentance and liberation of the heart but also the reformations, renaissances, and revolutions of external conditions. For Christian hope the world is not an insignificant waiting room for the soul's journey to heaven, but the "arena" of the new creation of all things and the battleground of freedom. Christian hope . . . must draw the hoped-for future already into the misery of the present and use it in practical initiatives for overcoming this misery. Through criticism and protest, on the one hand, and creative imagination and action, on the other, we can avail ourselves of freedom for the future.[39]

It remains now to suggest what all of this means for pastoral theology and pastoral care. For if Moltmann is correct in his construction of the eschatology of the cross and its consequences, then this body of work becomes a most significance basis for both criticism and reconstruction.

The Eschatology of the Cross and Pastoral Theology

My concern now is to identify the theological issues that arise for pastoral theology when it is brought into the light of eschatological thinking. The fact of death is reason enough to posit hope. The question is: Does hope have a ground, or is it just desire or wish? Further, the fact of human suffering is ethical reason enough to protest against and work to change social structures and economic conditions that make for this suffering. But is there any ground in God for a pastoral ministry of social righteousness that is other than an endless tilting at windmills, all effort without success against the power of the ways of the world? What does pastoral care of community look like? It is in the light of the resurrection of Jesus and the coming kingdom of God that we set death and present social, political, and economic reality in a redemptive perspective in which we criticize and mobilize against death and the deadly systems that kill and dehumanize people. Eschatology forces us to see that in ministry it is not enough to

39. Moltmann, *Religion, Revolution, and the Future*, 139–40.

care for people so that they can cope with the pressures and blows of common life. Neither is it enough even to understand what ails people in the context of their sociopolitical milieu. Union with Christ in his coming again creates in the present a restless, forward-looking way of life in which trust in God's promises motivates discipleship for action in such a way that every area of the world's life is seen in terms of Christ's rule. At his coming in the flesh, he took all things upon himself, and nothing is excluded from the sphere of his lordship. At his coming again, his reign over all things will be manifest. The question for pastoral ministry is this: What does it mean for ministry today to live within the context of the once and future advent of the Lord?

Moltmann's eschatology of the cross is one attempt to characterize theologically both God's own protest against death and deadliness in the world and his promised victory over them. I present it here in light of the fact that pastoral theology today is characterized by a lack of attention to eschatology, and thus has ill equipped pastoral work to deal seriously with forsakenness, death, and the deadly systems of the world. Without a thoroughgoing eschatology, pastoral theology will lead to a form of pastoral work that bears the marks of a generalized Docetism—a lack of concern for the physical, political, and economic side of suffering. The collapse of pastoral work into forms of psychotherapy or, more generally, into solicitous but privatized care has meant a nonphysical and noncorporate kind of pastoral work that at its worst is a flight into self-centeredness.[40] Pastoral work then becomes a validation of the flight into interiority, personal peace, and well-being in a world that is continually being ripped apart with violence, vastly unequal distribution of resources, and dehumanized living for the great majority of people on the planet. Specifically, we must ask what role the resurrection of the body must play in pastoral work, for it means a future for the person as embodied and a future for heaven and earth, both of which are the meaning of the reign of God. This means we must ask about the relationship between the sociopolitical imperatives of the gospel and pastoral work

The reason these questions are necessary is found in the very nature of Christian theology itself. The central problem is: Who is Jesus Christ? Christian theology exists only in relation to Jesus Christ. As such, theology is forced to consider the problem of the future, for not only must it be made clear who he was and is, but also who he will be and what is to

---

40. See C. FitzSimons Allison, *The Cruelty of Heresy: An Affirmation of Christian Orthodoxy* (Harrisburg: Morehouse, 1994), 27–28.

be expected from him. Theology moves within the space opened up between the life, death, resurrection, ascension, and parousia of Jesus. Perhaps Moltmann's most helpful contribution, then, has been to see the dialectic that historical-eschatological thinking about Christ demands. This dialectic forces us to think eschatologically about Jesus' life and death, and historically about his resurrection. It is the task of pastoral theology to demonstrate what this means for the ministry of the church in the face of death and deadly forces at work all around us.

Having put pastoral theology into the orbit of the eschatology of the cross, we may draw some conclusions. The eschatology of the cross has been developed in such a way that it stimulates a hope that is compelled to live in historical anticipation of the fulfillment of the promises of God. Whatever pastoral work should look like in the light of these promises, it must include living in hope that is *both* a personal *and* an historical and political reality. That is, Christian hope is hope that is concrete regarding actual people. It is not wishful thinking. It is a way of living in the present in the light of the coming, promised future that both criticizes the present insofar as it is not yet the kingdom of God, thereby demythologizing all nations and politics, and mobilizes people for action in work that anticipates the coming community of love and freedom. Thus there can be no stepping back from the eschatological imperatives of the kingdom of God into the immanent prospects of secular deliverance, whether through psychotherapy or political ideology, and neither can the church address only a private, personal sphere of existence. Insofar as much twentieth-century pastoral work has been dominated by individualistic and developmental psychotherapeutic categories, eschatological faith calls such domination into question and insists on a broader perspective in which we must address death and the conditions that make for death. To put that in a different category, eschatological faith insists upon a soteriological understanding, but in such a way that ministry and faith are both a present protest and movement against the forces that make for death *and* a living in hope that these forces do not have the last word, for God will save. That is, there is both a future indicative and a present imperative suggested by the nature of the gospel.[41] This is the eschatological meaning of union with Christ.

Moltmann is critical of what he calls "the pastoral church," the church that looks after people.[42] His critique is helpful, though potentially unbalanced.

---

41. This wording is suggested by Stanley J. Grenz, *The Social God and the Relational Self: A Trinitarian Theology of the Imago Dei* (Louisville, Ky.: Westminster John Knox Press, 2001), 18.
42. Moltmann, *Church in the Power of the Spirit*, xvi.

It is necessary to understand pastoral work in terms of ecclesiology and to relate it to the wider mission of the church as that meaning is given by the gospel. We have seen how easily the church slips into playing a role in society in which the question of God is allocated to a personal and private realm of existence. Religion and, by implication, pastoral work serve as a vehicle of inner unburdening, while external conditions are left as they are. Stabilizing inhumane social conditions by providing the inner life of the heart with the things it has to do without in public life, the pastoral church in effect ratifies the present social order. When Christian faith and pastoral work give up the eschatological imperative to anticipate in action the coming of the promised kingdom of God, they become instead a dialectical counterbalance to society. Society remains largely untroubled by Christianity, and pastoral work becomes a means of helping people to adjust, failing thereby in its eschatological calling. The church's quiet acceptance of this privatized pastoral care is inconsistent with eschatological faith. Eschatological faith calls into question the individualism of much pastoral practice and replaces it with an understanding of human existence in line with the announced coming of the kingdom of God. In other words, the primary anthropological categories are social and relational as well as personal. This means that pastoral work must be related (1) to the congregation, and therefore to worship and community, and (2) to the society, and therefore to political and economic life.

There is still a place for the personal issues of life. We each die our own death. Moltmann acknowledges that while the kingdom of God is political, politics is not the kingdom of God. It is also necessary to insist that the kingdom of God is personal, and in such a manner that there is hope for each one of us in our actual personhood. His scheme, for all its strength, runs the danger of subsuming the person into the political. It is precisely a pastoral church that acts against such a mistaken view of Christian ministry and hope.

Thus eschatological faith forces upon us two perspectives: a direct word concerning death, and the need for what we rather clumsily can call a sociopolitical pastoral theology. In this way, pastoral theology can address both the processes in society that make for death, that stand counter to eschatological expectation, *and* the persons affected by these processes. As such, pastoral theology can help build the argument that encourages those involved in pastoral care to move away from the limited clinical and individualistic approach of the last eighty years. Christian faith implies both believing and living a fellowship of reconciliation—with God, within the church as the body of Christ, and within society—because God has promised a new heaven and a new earth. A resurrection-sociopolitical pastoral theology is both critical and constructive, as I have suggested, and as such it is inclusive of eschatological faith in a way that opens up pastoral work to new meaning and expectation that includes both the person and the society as we anticipate a new heaven and a new earth.

The subject matter of this chapter influences most directly chapter 10, on the ministry of the reign of God, considering hope and social right-eousness within the framework of pastoral work as we try to pull together what the theological curriculum most usually separates. We must not ghettoize eschatological faith, however. As far as possible we must think it into all the areas of ministry, just as we must think the historical and ascended life of Jesus into the meaning of eschatological faith. It is to the meaning of all that has been said so far in this book that we now turn, look-ing at representative ministries of God in which by grace we participate.

Part Two

Ministry in Union with Christ

I n part one I argued that the ministry of God in, through, and as Jesus Christ is the proper foundation for the understanding and practice of pastoral ministry. Thus I have been concerned with God's practice, the ministry or mission of God, which was and is and ever will be actual, and therefore relevant and appropriate because it is God's ministry. The church's ministry is a participation in that ministry, not something new of the church's invention to meet some present need or circumstance, or a vague imitation of Jesus Christ but doomed to failure because we are not messianic. It is not an ideal ministry yet to be made practical; it is the actual ministry of God, rather, which makes the church's ministry practical, relevant, and appropriate. The danger is always that a pragmatic impulse might take over under the felt ministerial pressure of meeting needs. Were this to happen, the profoundly practical theological grounding for ministry would be lost and we would be back once again with the old problem of pastoral care validated by successful "works."

The task in chapters 7–10 is *not* to apply this argument, as if all that has gone before is some kind of theological theory that must be made relevant and appropriate to the present praxis of the church in some specific world context. Rather, the task is to think through the content and meaning of our participation in the apostolic priesthood of Jesus Christ in its past, present, and eschatological dimensions in such a way that the shape of ministerial practice becomes clear in concrete ways as we move from discussion in an indicative mode to an imperative mode. The issue is the locus or place of Christ's apostolic priesthood in the world today[1] as that is the truth of our life because Christ is in us and works through us, and we are in him. The concern is to illustrate the pastoral practice of our participation in Christ in some specific regards. David Hansen's thesis, referring specifically to the work of pastors, "that people meet Jesus in our lives because when we follow Jesus, we are parables of Jesus Christ to the people we meet,"[2] is an illustration of what is intended as long as it is understood to mean that it is God who is the actor, and our action of following Jesus is not an *imitatio Christi* but a *participatio Christi*, a response enabled at all points by the reality and power of his vicarious humanity to which we are joined through the Holy Spirit. Nevertheless, in the church's ministry people should expect to meet Jesus, neither party existing in the abstract, but in the concretion of life and death.

To argue for a *God*-actualized approach is clearly counterintuitive in a *self*-actualized and needs-responding ecclesiastical and social culture. But with regard to ministry, that surely is the challenge of Romans 12:2, "Do not be conformed to this world, but be transformed by the renewing of your minds." In other words, our understanding and practice of pastoral ministry must be converted from pragmatism to sharing in the work or ministry of God in, through, and as Jesus Christ. On this stands or falls all the practice of Christian faith: "for you have died, and your life is hid with Christ in God" (Col. 3:3, RSV).

In chapters 7–10 I discuss four areas of ministry—the ministry of the Word of God, the ministry of the grace of God, the ministry of the presence of God, and the ministry of the kingdom of God. They overlap, for it is the ministry of the one Jesus Christ; but considered from these four perspectives we unfold the meaning of Christ's ministry today. It would be possible to consider other aspects of the full ministry of Jesus Christ in which we participate by grace, for example, the ministries of the peace of God, of the freedom of God, of the love of God, of the joy of God, of the way, truth, and life of God, and so on.[3] But these four aspects of ministry illustrate the trajectory of approach to ministry entailed by this theological perspective. These themes—the ministries of the Word, grace,

1. This too is the issue raised by Christian D. Kettler, *The Vicarious Humanity of Christ and the Reality of Salvation* (Lanham, Md.: University Press of America, 1991), 231. While I agree significantly with his conclusion, what follows here I develop in a totally different manner.

2. David Hansen, *The Art of Pastoring: Ministry Without All the Answers* (Downers Grove, Ill.: InterVarsity Press, 1994), 11.

3. Already in an earlier book, and in more rudimentary theological fashion, I have discussed our participation in the ministry of the compassion of God. Andrew Purves, *The Search for Compassion: Spirituality and Ministry* (Louisville, Ky.: Westminster/John Knox Press, 1989).

presence, and reign of God—are also especially pertinent to the core work of pastoral care.

Unarguably, the Reformation tradition posits the primary threefold theological categories: Christ alone, Scripture alone, and grace alone, that is, Jesus Christ is the Word of God, attested by Scripture, the content of which or of whom is the grace of God. Christ, Scripture, and grace belong together, but the first is the subject matter of the second and third. Were this not the case, an abstract Scripture principle or the abstract noun *grace* would control Christian identity, and Christ would be a member of a list, albeit the first item, of so-called essential doctrines. The point is: the whole of Christian faith and life, everything in discipleship and ministry, is the explication of Jesus Christ and faith in him, which means a sharing in his *life*. He is not one "doctrine" among others; all other doctrines are expression of or elements in the one faith in Jesus Christ.[4] Thus in all aspects of Christian life and ministry, in everything that is said and done, Jesus Christ in his living personhood is the principal actor, the "thing itself," in whom we live and whose ministry we share. He is not a point of reference, or even the most religious of all ideas, as though that which is Christian is somehow at a distance from him. Neither is he a principle for action derived from his life, a kind of timeless ethical directive to be followed. Everything *is* the "speaking" of God's own Word and Truth who is Jesus Christ in his actuality, and as such, he is inherently and irreducibly a practical and personal Truth. Whatever else pastoral work is about, if it would be Christian it concerns directly Jesus Christ as the living and personal Word of God. Pastoral work has no other basis or validation than Jesus Christ; he alone is its self-sufficient basis.[5]

Let us look at this same point from a different perspective. John Calvin called pastoral work (or, in his language, church discipline) the ligaments that connect the body of Christ together (*Inst.* 4.12.1). Pastoral work is understood in terms of Jesus Christ, the Word of God, given to the congregation in sermon and sacraments, which are the ordinary means of grace, and as such the "soul of the church," but now as individual counsel, what Calvin called *admonitio privata*. Pastoral work is not then some other thing that now is different than that (or he who is) given in sermon and sacrament. Rather, it is the same Lord Jesus Christ who is given but

---

4. Thus Emil Brunner, *Dogmatics*, vol. 2: *The Christian Doctrine of Creation and Redemption*, trans. Olive Wyon (Philadelphia: Westminster, 1952), 239.

5. For some of these thoughts, see Eduard Thurneysen, *A Theology of Pastoral Care*, trans. Jack A. Worthington et al. (Richmond: John Knox, 1962), chapter 1.

now to the person directly. This is why pastoral theology has the same content as any other branch of theology, although its goal or focus is different. And it is this present Lord who distinguishes pastoral work from all other forms of personal care of the soul, "natural" forms, we might say, based upon psychology or common sense.[6] Pastoral care has no other content or legitimization than Jesus Christ. What follows over the next four chapters tries to make this explicit for the concrete practice of pastoral ministry.

6. Ibid., 51.

Chapter 7

The Ministry of the Word of God

Long ago God spoke to our ancestors in many and various ways by the prophets, but in these last days he has spoken to us by a Son, whom he appointed heir of all things, through whom he also created the worlds. He is the reflection of God's glory and the exact imprint of God's very being, and he sustains all things by his powerful word.

Hebrews 1:1–3

In the beginning was the Word, and the Word was with God, and the Word was God. . . . And the Word became flesh and lived among us.

John 1:1, 14

Pastoral care exists in the church as the proclamation of the Word of God to individuals.

Eduard Thurneysen, *A Theology of Pastoral Care*

They share, they really share, Christ's conflict and His triumph. Not only is it true that the law of life that is in Christ Jesus makes them free from the law of sin and death, but they partake in His service to the world. As members of His body they are His hands and His feet, doing His will for men.

H. R. Mackintosh, *Some Aspects of Christian Belief*

I n this chapter I follow the threefold development presented in chapter 3, where I discussed Athanasius's treatment of the Word of God spoken, heard, and obeyed. Jesus Christ is the one who is the speaking forth of God. He is also the man who hears this Word and responds to it on our behalf. Through our union with Christ we share in his threefold ministry of speaking, hearing, and obeying or responding to God's Word.

155

As such, the church's ministry is inherently an apostolic and priestly ministry grounded at all points in the vicarious humanity of Christ and enabled, as it were, through our union with Christ by the power and act of the Holy Spirit. The most obvious beginning point is to reflect upon the preaching of the Word of God, considering how the ministry of the spoken Word of God shapes the practice of pastoral care. Then I consider the ministry of the heard Word of God. Finally I address our sharing in Christ's response to the Word of God.

The Ministry of the Spoken Word of God

Preaching

Through union with Christ we share in his speaking forth the Word of God, for we share in him, in the life of the one Word of God. The difficult point to catch hold of here is that the reality, truth, and power of the actuality of our preaching is the Word of God addressed to a congregation, not an illustration of it, or some kind of practical application. We must attest to the reality, truth, and power of the Word of God as the sermon apart from homiletical techniques, rhetorical strategies, or even theological acuity, as if we might thereby exercise control over the Word of God. Through union with Christ, the proclamation of Christ Jesus as the living Word of God to and for us speaks on its own terms as Christ's Word. Thus, according to the Second Helvetic Confession, "The preaching of the Word of God is the Word of God" (1.04). This, without doubt, is a gift of God's freedom and will to "speak" through the preaching of the sermon. This gift is not within our power to engender or manipulate. It means that preaching is a truth that is not ours to invent; it is a happening that is not ours to control. We must surely pray for God to speak through this human instrument of the sermon and prepare for preaching with the expectation of God's blessing. But we do so resting content with this ordinary means of grace as a human act becomes a divine act when and as God wills that it be so. N. T. Wright has said this most clearly in a summary of Paul's preaching:

> Paul discovered, at the heart of his missionary practice, that when he announced the lordship of Jesus Christ, the sovereignty of King Jesus, this very announcement was the means by which the living God reached out with his love and changed the hearts and lives of men and women, forming them into a community of love across traditional barriers, liberating them from the paganism which had held

them captive, enabling them to become, for the first time, the truly human beings they were meant to be. . . . When Paul announced this gospel message, it carried its own weight, its own authority, quite independently of the rhetorical or linguistic skill of the herald.[1]

As the Torah is for Judaism what Wright calls "the living breath of the living God,"[2] so for Christians the proclamation of the Word of God through union with Christ is the living breath of the living God for all people. Accordingly the sermon has personal divine authority. Or, to put it more startlingly: through our union with Christ, whereby we share in the life of Jesus Christ, the sermon becomes a present form of the incarnation, an enfleshment in speech today of the once historical and always eternal and living one Word of God. The sermon *is* the Word of God. The basis on which all Christian ministries are built is this one Word of God, in which we participate and which must be proclaimed. Preaching, in other words, is a theological act in the true sense: it is an act whereby God "speaks," for it is God's address to the congregation, and not just a human reflective word concerning God. It is God's personal and actual Word of address to the people gathered through the voice of the minister.

Practically speaking, preaching is the announcement of the gospel message—the preacher tells about Jesus, Messiah of Israel, as he is attested by Scripture. The content of this message is summed up as the grace of the Lord Jesus Christ, the love of God, and the communion of the Holy Spirit (2 Cor. 13:13). That is the gospel that is incarnated, Spirit-conceived, in and through the speech of the sermon. That this announcement is in God's time God's Word, in which God is the speaking subject, is the foundation of the present being of the church.

In his *Church Dogmatics*, Karl Barth made four points to suggest the theological nature of preaching.[3] First, the Word of God preached means human talk about God on the basis of God's own direction, transcending all human causation.[4] Barth cites Luther, "Without God's sending cometh no Word into the world. . . . There is a vast difference 'twixt the Word that is sent from heaven and that which of my own choice and device I invent."[5] Second, Barth states that God's Word preached means human

1. N. T. Wright, *What Saint Paul Really Said* (Grand Rapids: Eerdmans, 1997), 61.
2. Ibid., 74.
3. Karl Barth, *Church Dogmatics*, I.1, ed. G. W. Bromiley and T. F. Torrance; trans. G. W. Bromiley; rev. ed. (Edinburgh: T. & T. Clark, 1975), 88–99.
4. Ibid., 90.
5. Ibid., 91.

talk about God on the basis of the self-objectification of God that is given in the freedom of God's grace insofar as and when God wills himself to be the object of this talk.[6] In other words, God, as it were, gives himself as the theme of preaching, a theme that is never in our possession, that is not a neutral datum of experience, yet that sets itself where and as God chooses. Third, the truth of preaching is not a judgment made according to an independent criterion or external principle of verification, especially, I might add, a religious and churchly criterion or principle. Rather, the Word of God preached means human talk about God that is true because it is under the control of God's own judgment and as such must be heard and obeyed.[7] Fourth, centrally, and in order to allay any sense that preaching's truth is in any way the result of something the preacher does, Barth insists that preaching is primarily and decisively God's own act.[8] Human talk as preaching is God's own speech, and God's free act. The human is part of the process as both preacher and listener, but God is the primary acting subject from whom preaching receives ever anew and afresh its true name.[9] The actuality of God's Word makes the human word possible: "The Word of God preached means in this fourth and innermost circle man's talk about God in which and through which God speaks about Himself."[10]

Barth published these thoughts in 1932. In 1953, he summed up the main point at the beginning of his exposition of the doctrine of reconciliation: "He, Jesus Christ, is Emmanuel, 'God with us.' How else can He be proclaimed except as the One who proclaims Himself?"[11] Everything said, done, and thought with regard to preaching, I might add, is in view of this singular and remarkable truth.

Consider Barth's points in the context of preaching ministry today. The professional pressures on ministers today are immense. At the level of practical theological argument, the case can be made that to understand the burnout rate among ministers and the lack of vocational fulfillment that many ministers experience we must also recognize the decision we may have made to turn away from this theological and practical foundation for ministry in general, and preaching in particular. We must consider this turn because it signifies, as I have argued throughout, the introduction

---

6. Ibid., 92.
7. Ibid., 93.
8. Ibid., 93.
9. Ibid., 94.
10. Ibid., 95.
11. Karl Barth, *Church Dogmatics*, IV.1, ed. G. W. Bromiley and T. F. Torrance; trans. G. W. Bromiley (Edinburgh: T. & T. Clark, 1956), 18.

of a countergospel basis for ministry and means here that preaching becomes something we do, something that we must make effective. Preaching becomes the minister's burden, a new law, the consequence of which is a kind of ministerial Pelagianism in which there is now a strictly human, albeit religious or churchly, criterion of success. Bluntly put: this turn means that it is up to the preacher to make preaching effective.

Without doubt there are both peer- and denomination-driven demands for congregational growth and revitalization that place enormous pressures on preachers. Demanded of preachers are sermons that have contemporary appeal. Books and programs abound to help ministers to connect with and attract potential converts through preaching and worship styles that are measurably successful. These aids to ministry are practical, pragmatic, and purposeful. In fact, the professional ministerial agenda today is filled with aids (to help us do what we now doubt any more the preaching of the Word of God can do?). I put the qualification in parentheses and with a question mark to suggest hesitantly a genuine, not uncommon, but overwhelming experience. I risk hyperbole to make a point: the crisis in ministry is in part the lack of confidence in the efficacy of Word and sacraments to do what has been claimed for them, namely, to be the present form of Jesus Christ, the Word of God, in truth and power. If we doubt the efficacy and truthfulness of the sermon as the one Word of God, and God's free and gracious address, through our union with Christ, what else is left us but the "management" of religion and the construction of ministries that draw their appeal from somewhere other than the faithful preaching of the Word of God? If God is (apparently) not productive in his Word, what now? Solomon Stoddard's words of warning to his clergy in 1703 in Boston concerning being too much attracted to the spirit of the times are a relevant word of warning for today: "ministers living in an infectious air, are in danger to be infected also."[12]

The drowning minister turns to places of rescue that, tragically, may be no rescue at all. Much in biblical studies today is arcane, dense, academic, and often beyond the reach of many, at least in terms of their available time to master difficult material. Theology too by its nature is more or less a technical discipline, and is often judged to be irrelevant to the practice of ministry. The tag "mission unites, theology divides," while perhaps at times true, is often taken to be a rationale to abandon theology for (an atheological?) practice. The turn toward developing pragmatic skills for

---

12. Cited by George M. Marsden, *Jonathan Edwards: A Life* (New Haven and London: Yale University Press, 2003), 13.

preaching, when it means turning away from the proper theological foundation—that is, an understanding of what really happens in preaching—is a turn toward the death of ministry because it is a turn away from the Word of God on its own terms. To put this in a positive way: homiletical skills must at all points be controlled by the subject matter, the gospel to be proclaimed, that by God's grace is proclaimed, and that is the content of God's address whereby people are brought to faith and into the church.[13] Preaching is preaching only as it is the present and efficacious Word of God. Karl Barth said, referring to Jesus Christ, "it is not He that needs proclamation but proclamation that needs Him."[14] Because preaching is by its nature a theological act, the primary responsibility of the preacher is a theological responsibility: to hear the Word of God and to preach that Word trusting that God honors the divine commission that God gives himself to be its theme, judges its truth according to God's truth, and exalts the human word so that, as Barth puts it, "'preached' belongs to the predicate."[15] The Word of *God* is preached.

Pastoral Care

Regrettably, only rarely are preaching and pastoral care considered together. Eduard Thurneysen, the author of arguably the most important Reformation-based pastoral theology published in the last half of the twentieth century, *A Theology of Pastoral Care*, has done just that. Thurneysen has been rightly brought to task for being overly didactic and homiletical in his approach to pastoral work, making it appear as a subset of preaching. Yet, while pastoral work is not reducible to proclamation, it is because Jesus Christ is the Word of God spoken in our midst that pastoral work must find a place for the Word of God addressed to us. Where such pastoral work is lacking in some way, the true church does not exist with health, for then the evildoer will work without reprimand, members will not be protected, and sinners will not personally be led to repentance and amendment of life.

Programmatically, Thurneysen states that "pastoral care exists in the church as the communication of the Word of God to individuals."[16] It can hardly be put any plainer. This is the intrinsic foundation of pastoral care,

13. Wright, *What Saint Paul Really Said*, 116.
14. Barth, *Church Dogmatics*, IV.1, 227.
15. Barth, *Church Dogmatics*, I.1, 95.
16. Eduard Thurneysen, *A Theology of Pastoral Care*, trans. Jack A. Worthington et al. (Richmond: John Knox, 1962), 11.

and built on this foundation pastoral care "must correspond to the event of God's own speaking in the form of his living Word."[17] In this way, from the very beginning, pastoral work is cast back upon its own true foundation and proper object, the Word of God, which is, of course, a Word other than our human word. It is, says Thurneysen, a *verbum alienum*, an alien and not a natural word. "It is a Word entirely of its own order, and it is never in our power to speak it. It is a Word which in its own power and majesty stands against all our words."[18] It is a Word from outside our sphere of possibility and understanding; it is the antithesis of human capacity.

The distance between the assumptions of empathic and eductive pastoral counseling and classical Reformation teaching could hardly be clearer. With the former, represented, for example, by the work of Seward Hiltner, resources for healing are believed to lie latently within a person, to be drawn out by the good work of the counselor. By implication, eductive counseling in a Christian context assumes that God is immanent within the created process, a force for healing and blessing more or less incognito. Thurneysen's subscription to Reformation theology, in contrast, leads him to argue that there is no bridge, no point of contact, between God and us, *unless God builds it*, which he does through and as his Word, Jesus Christ. God must come to where we are, into our sphere, to make connection with us. Insisting upon the absolute distinction between the Creator and his creation as regards salvation and knowledge of God as a saving God, Reformed theology posits a corresponding distinction between grace and nature that guards the "Godness" of God and the "naturalness," or createdness, of creation (although without danger of imputing a deistic disjunction into the frame of understanding that would mean that God cannot act within creation). Accordingly, the only foundation for positive theology is the revelation of God by, through, and as a Word that is God's Word, which comes to us in its own freedom, power, and grace. According to Thurneysen, God does not establish contact; God re-creates contact.[19] As such, we are born again from above.

Because this is the same Word preached in the sermon and celebrated in the sacraments, pastoral work comes from sermon and sacrament and returns to sermon and sacrament. It happens within the bookends of the church's worship. In this case, pastoral work happens within the Christian community and seeks to preserve people in it[20] or bring them to it. In

17. Ibid., 12.
18. Ibid., 106.
19. Ibid., 83.
20. Ibid., 32.

either case, pastoral work is a ministry of the church and as such shares the same ground as the church does—the Word of God. There is no sense in which or way by which pastoral work can be cut loose from the ordinary means of grace by which God builds up his church through his Son and in the Spirit.[21] In summary: "pastoral care can be nothing else than a communication of the Word of God *in a particular form*. Hence, pastoral care can be concerned with nothing else than the proclamation of forgiveness and the sanctification of man for God."[22]

According to Thurneysen, pastoral work happens in the form of a conversation in which both parties listen to and respond to the Word of God, for it is God's Word alone that ultimately interprets and heals the human situation. The goal is not to join the parishioner on the ground of his or her feelings and thoughts (although that is a good and right place to start—thus there is always a case to be made for empathy as a kind of preparation for pastoral work in which we project ourselves into the feeling world of a parishioner), for that would be to cast people back upon themselves, an action that is ultimately cruel and fruitless and hopeless. The goal with a parishioner is to build on the ground of his or her baptism, which is the ground that the whole person has died and been born anew and claimed by Jesus Christ, in union with whom is identity and life. In this case, in pastoral work pastor and parishioner become servants of this Word for one another. In the case of pastoral work with unbelievers, the pastoral imperative might focus on evangelism, as classical authors like Martin Bucer and Richard Baxter have made abundantly clear.[23] The point is: in either case the person is cast back upon Jesus Christ, who comes as he is, the Word of God, attested by Scripture.

In his teaching, my colleague Dr. Craig Barnes uses a powerful metaphor to describe the direction of pastoral work. While the pastor begins with the presenting problem, the crisis of some kind that the parishioner brings to us, and listens carefully, relates empathically, and responds helpfully, the primary job is not to fix that problem. In fact, a host of properly trained professionals will do a better job in that regard than the pastor. The pastor's primary job is to listen for what Barnes calls "the entrance ramps" that lead us from the presenting problem to a discussion of the real truth of the person's life, which is the person's union with Christ. It is likely that

21. Ibid., 33.
22. Ibid., 52, emphasis added.
23. See Andrew Purves, *Pastoral Theology in the Classical Tradition* (Louisville, Ky.: Westminster John Knox Press, 2001).

the parishioner may have little language or framework by which to speak of this deepest truth of his or her being. Yet buried behind the presenting drama there is the divine drama in a person's life, which is the deepest truth, and as this truth it will properly interpret the presenting problem. As the pastoral conversation proceeds, says Barnes, the Holy Spirit provides many opportunities to turn the parishioner via an entrance ramp to the real reason that brought the parishioner to the pastor in the first place. (Don't worry if you miss it the first or second time around; you will have many opportunities later.) Thus the pastor moves the conversation away from inner resources or external fixes to a ground in the gospel.

A simple and common illustration: a woman drops by to talk about a relationship problem: "Should I marry him?" Unarguably the one thing a pastor must never do is answer that or a similar type of question! The pastoral challenge is to listen for and then take the appropriate entrance ramps that will move the parishioner's reflections onto the ground of her union with Christ. Initial listening skills and communicated empathic sensitivity are always necessary; they help initially to build confidence with the person and aid in self-reflection and self-understanding. But thus far, pastoral care has not yet really occurred. It does not properly happen if the pastor works only at a psychological, therapeutic, or self-insight level of ministry—although that kind of ministry may at some point be required by an appropriately trained family therapist, for example. The task of the pastor, *specifically* as pastor—and what makes pastoral work pastoral *as Christian*—is at some point to move the conversation onto the ground of the Word of God and to allow their mutual listening to that Word to interpret and transform the parishioner's experience of the situation that confronts her. Keep in mind that the parishioner has come to the pastor for help. She is a Christian who wishes, perhaps as yet still in a hidden way, to have her relationship and potential marriage reflect her faith. Simply put: Is there a Word from the Lord? Thus the pastor might invite the person to reflect on biblical passages that seem to be appropriate, enter a season of focused prayer, or attend a marriage preparation class with instruction on Christian marriage.

What makes pastoral work *Christian* pastoral work is not helpfulness as such—and counseling helpfulness in particular—but specifically moving the pastoral conversation onto the ground of the Word of God, identifying Jesus Christ as the one in terms of whom this issue will be explored and from whom help is asked. To return to Thurneysen: "the form of pastoral conversation is determined by its claim to see even the remotest human concern in its relationship to God and his Word established by the incarnation of Jesus Christ. . . . It is a constant listening to the Word of God and constant listening to man who only in the light of this Word can come to a true understanding of his life."[24] Clearly, this very definite assumption—that only the Word of God, Jesus Christ as he is attested in Scripture, reveals and heals the human condition, even in its little pains and frailties—takes us to the heart of an evangelical pastoral practice at a point where the faith itself stands or falls. No reference here to an implicit Christ or to a silently immanentist Christology. The reference is direct, explicit, and intentional. According to Thurneysen,

> The christological statement of the *assumptio carnis* delineates the proper and ultimate background of the form and effectiveness of pastoral conversation. All things stand in relation to the Word of God and can be lifted up and sanctified by it not by nature nor by virtue of an indwelling analogy to the divine, but because God's Word in its *incarnation* has accepted all things. Because Jesus Christ has become flesh, there is now nothing fleshly and human, however sinful and corrupt it may be, that cannot be reached and grasped by the Word of God and translated into God's own. . . . There is no problem, no sorrow, no sin, no pain, and no death over which a word of judgment and of grace cannot and must not be pronounced in the power of this name. All valid pastoral care refers to and claims this prerogative when it engages in conversation about any worldly subject. To practice pastoral care indeed means to take nothing seriously except the sovereignty of Christ in the midst of the distant and dark realms of human problems, into which the pastoral conversation inevitably leads us.[25]

This magnificent pastoral vision is nothing other than the affirmation of the Apostles' Creed: "born of the Virgin Mary, suffered under Pontius Pilate, was crucified, dead, and buried. He descended into Hell; the third day he rose from the dead, he ascended into heaven, and sitteth on the right hand of God the Father." Everything is seen from the perspective of the vicarious humanity of Christ in which he assumed our place, our suffering, and our death, in order to bring us to the Father through our participation in him, in his life. It means that pastors listen to their people in the context of the Word of God and seek always to return them to that Word.

24. Thurneysen, *Theology of Pastoral Care*, 115.
25. Ibid., 118.

Notice what Thurneysen has done. For this form of pastoral care to happen there is the necessity for what he calls a breach in the pastoral conversation. This is the heart of his pastoral praxis:

> Pastoral conversation places under the judgment of the Word of God the whole field of human life with all the psychological, philosophical, sociological, and ethical explanations and critical interpretations pertaining to it. Therefore, a breach runs through the whole conversation which indicates that although human judgment and evaluation and the corresponding behavior are not invalidated here they are recognized as provisional.[26]

While the pastoral conversation takes up any fact, problem, or concern, and understands it with the help of psychological, philosophical, or sociological analyses, the Word of God eventually surpasses these preliminary perspectives. A Christ who is incognito or assumed panentheistically to be incarnate in healing processes is simply just not specific enough at this stage. In other words, there is a movement at this point from acceptance to exposure. This is where pastors really do their job! Thurneysen is not saying that psychological and other analyses are not important; pastoral work needs psychology as an auxiliary discipline. Rather, he is saying that pastoral work is not built upon the foundation of psychology and is not to be held accountable to it. Rather, "in a very fundamental way, we assert the primacy of the Holy Scripture over psychology and its knowledge of human nature. . . . The Word of God is not one source of knowledge among others."[27] The reason for this conclusion is clear: for Thurneysen, pastoral care built upon the Word of God travels into territory where psychology cannot go, namely, the ultimate mystery of the human condition and its redemption in, through, and by Jesus Christ.[28] There is argument, though, for a Christian use of psychology. In the last analysis, pastoral work stands or falls with the biblical attestation to Jesus Christ, Lord and Savior.

There comes a time, therefore, when the minister must move from the ground on which the parishioner stands in his or her own humanity (and its appropriate self-understanding) in order to see the person and help the parishioner see him- or herself in the light of the Word of God ("In your

26. Ibid., 131.
27. Ibid., 206.
28. Interestingly, and from a quite different perspective, a similar conclusion is arrived at by the psychiatrist Gerald May in *Will and Spirit: A Contemplative Psychology* (San Francisco: Harper & Row, 1982), vii, where May argues for the need for psychology to recognize its limits.

light we see light," Ps. 36:9). It is this movement onto another ground, onto this "alien" ground of the Word of God, that entails the breach in the pastoral conversation, and that actually constitutes the pastoral conversation as such. There is, then, a "great pastoral turning point, the disturbing and breaking of the conversation by the hearing of the Word of God."[29] And because this breach enters into the conversation, forced, we might say, by this "alien" Word, and because of the nature and content of this Word (an issue I address in the next chapter), this Word is to be heard and acted upon. A decision is called for. The parishioner will have to respond for or against grace, for or against Jesus Christ, who, as we shall see, already both hears and responds on his or her behalf. The breach in the pastoral conversation leads to a struggle with Jesus Christ.

This is the climax of everything that has been said thus far, for the whole argument, at its simplest, is that pastoral work does its job when a person is confronted with Jesus Christ. Through union with Christ, God, in the grace of the Holy Spirit, uses the church's pastors, and many others also, no doubt, to speak the Word of Christ to his hurting, sad, and lost people. There is then this breach in the pastoral conversation, this taking the entrance ramp to go to another place. It cannot be otherwise. Much of what follows in this and the remaining chapters unpacks what this involves from a series of perspectives.

The Ministry of the Heard Word of God

As noted in chapter 3, Jesus Christ is not only the Word of God to humankind but also humankind itself, in the actuality of the one man Jesus of Nazareth, hearing that Word on behalf of all people. There, we noted Athanasius's argument in *Contra Arianos* that Jesus Christ not only gives or speaks God's Word to and for us, but also as a man he hears and receives God's Word on our behalf: "giving as God's Word, receiving as man. . . . For when he is now said to be anointed in a human respect, we it is who in Him are anointed; since also, when He is baptized, we it is who in Him are baptized" (1.48). Athanasius did not regard us as having a free mind (2.56), but as being people under sentence of death (2.69). Further, we could not become sons and daughters of God other than by receiving the Spirit of the true Son (2.59; 3.19). Even were God to speak, without the Spirit of the Son hearing on our behalf, we would not hear and receive that Word, for we are not children of the Father by nature, but only in the Son, and

---

29. Thurneysen, *Theology of Pastoral Care*, 138.

only the Son can hear the Word of the Father. See, for example, the realization in the Old Testament at Psalm 40:6b (RSV margin), that it is necessary for God to dig out ears for us to hear the Word of God. In Christian terms, Christ is our newly dug ears. So Christ received the Word of God when he took flesh, not for his own sake but for us (3.39). In so receiving, Christ as the Word of God received nothing that he did not possess before; it is in the flesh, as the man for us, that the one who is the Word of God received that Word in his humanity for us (3.40). Jesus Christ then is both speaking God and a hearing man, and this for us. "For He who is the Son of God, became Himself the Son of Man; and, as Word, He gives from the Father, for all things which the Father does and gives, He does and supplies through Him; and as the Son of Man, He Himself is said after the manner of men to receive what proceeds from Him, because His Body is none other than His, and a natural recipient of grace" (1.45).

This Athanasian theological perspective could be illustrated in a general way with regard to any person, and its applicability shown to be universal. But it is especially relevant in two areas of pastoral ministry—ministry to preverbal children and ministry to persons with Alzheimer's disease—showing that at all points the ministry of the gospel *is* a ministry of God's grace. Both situations present insufficient cognitive functioning, one undeveloped as yet, the other having declined, and neither the infant nor the ill have the capacity to hear the Word of God and respond in faithful obedience. While these examples do not limit the range of application, reflection on them illustrates the grace of God in hearing for us the Word that we cannot or do not hear, and to which vicarious hearing pastoral work can bear witness.

Consider a minister, attempting to resist young children receiving Holy Communion, writing in the announcements one Sunday morning that they would not be welcome because they did not understand enough about the sacrament to receive it meaningfully. There has been a long-standing assumption certainly within Reformed theology that full participation in Christ involves, among others things, both a cognitive understanding of the meaning of the gospel and responsible assent. The problem is that this understanding of Christian tradition implies that the gospel is only fully applicable for full-functioning adults. The issue here is not to debate the merits or necessity of confirmation or preparation for a first communion but to inquire into a deeper theological question: In what sense, if at all, can we speak of a child "in Christ" when that child has not "made her decision for Christ" or come to understand in some appropriate sense the meaning of the gospel? Indeed, that child has no capacity whatsoever to grasp the meaning of the primary Christian affirmation: Jesus Christ is

Lord. In what sense, we might ask, is it even possible to speak of the assurance of salvation in the case of a child?

Hearing the Word of God, already for Israel, was an act of God. As noted above, Psalm 40:6b reads literally, "ears you have dug for me." God, as it were, has to open the natural ear so that the Word of God may be heard. In the Christian perspective, as the truly human one Jesus Christ, as baby and as adult, has heard the Word of God in our place. This Athanasian theology radically undercuts the scholastic precondition for faith and salvation that wraps around much Protestant practical theology. Not only when we do not hear, but also—and this is the point—when we as yet have no ability to discern what we hear, Christ has heard for us. His was a vicarious hearing such that the child's inability to hear that in Christ God loves her and has claimed her for herself is displaced and Christ's own hearing of God's Word is substituted in its place. That which the child cannot do for herself Christ does for her. This is a soteriological displacement, for it is a saving hearing that, through union with Christ (the work of the Holy Spirit), means that the child has been addressed by and has heard the Word of God for her. The remarkable and (for adults) humbling conclusion can be drawn that in this case the precognitive child is indeed a hearer and thereby a bearer of the Word of God: "At that same hour Jesus rejoiced in the Holy Spirit and said, 'I thank you, Father, Lord of heaven and earth, because you have hidden these things [God's plans and purposes] from the wise and the intelligent and have revealed them to infants" (Luke 10:21). Commenting on Karl Barth's teaching on the knowledge of God in the *Church Dogmatics*, John Webster notes quite plainly: "Our knowledge of God is thus not a function of any cognitive capacities which we may possess, but of the fact that, in Christ, we have peace with God."[30]

That which has been heard vicariously can by God's empowering Spirit be heard by us for what it is, the Word of God with its claims upon that person's life. Yet even then, let there be no doubt, that later hearing is itself a hearing "in Christ," a hearing, that is, in which as an adult the person participates in that which Christ has already heard on her behalf. Even then there must be no going back behind the lordship of Christ as if with cognitive development one developed a human capacity to hear the *verbum alienum*. Our human hearing of the Word of God always happens in union with the actuality of Christ's hearing for us, so that the hearing of the Word of God is, as with everything else, a gracious gift of God in and through Jesus Christ.

---

30. John Webster, *Barth* (London and New York: Continuum, 2000), 81.

Turning now to persons with Alzheimer's disease, perhaps all that I need to say is to make specific the by now obvious point of Christ's vicarious hearing of the Word of God. But it is worthwhile to stay with the issue a moment longer, not only out of respect for persons who suffer and their families, but also out of recognition that as the general population ages we can expect an increase in the amount of time pastors will spend with such persons. Absent a proper theological perspective, this time will undoubtedly become increasingly tiresome and unproductive.

Alzheimer's disease is a brain disorder in which nerve cells die. Brain signals cannot be transmitted properly. The disease leads to impairment of memory, judgment, and thinking. Generally a person becomes progressively confused, and routine practical matters are increasingly difficult to negotiate. Changes in personality and behavior occur; a patient may become withdrawn, find difficulty with language and communication, and lose motivation or initiative. Between 5 and 8 percent of adults over age 65 suffer some form of dementia. This number doubles every five years. Perhaps about half of persons in their eighties suffer from dementia.[31]

In view of these circumstances, where a person can no longer participate in a knowing way in the life of the faith, or where a person has never come to confess faith in Jesus Christ and so is unable to make a confession of faith, what is the Word of God, of his love, care, and grace, for such people and their families?

A caution: those of us standing on the outside of Alzheimer's disease can never know for sure what goes on in victims' hearts, minds, and spirits. Let us be slow to say what God might or might not be doing secretly within them.

What assurance can we give to those who love such persons? The principal Reformers believed in the assurance of salvation. The ground of this assurance lies in the confidence that salvation is God's work, not ours. While a response is called for, we are saved by God in, through, and as Jesus Christ. This means that the hope of salvation rests in God's goodness, not in a required response or form of behavior impossible for those who suffer from serious brain impairment. Thus the hope for the successful completion of a soteriological formula is both cruel and theologically invalid. The good news is that Jesus Christ hears on their behalf; Jesus Christ also responds on their behalf. Does that mean, at least with regard to persons with Alzheimer's disease, that we are theologically obliged to turn and move in a universalist direction? If that is what is

---

31. These details were taken from MSN Health, "Alzheimer's Disease," http://health.msn.com.

demanded by the gospel of Christ's hearing and responding on behalf of those who cannot hear and respond for themselves, so be it! Let us not be afraid of such a conclusion—it is a joyous and glorious affirmation of a grace and love that is far, far greater than our puny piety. That is not to say that those who in Christ can hear and respond have no responsibility. It is to say rather that the gospel of the good and merciful God surely cannot be construed in such a way that there is a double jeopardy for those aging persons who are progressively losing cognitive functions—they lose both the capacity for faithful response to the gospel and God's salvation. The pastoral word of comfort here is the affirmation of the gospel: Christ has heard God's Word and said yes for this person.

The Ministry of Christ's Response to the Word of God

We move easily from Christ as the hearer of the Word of God to Christ as the one who in our place responds to the Word of God, for, as just illustrated, these are distinguishable but not separable aspects of the one ministry of Jesus Christ. There is a sense in which everything that has been said over the previous chapters refers to Christ's response for us. Now in order to illustrate my general point with regard to pastoral ministry I narrow the focus to consider briefly what it means that we are joined to the faithfulness of Jesus Christ in two regards, faith itself and worship.

Faith

The Latin theological tradition, especially since the Reformation, has tended to emphasize heavily the faith of the believer. North American evangelicalism today is a case in point, where faith is seen as a necessary condition for salvation. This faith includes some combination of cognitive assent as belief, and trust in the merits of Christ. The pastoral problem is easily identified: What is a minister to say when a parishioner asks if she or he has enough of the right kind of faith to be assured of salvation? The faith in the question is a definitionally slippery, near-quantitative human condition that is the fruit of the will; at the last everything in salvation now appears to depend upon a human decision and an experience of trust in God. Christian faith, when faith is the necessary condition for salvation, becomes the religion of a new conditionalism. In this case faith functions as part of a causally construed soteriology: Christ does his part, but a human component appears to be required, for we must have faith in his part. Even when the work of the Holy Spirit is slipped into the equation as the primary actor in a person's coming to have faith—a factor that is appropriate for a full understanding of faith—and assent and trust thereby are properly understood as the gifts of God that constitute a person's having faith, the pastoral problem remains. No minister has access to another's human experience. (Is asking the question in the first place a sign of faith or of its lack?) The problem is that if the minister tends to look for the meaning and significance of faith in the wrong place, he or she has no assurance to give.

A fully evangelical perspective on faith does not cast persons back upon themselves, whether upon religious experiences of some kind or the assent given to statements of belief. Here, as at all other points of Christian faith and experience, the primary reference is to Jesus Christ as the one who stands in for us, doing for us what we do not and cannot do for ourselves. In this case, Jesus Christ is the one who, in the flesh of our humanity, hears and responds believingly and faithfully to the Word of God. Before we have faith, he is the believing human into whose faith we are engrafted, so that at the last we are cast upon his faithfulness and not our own. This is not to dispute the faith that grows within, which is the Spirit's gift. Neither is it to say that in the freedom of Christ's faith for us to which we in the Spirit are engrafted we may not with perversity and ingratitude walk away from faith in unbelief to our judgment. This is surely a great mystery. Nevertheless, the whole movement of the gospel is away from us and toward Christ, in whom we have faith.

Faith involves our trust in God's gift rather than confidence in our choices. But this gift of faith has a special characteristic that marks it as Christian: faith is established at God's initiative by the special work of the Holy Spirit, who joins us to Jesus Christ, to share in his communion with and mission from the Father.[32] In union with Christ, that which is his becomes ours. His Father becomes our Father. His knowledge and love and service of the Father become, in union with him, our knowledge and love and service of our Father. In other words, Jesus Christ and our union with him through the Holy Spirit determine Christian faith so much so that our union with Christ is the proper framework within which we understand the meaning of Christian faith in all regards. This is what Paul teaches in verses like: "In him we live and move and have our being" (Acts 17:28), and "Your life is hidden with Christ in God" (Col. 3:3).

The pastoral response is profoundly shaped by the *Christian* truth that in all things we do not stand before God on the strength of our own piety, faith,

---

32. This formulation is found in James B. Torrance, *Worship, Community and the Triune God of Grace* (Carlisle: Paternoster, 1996), 19.

good works, and the like. Rather, because the Holy Spirit joins us to Jesus Christ we share in everything that is his. In and through him we are children of the Father, sharing in his own life as, in, before, and from God. Joined to Jesus Christ we share in the communion and mission of the Holy Trinity. We stand before God in Christ's name alone, and we serve in his name alone. The real meaning of the Christian's faith is the trust that "for Christ's sake" we are enfolded into the inner life of the Holy Trinity, to share in our Lord's communion with the Father and in his mission from the Father.[33]

These points are difficult to establish with quick biblical reference. Let a brief discussion of Galatians 2:16 suffice. In Galatians 2:15–21 Paul is discussing that Jews and Gentiles are justified through Christ's death. At verse 16 Paul states that "we know that a person is justified [or reckoned as righteous] not by the works of law but through the *faith of* [rather than *faith in*] Jesus Christ." The translation of that last phrase, *dia pisteos Iesou Christou*, is the subject of considerable scholarly debate.[34] Nevertheless, a reasonable translation indicates that salvation is the result of the faithfulness of Jesus Christ, given in his death for us, in which we trust. Thus the emphasis is turned away from our faith in the gospel—a good and necessary thing in its proper place—to the more basic or foundational affirmation that everything depends upon Christ's faithfulness unto death for us. Similar renderings can be found at Galatians 3:22; Romans 3:22; 3:26; and Philippians 3:9. The point is that Jesus has offered the Father the faith that we do not have. Assurance of salvation is found, therefore, in pointing people away from themselves and toward Christ, in whom alone is our hope.

This pastoral theology received classical expression in the opening question of the Heidelberg Catechism. "What is your only comfort, in life and in death? That I belong—body and soul, in life and in death—not to myself but to my faithful Savior Jesus Christ."

Worship

Congregational struggles over worship now occupy a huge amount of ministerial time and energy. Whether there is debate within a congregation between supporters of contrasting styles of worship, or more individually

33. For a fuller discussion of these points see Andrew Purves and Charles Partee, *Encountering God: Christian Faith in Turbulent Times* (Louisville, Ky.: Westminster John Knox Press, 2000), chapter 2.

34. For a handy reference to different perspectives see Richard B. Hays, "The Letter to the Galatians: Introduction, Commentary, and Reflections," in *The New Interpreter's Bible*, ed. Leander E. Keck et al., vol. 11 (Nashville: Abingdon, 2000), 240 n. 112.

dealing with persons who find preaching and worship to be unfulfilling or lacking in meaning, pastors today confront "the worship wars."

My intent here is not to outline an entire theology and practice of worship. One point both illustrates the general theme of this chapter and suggests a way beyond the current distress over worship. The point is this: before we have entered a sanctuary, sung a hymn, said a prayer, or listened to a sermon, Christ, clothed with the flesh of our humanity yet in the intimate holiness of God, stands in for us, offering his own praise of God, in which praise we, by the Spirit's act, are graced to share. Already on earth Jesus lived a life of worship and service of the one he called "Abba." Not only in the synagogues of Galilee but also in the temple in Jerusalem, not only alone on the hillside but also with his friends in houses, he was a man of worship who led his people in that way of life. Do this, he said, remembering me. But not only after his example, but also as the living and reigning Lord, Christ is the *ton hagion leitourgos*—the minister of the holy things (or holy place; Heb. 8:2). Enthroned at the right hand of the Father, Christ, our great high priest, eternally discharges his ministry of praise. While Christians rightly worship Jesus as Lord, they also perhaps more so worship God, Father, Son, and Holy Spirit, *through* the same Jesus Christ, sharing in his intra-Trinitarian praise. Through union with Christ we are, as it were, enfolded into the communion of the Trinity, to share by adoption and grace what is his by sonship and nature. Thus all worship (and prayer) is through Jesus Christ our Lord. There is arguably no more urgent pastoral task today, in view of the worship wars, than helping people to understand and participate in worship that is rightly conceived and constructed according to the soteriological priesthood of Jesus Christ. For only in and through him will we worship as the Father desires.

The source of Christian confidence in worship lies in both the completed work of Christ on the cross and his present ministry before the Father on our behalf by which he continually presents himself to God in and through his own self-offering. What does this mean? When he died on the cross, he died for the forgiveness of our sins. He offered himself to God for our sake. The lordship of Christ yet means more. The irresistible conclusion that takes us into the evangelical heart of the gospel is this: because the life he carried with him into the heavenly sanctuary was not only of God, but also of humankind, we now in union with him are offered to the Father "holy and blameless before him in love" (Eph. 1:4). In other words, salvation does not mean that our sins have been forgiven; we must still be brought into communion with the Father. Thus he is not only the ground of forgiveness of sins but also he presents us to share in his communion with the Father. Thus in union with Christ God has "seated us with him in the heavenly places" (Eph. 2:6). The result, according to Calvin, is "that we do not await heaven with a bare hope, but in [Jesus Christ] our Head [we] already possess it" (*Inst.* 2.16.16). As Christ ever lives to love and praise the Father, we, in union with him, "in the midst of the congregation" (Heb. 2:12), will love and praise God.

Chapter 8

The Ministry of the Grace of God

Pastoral conversation has as its only content the communication of the forgiveness of sins in Jesus Christ. For it is the conversation in which man in his totality is addressed with full authority as a sinner under grace.

Eduard Thurneysen, *A Theology of Pastoral Care*

When Jesus saw their faith, he said to the paralytic, "Son, your sins are forgiven."

Mark 2:5

It is not at all the case, then, that the being of saints is compromised by their being as sinners. On the contrary, their being as sinners, their life in the flesh, is overwhelmingly and totally compromised by their being as saints.

Karl Barth[1]

Through Christ's union with us and our union with Christ we are recipients and bearers of the grace of God. This means two things. First, in and through Jesus Christ, through his union with us in our sin, we are forgiven by God and brought to share in the life of God. We are enfolded into the life of the Trinity, to share in Christ's communion with the Father in the Holy Spirit, so that worship is the true expression of being human in Christ. Second, we share in Christ's responding human life of obedience, his ministry from the Father, so that vocation is the

---

1. Karl Barth, *Church Dogmatics*, IV.2, ed. G. W. Bromiley and T. F. Torrance; trans. G. W. Bromiley (Edinburgh: T. & T. Clark, 1958), 526.

counterpart of worship. In this chapter I examine pastoral ministry in terms of (1) the ministry of the grace of the cross of Christ and (2) a new life of holiness lived graciously as Christian vocation and understood as a sharing in his ministry to the glory of God for the sake of the world. The discussion includes pastoral theological reflection on justification and sanctification as inherently practical and pastoral doctrines that bear witness to the reality of the life of Christ for, in, and through us.

The understanding of the ministry of the grace of God begins with a most important initial pastoral affirmation: the indicative "you are forgiven" (this is Thurneysen's principal insight, as we shall see). Pastoral work thus is shaped by the implications of justification. But pastoral work must move more deeply into the gospel by pushing beyond even such forgiveness, to include the affirmation of restoration to communion with God. The operating vision of pastoral work is the announcement of a restored relationship with God as an actuality that already exists from God's side, and the more the proximate grace of forgiveness of sins is itself qualified by this reality.

Pastoral work must also be understood in terms of sanctification, as a gracious—that is, God-given—sharing in Christ's human response to the Father so that the indicative of grace is balanced with the imperative of grace. As Karl Barth has made so clear, "I will be your God" calls forth the corresponding, "Ye shall be my people."[2] In particular, pastoral work must have the call to discipleship as vocation clearly in mind—that is, living in all things to the glory of God for the sake of the world, and the ministry of the grace of God becomes the place where we hold together two seemingly different but necessarily conjoined aspects of Christian experience: pastoral care as the announcement of forgiveness and communion, and the grateful call to discipleship as lived Christian vocation.

The Ministry of the Forgiveness of Sin and Communion with God

The theme of reconciliation with God is the heart of the gospel message and, therefore, of the church's faith and ministry. As Barth has made clear, reconciliation is primarily an affirmation concerning the act of God and his covenant faithfulness to be "God with us."[3] As such, however, it also

---

2. Ibid., 499.

3. For the following, see Barth, *Church Dogmatics*, IV.1, ed. G. W. Bromiley and T. F. Torrance; trans. G. W. Bromiley (Edinburgh: T. & T. Clark, 1956), 3ff.

tells us about ourselves. Reconciliation is the truth of our history and being, for God does not wish to be God apart from us. Whatever else they must consider, pastoral theology and pastoral work must consider the truth of the gospel that in and as Jesus Christ God has entered into our history in such a manner and to such a purpose that henceforth, in and through the same Jesus Christ, that which has separated us from God has been overcome and we may now participate in God's life as beloved children of the welcoming Father. God with us means us with God.[4] Emmanuel means homecoming. This is more than a forensic justification, for reconciliation includes the restoration to communion, which is a sharing in God's life and is the ground and possibility of our true human being, our life, the response to which is gratitude. For this life with God we have been created and redeemed, and everything else concerning our human being is to be understood and lived out in view of this. Pastoral work, which is always characterized by its focus on people in their neediness, must have as its central task, then, announcing this divine act of response to a yet more radical neediness in which God in, through, and as Jesus Christ undertakes to do for us what we cannot do for ourselves, arresting and reversing the dire human course unto eternal death.[5] Whatever the present suffering, Jesus Christ is attested as the one in and through whom we have human life in fullness through forgiveness of sin and restoration to communion with the Father.

Forgiveness and communion should not be separated, as if we might foolishly choose the one without the other. Because there is an appropriate theological movement from forgiveness to communion I consider them in that order. Even the declaration of the forgiveness of sins cannot be the first pastoral act, however, for it has its own ground in the love of God, in God's will to be in communion with us.

The Ministry of the Forgiveness of God

Atonement is a divine sovereign act of grace, an actuality in, through, and as Jesus Christ, not a human insight or idea drawn from his life. It is rooted entirely in the freedom of God to save and, as such, in and as the act of Jesus Christ. That we stand in need of God's mercy and forgiveness is not, however, a knowledge that we are naturally capable of gaining, that needs only to be awakened somehow into a religious, spiritual, or moral

---

4. Ibid., 14ff.
5. Ibid., 213.

sensibility.[6] Standing in need of God's forgiveness is not the same as having a bad self-image or feeling basic guilt. The paradigmatic biblical teaching is Psalm 36:9, "In your light we see light"; otherwise, all is darkness, even the most sublime religious, spiritual, and moral striving of which we are capable. It makes no sense therefore to begin with human sin and the resultant separation from God. It makes even less sense, if that were possible, to begin with the judgment of God upon us. Apart from a knowledge of and relationship with God for us in and as Jesus Christ, knowledge of ourselves as saved sinners is not a possibility. We can only come to this knowledge in view of true knowledge of God and especially of the love of God that has searched for, found, and forgiven us in Christ. Thus, even before we declare, "in the name of Christ, you are forgiven," which implies an awareness of ourselves as sinners and some view of the atonement, we must first declare who the God is who forgives us and what this God is about.

There is a dual and contrasting religio-cultural context for this first pastoral movement of declaration: (1) the prevalence of a vague theism or deism among those who are not Christian or are only nominally Christian, and (2) among Christians, the belief in God as a God of law, anger, and judgment. We cannot assume that people know God. The problem is that they think they do, so that the word *God* is part of public and political discourse.

The content of generic theism exists as God's mild though distant benevolence. This deity gets tangled up in civil religion ("In God we trust"), being a God who in some undefined (and the more undefined the better) way blesses the country. This God is invoked by civic and religious leaders at all levels and is inclusive of all religious beliefs and none. The particular name of God according to any specific creed is merely incidental, a partial expression of a God who transcends religious traditions. This is a kind of "many ways, one god" theology. In contrast, some Christians know God as a judge quick to anger, whose word is law; grace is conditional on human response. My own pastoral experience suggests (somewhat unscientifically) that one does not need to scratch much below the surface of many Christians to find either a fatalism that comes from believing in a God whom they knew would eventually find them out in

---

6. According to Barth, "That we are sinners, and what our sin is, is something we can never know by reflection about ourselves in the light of a standard of good and evil which we have freely chosen or discovered. This is made impossible by the fact that with [Christ's] coming we are displaced from the office of judging." Ibid., 240. Further, "access to the knowledge that he is a sinner is lacking to man because he is a sinner." Ibid., 361.

the end and deal with them accordingly, or a profound confusion because they thought they had been good or pious enough only to be proved wrong in the end.

All pastoral work begins within the framework and announcement of the love of God, for God is love (1 John 4:8). The gospel begins from the standpoint that God so loved the world . . . (John 3:16). We must first approach people not with God's judgment, or even with God's forgiveness—for we cannot assume that a person knows who the God is who judges or forgives him or her—announcing and bearing the love of God. This is the frame within which all pastoral work is rightly cast. (I have discussed the love of God in chapter 3 and need not repeat it.) It is important to say that God's love is neither some vague and pleasing affective or ethical attribute of a distantly benevolent God, nor is it a liberal philosophical counterpoint to the scholastic Calvinist God of judgment and anger. God's love has its specific content precisely and actually in the fact of Jesus Christ, and thereby has a uniqueness, singularity, and particularity that scandalizes the human religious sensibility that sees Christianity as one expression among many others of faith in God. Thus the first pastoral movement of the ministry of grace must be, quite simply (although of immense significance), the announcement: "Jesus Christ is Lord, and this Jesus who is God loves you." This statement stands over and against all other claims to divinity and all other definitions of deity, for here the claim is made that this man, who died on the cross of Golgotha, and this man only, is as such the revelation of God and the event of the love of God for us. It is the announcement of the human reality as Paul saw it: "for you have died, and your life is hidden with Christ in God" (Col. 3:3). God's love in Jesus Christ means that we have been claimed by God, and now nothing "will be able to separate us from the love of God in Christ Jesus our Lord" (Rom. 8:39).

To make the point plainly: pastoral work that is Christian is explicitly in the name of Jesus Christ. He is its content and goal. Without explicit grounding in Jesus Christ, an explicit sharing in his life and ministry, pastoral work accommodates itself to ideologies or theisms, becoming a cultural expression of care (not necessarily uncaring in itself, but not *pastoral* care), but bereft of the truth and power of the gospel. Even the appeal to an implicit Christ (for the word *incarnation* has only one subject, referring to a specific event within history) becomes the appeal to a spiritual or ethical Christ-principle; this, however, is not the explicit *Jesus* Christ, in whom alone God has come among us to heal and to save, who alone *is* the grace of God. Pastoral work that is Christian has no ground and no hope other than Jesus Christ, who is the love of God for us. Thus the first pastoral act of the ministry of the grace of God is this announcement: "Jesus Christ is Lord; Jesus who is God loves you."

This attestation that Jesus is the Lord who loves us becomes specific now, first of all, in the declaration of the forgiveness of sins. Love remains disconnected to the true human condition without it. With the caveat of the previous paragraphs, we can now agree with Eduard Thurneysen, "Pastoral conversation has as its only content the communication of the forgiveness of sins in Jesus Christ. For it is the conversation in which man in his totality is addressed with full authority as a sinner under grace."[7] While Thurneysen is in danger of collapsing the gospel into the forgiveness of sins, pastoral mediation of the gospel must include a central role for the announcement of the forgiveness of sins because the content of pastoral work is the nature and substance of the gospel. It can have no other ground. In order now to understand what Thurneysen has in mind, we must see the forgiveness of sins as it was understood in the sixteenth century, for he takes his orientation from the principal Reformers.

The primary focus of attention among the fourth-century Greek fathers of the church was concern for the identity of Jesus Christ. This concern was resolved with the Nicene theology that the Son was *homoousios to Patri*, of one substance with the Father. The primary focus of the Reformation age was on the mighty acts of God, demonstrated especially in the forgiveness of sins and the great evangelical doctrine of justification by grace alone through faith. For the Greek fathers, the concern was Christology; for the Reformers it was soteriology. From this conjoined history we learn that the being and act of God must be held together: incarnation *and* atonement. While Thurneysen's focus is on the act of God in and as Jesus Christ, we keep the whole field in view—the person of Christ in his acts, and the acts of Christ as the truth of his person.

Thurneysen begins his exposition of the mighty act of God with a citation from Luther's Shorter Catechism. "I believe that Jesus Christ, very God, born of the Father in eternity, and also very man, born of the Virgin Mary, is my Lord, who has redeemed me, a lost and damned man, and has won and delivered me from all sins, from death, and from the power of the devil."[8] This is not intended to be metaphorical language; its intent

---

7. Eduard Thurneysen, *A Theology of Pastoral Care*, trans. Jack A. Worthington et al. (Richmond: John Knox, 1962), 147.

8. Ibid., 151.

is bluntly realist, and as such, pastorally practical and relevant. There is no deeper truth concerning a person. Humankind is lost, condemned in sin, belonging no longer to God but to death and the devil. To such a lost condition the word of grace is: "redeemed, delivered, won!" How is this possible? The answer is that Christ has taken our place, the death of Christ for sin once (*ephapax*) for all (Rom. 6:10; Heb. 7:27; also 1 Pet. 3:18), wrenching us thereby from the province of death and putting us into the kingdom of God, no longer subject to the alien powers. Thus, according to Thurneysen, "the whole work of redemption is thereby described as the work of the *forgiveness of sins*."[9]

Calvin sees the matter similarly. Christ has won our redemption through the shedding of his blood, and because we are washed with this blood in the power of the Holy Spirit, a real change takes place in our lives. Knowledge and feeling of the power and benefits of Christ are born in us. As Thurneysen puts it, "a new man is created—through what? Through the blood, and this again means through the forgiveness of Jesus Christ. . . . To live in the church means precisely to participate in the forgiveness of sins. The forgiveness of sins thus becomes the one and only content of the Christian faith as it lives in the church."[10]

Thus did the principal Reformers understand the human situation in the light of the gospel. Our whole life is in thralldom to sin and death. Our whole life is liberated from this deadly situation by Jesus Christ. Especially Calvin is aware of the need for a subjective appropriation of this fact. At the core of the biblical message and the pastoral care that is faithful to it is the question: Are you at peace with God? But this supreme pastoral question is only rightly asked and heard when it coincides with the question: Do you know that your sins are forgiven in Jesus Christ? To Thurneysen, this is *the* question for pastoral work.[11] "Pastoral care means and primarily functions as *care about such peace*. Its practice consists in man's being regarded and addressed in the pastoral conversation as one on whom God in Jesus Christ has laid his mighty and merciful hand."[12] This forgiveness of sins, however, has the force of real liberation only when it is communicated as what it is, an unconditional act of God's grace. It is announced under no provisos. There should be no fear of being too generous with the announcement. Indeed, withholding forgiveness

9. Ibid., 151–52.
10. Ibid., 152.
11. Ibid., 154.
12. Ibid., 155–56.

signals some kind of legalism. According to Thurneysen, "grace and only grace awakens the ethical decision and will power of man. . . . Grace must be able to flow unhindered in order to be effective and healing."[13]

What does this pastoral care look like? First, it is an orientation. Second, it assumes a definite hermeneutical perspective. Third, it is a practice. We will look briefly at these three perspectives.

1. Pastoral care as a sharing in the ministry of the grace of God is an orientation. Here we think especially of the basic theological perspective of the caregiver. It is no slight thing to say that ministers especially must undergo a profound and continuing transformation of mind and perspective in order to see the people given into their charge bathed in the love and mercy of God. This was the point made by the Strasbourg reformer Martin Bucer in his *Von der waren Seelsorge*, published in 1538.[14] For example, Bucer interprets Luke 15:4–6, from the parable of the Lost Sheep, to mean that whatever is necessary must be done as a matter of highest priority in order to win back for Christ those who once acknowledged him and are still his. Imaginatively, Bucer uses Galatians 4:19–20 to interpret the effort involved. He likens the work of restoring the wayward to the communion of Christ to an anguished childbirth (156, 18). Describing those pastors who go in search of Christ's lost lambs, Bucer uses a striking series of images: they leave everything to search for, find, and bring home the persons who have wandered from Christ; they do this not only by direction or coercion, but also by carrying them home on their shoulders; and like mothers, in a sense they give birth again, with much pain, though also with great gentleness (157, 3–4). This ministry of care is above all else a ministry of love (224, 13). Neither domineering (*herrisch*) nor unfriendly, the caregiver acts humbly and like a mother (*mütterlich*), like a nurse with her child (225, 11). This is a most interesting series of German words to use in describing the appropriate attitude to take in pastoral care.

2. Pastoral care as a sharing in the ministry of the grace of God assumes a definite hermeneutical perspective. Here we think especially and specifically of looking upon a person—interpreting a person—in the light of the

---

13. Ibid., 165.

14. Martin Bucer, *Von der waren Seelsorge, Martin Bucers Deutsche Schriften*, vol. 7: *Schriften der Jahre 1538–1539*, ed. Robert Stupperich (Gütersloh: Gütersloher Verlagshaus Gerd Mohn, 1964), 90–241. Citations from *Von der waren Seelsorge* give the page number from the German edition and the line on which the citation begins. For a presentation of Bucer's pastoral theology, see Andrew Purves, *Pastoral Theology in the Classical Tradition* (Louisville: Westminster John Knox Press, 2001), chapter 4.

fact that Jesus Christ lived and died for this person, who, therefore, has been forgiven and restored to fellowship with the Father. In Jesus Christ this person has been elected to be God's friend, and is now called through the Holy Spirit correspondingly to live this truth. God has really acted in this person's life, and his/her situation has been altered from enmity toward God to peace with God. In baptism this person has died to sin to walk now in newness of life (Rom. 5:4). For all that a person before us is physically, psychologically, and sociologically, that which a person *is* and which expresses the truth of that person not in any theoretical or merely spiritual sense but actually, is that he/she is forgiven and restored to communion with God. The physical, psychological, and social dimensions of human experience are brought under the fact of the gospel and are, finally, understood in terms of it, for we hope for the resurrection of the body and a new heaven and a new earth in the reign of God's victory over all that separates us from God. Thus the forgiveness of sins is the irreducible interpretative framework by which we consider a person.

3. As a practice, all of this means seeing and understanding the person before us as God's person, who has been irrevocably claimed and dealt with by God, even if he or she does not yet know it. This hermeneutical perspective leads us to act in a certain way. The person before us may rebel and lie and live in fear, but we now know this is in impotent conflict with the truth of his or her being.[15] Whatever confronts us pastorally concerning this person, we must think of him or her and respond in terms of the fact that he or she has been reconciled with God in Jesus Christ. Even when this truth is still hidden or denied, Christian pastoral care knows the truth, seeks to announce it, and to call forth the amen of faith. Pastoral work makes attitude and perspective concrete in actions that embody gracefulness, love, forgiveness, restoration, and peace.

Regarding a person burdened by sin, there is no better statement of the *movement* of pastoral care that shares in the ministry of grace than Thomas Cranmer's prayer: "The Almighty and merciful Lord grant you absolution and remission of all your sins, true repentance, amendment of life, and the grace and consolation of the Holy Spirit." Pastoral work can be greatly guided by the theological movement of this prayer in its counsel of sinners. The theology of this prayer moves graciously from the indicative to the imperative of grace. Absolution and remission of sin are prior to repentance, following Calvin's teaching. But without doubt repentance and amendment of life are called for in the grace of the Spirit.

---

15. Barth, *Church Dogmatics*, IV.1, 91.

Regarding a person who might be found on a range of experiences from doubt and loss of faith to apathy and disinterest to rebellion against God, the practice of pastoral care is guided and sustained by the knowledge that this person's life is hidden with Christ in God (Col. 3:3). Assured that this person's life in Christ is not up to us, or even up to him or her, but is God's business, with confidence we bear witness, listening for the movement of the Holy Spirit who awakens a person to conversion, and waiting calmly and discerningly—it might take years!—for the right moment to offer the appropriate word of Scripture and assurance.

The Ministry of Communion with God

Galatians 4:5 provides the frame of reference: God sent his Son "in order to redeem those who were under the law, so that we might receive adoption as children." John McLeod Campbell rightly notes that theology has often attended to the former—redemption from the law—and paid less attention to the latter—our adoption and homecoming to God[16]—substituting a legal standing for a filial standing before God, thereby undercutting the great promise of the gospel.[17] Those who thus undercut the gospel emphasized God's attention in Christ only to the turning from God by humankind, leaving aside the turning to God that is also the work of Christ for us that is implied in the restoration to fellowship. In our discussion of Christ as the apostle and high priest of our confession, I examined McLeod Campbell's position. In summary, he argued that the atonement is a sharing not just in the grace of Christ's benefits, but in the grace of his filial love for the Father, in his *life*, and in a relationship that is uniquely his. Jesus reveals God precisely as Father, and only in that revelation do we know who the Father is and what the desire is of the Father's heart. This knowledge teaches us of our loss through sin and of the Father's will to restore us from our orphan state to communion through adoption. To do this, Christ, who has made the perfect confession, now expresses his own righteousness in humanity as perfect love toward and in service of God. Christ has consecrated a way into the holy company of God through the purification of his blood, enabling us, in his name, that is, in union with him, not only to worship God in truth and to draw near to God, crying, "Abba, Father," but also to serve God as we are called to

---

16. John McLeod Campbell, *The Nature of the Atonement* (1856; reprint, Grand Rapids: Eerdmans, 1996), 50.

17. Ibid., 76.

do. We come to God only as God's children, or not at all,[18] and we do it alone in union with the priestly sonship of Jesus Christ, in his revealing of the Father as our Father, and in his offering of us in his own humanity to share in his divine sonship.

This argument has two important implications for pastoral work: (1) worship is the starting and ending point of all pastoral work, as has already been noted; and (2) the ultimate framing of all Christian counsel is peace with God, announced not just as forgiveness of sins, but also as restoration to relationship with God.

1. Worship. Building again on the gospel indicative that our life and the life of those for whom we have pastoral oversight is hidden with Christ in God (Col. 3:3), we must press the point that the fulfillment of human personhood is the right worship of God. This is what it means that we share in the Son's communion with the Father. "But the hour is coming, and is now here, when the true worshipers will worship the Father in spirit and truth, for the Father seeks such as these to worship him. God is spirit, and those who worship him must worship in spirit and truth" (John 4:23–24). The truth of our life is that, through union with Christ, and in the Spirit, we are enfolded to share in Christ's communion with the Father—that is, we share in his sonship. The center of life is to live this communion in a life focused on the worship of God. This is what it means to share in the response of the Son to the heart of the Father.[19] Worship means that we recognize the truth of our humanity before God in Christ that life is lived gratefully through Christ and in the Spirit before God. Life lived without the worship of God in spirit and truth is life lived both incompletely and falsely, a life against the truth of who we are in Christ. Participation in Christ's divine sonship means moving from a soteriology of imputed righteousness to one of filial relationship with God, the heart of which becomes our crying out, "Abba, Father." This is the proper theological goal and meaning of all human life.

Classical theology and pastoral care viewed worship and ministries of care as unsunderably connected. All pastoral work comes from Word and sacrament and returns to Word and sacrament, which means that pastoral work legitimately seeks to bring people into worship. This should be the highest goal and always in mind, no matter the presenting issue. It means also that pastoral work is rightly liturgical work, in which caring is both worshipful in attitude, for it is to the glory of God, and ever ready to be

18. Ibid., 243.
19. Ibid., 144.

worship in act. Thus pastoral work directly involves the anointing of the sick and the laying on of hands, the celebration of the Holy Communion and prayers, the reading and interpretation of Scripture, the confession of sin and absolution, singing of hymns and psalms and canticles. Too much in recent times pastoral work has become a reflective listening exercise only, using liturgical "resources" only rarely. To ensure the closest possible connection between worship and pastoral work, pastoral care should express itself in worshipful acts regularly rather than just occasionally.

Worshipful pastoral work can undoubtedly become routinized, but I suspect that the problem is elsewhere. Allow, please, a personal reflection to make my point. During my recovery from and extended hospitalization after cancer surgery, in the midst of completing the first draft of this book, I was struck with two observations. First, I was surprised to notice how few patients received visits from clergy. Lack of spiritual comfort may be a sad fact of hospitalization for many people. At the very least there is the need for adequate chaplaincy services, yet they are often the first to go during the economic downturns. But parish ministers too must be mindful of their responsibility to visit the sick. The church needs to be in the hospital. Second, fortunately, many ministers made me brief visits. Some prayed with me, a few read Scripture, but none anointed me with oil, or engaged in brief liturgical acts attesting forgiveness of sin, or offered to celebrate Holy Communion. I am very grateful for the warmth of the affection that these visits indicate, and for the piety usually expressed—in fact, I am grateful beyond telling, and do not intend personal criticism. I merely observe how far Protestant pastoral care has moved away from seeing worship close to the center of its work. The most profound "pastoral" experience during these long and difficult days was my wife and me—at her insistence—reading morning and evening prayer or compline together. This became the anchor of my days, giving me both a context within which to reflect upon my illness and a sure sense of hope. Especially lost to mainstream Protestantism, I fear, is the liturgical rhythm of the classical daily liturgies, the reading of the daily lectionary, and the singing of the great canticles of the faith—the *Venite, Jubilate*, and *Te Deum laudamus*, for example. Lost also, I suspect, is the glorious comfort of compline at day's end, and of the repeated antiphon of assurance: "Guide us waking, O Lord, and guard us sleeping; that awake we may watch with Christ, and asleep we may rest in peace." I have the hesitant hunch that many of my Presbyterian brothers and sisters in ministry simply do not know this material exists, and if they did, what they would do with it.

2. Peace with God. It is important that the proper place be given in pastoral work to assurance of salvation and restoration to communion with God. (In that this is also part of the doctrine of hope, I develop this idea further in the final chapter.) Here it is enough to note that the grace of God in the atonement confers something good for us now, namely, life in communion with God. This life means a life of prayerful and worshipful trust, expecting the life of Christ to be made perfect in our weakness. It means living in God's favor and oneness of mind with Christ. It means knowing and enjoying God as Father who has received us as his own, having access to God as the Son has access to the Father. It means our access into the holy of holies, and it means that the love with which the Father loved the Son might also be in us. It means that the desire of the Father's heart for us is now fulfilled in us. It means the amen of a person to the amen of the Son to the mind and will of the Father in relation to us. All of this is in the fellowship of Christ's own sonship that he shares with us, so that what is his becomes ours.[20]

Pastoral work never enters the fray, or contends for people's lives before and with God, with no resources at hand, because Christ is already and always the minister both *from* God as God in and as the man Jesus of Nazareth, and *to* God as wholly human in our stead. Indeed, pastoral work is abundant in giftedness, for the whole range of the gospel promise is ours to attest—namely, that we participate in Christ as the minister of the grace of God to us and as the minister of obedience to the grace of God to God. He gives us God's grace; and through him we too live in God's grace. We can sum up what this means in simple terms: pastoral work has the extraordinary privilege of being able to say to all manner of people in all kinds of situations, "You belong to God; God has made you the beloved through Jesus Christ and restored you to fellowship with God. Receive who you are, and rejoice."

The Ministry of the Grace of God as Vocation

To participate in the life and ministry of Jesus Christ is to share in his life as the grace of God, from God, to and for us. That discussion is now behind us. It is also, however, to share in the grace of God, to God, for the sake of the world; for as we have seen, Christ ministers both the things

---

20. All of these images are taken from ibid., which are scattered throughout the book, many of which are frequently repeated.

of God to humankind for us, and the things of humankind to God for us. This is no less a ministry of the grace of God, for it is also for us. Thus in Christ Christians (to borrow again James B. Torrance's felicitous formulation) share in Christ's communion with the Father, and share in his mission from the Father. Both aspects are a ministry of grace, both are for us, and both are to the glory of God.

Before discussing the pastoral theological perspective on vocation, an illustration, again drawn from my hospitalization, might be helpful. I offer this aware of the danger of both generalizing idiosyncrasy and of seemingly self-congratulatory piety. Yet the source of the ministry I here briefly describe, God knows, is solely the Holy Spirit, and I take it to be normative that everyone in Christ in some way shares in his ministry to the glory of the Father for the sake of others, no matter their present situation. This applies no less to recipients of pastoral care than to any other Christian person.

Immediately after surgery I was removed to a recovery room for a few hours. As I slowly woke up and gradually regained some functioning level of responsiveness, in spite of abundant morphine, I became aware of people lying on either side of me. I have no knowledge of their identities or circumstances, other than that they too were recovering from surgery. Quite unexpectedly, and without any virtue of decision or intention as far as I recall, I started praying for my companions in recovery. The sense of this intercessory praying—the imperative to do so lying upon my heart— was very powerful. This was something I could do, something perhaps I was compelled to do. Afterward, I was deeply struck that God would use me, feeling helpless, in pain, and very needy, for a work of grace. Periodically over the next two weeks I found the same yoke of Christ upon me, as I was led by the Holy Spirit to pray for my neighbors in the room in the bed alongside mine as we shared in the peculiar intimacy of hospitalized semiprivacy.

No one is too weak, too dependent upon the ministrations of others, or too woebegone to be outside the grace of participating in Christ's ministry from the Father. To suggest otherwise is to say that Christ's grace as the call to vocation depends upon prior human availability or necessary human possibility. It is to say that Jesus Christ is not wholly adequate to transform every human situation and circumstance and to bless every person for ministry. It is to say that participation in Christ is only for the hale and hearty. The grace that is for all, however, means both the mercy of God and communion with God for all *and* the vocation given to all who live in Christ by the act of the Holy Spirit. It means both that while we were weak, Christ died for the ungodly (Rom. 5:6), *and* that Christ's power is made perfect in weakness (2 Cor. 12:9).

My basic argument is that the Christian life is the vocational life as by grace and in the Holy Spirit it is a participation in the vocation of Jesus Christ. From this no one is excluded. Grace, and thereby call, is always for all. It involves a profound connectedness with the inner personhood and mission of Jesus himself as God with and for us, a connectedness that shapes us in every aspect of life, private and social, individual and communal. There is no reality of justification that is not also life in the Spirit, or sanctification. The Bible calls this being born again, and it leads to the Christian life as our life "in Christ" as opposed to our life "in Adam," as Paul expressed it. To understand the Christian life at all we have to understand it in such extraordinary and specific terms. The theology of the Christian life is not primarily concerned with the Christian's life as such, but with Jesus Christ, in relationship to whom singularly the Christian has a life. This means that pastoral work properly includes among its responsibilities the sounding of the call to vocation. From this call no Christian is excluded, for every Christian is called in virtue of the sanctity of the one who calls.[21]

Paul uses the phrase "in Christ" to designate or define among other things the Christian way of life. The Christian lives and acts "in Christ." This is the way salvation is lived out. So Paul instructs Christians to "rejoice in the Lord" (Phil. 3:1). Tryphena and Tryphosa "labor in the Lord" (Rom. 16:12). Christians are to trust (Phil. 2:14), stand fast (1 Thess. 3:8), be strong (Eph. 6:10), speak boldly (Eph. 6:20), fall asleep (1 Cor. 15:18), know and be persuaded (Rom. 14:14), and hope (Phil. 2:19) in the Lord. These lived virtues, attitudes, and activities are representative expressions in daily life of the redemptive reality of the Christian's status "in Christ." Our salvation through and relationship with Christ is lived out in concrete and practical ways.

A loose analogy for the sake of illustration can be drawn between this meaning of "in Christ" and marriage. Marriage is a status the couple enjoy. Yet marriage must also be worked at, struggled for, and lived into. The status of being married expresses itself in a particular orientation toward and discipline of life. Being married affects everything else, or at least it should. Working at a marriage does not mean that the couple attains a new status. Nevertheless, without working at it, the marriage will suffer. Similarly, persons "in Christ" have a status, but they also have an obligation to live and act in a way that is congruent with their status.

21. Barth, *Church Dogmatics*, IV.2, 528.

The analogy with marriage should not be pushed too far, of course, for the "sacred wedlock" (Calvin) between the believer and Christ is maintained from God's side and is not breakable in the same way that marriages are breakable. Christians are "in Christ" by virtue of God's unilateral decision and act, and are bound to that new reality by the work of the Holy Spirit. As such, they have the responsibility to live and act within that particular frame of reference. The superabundance of grace (Rom. 5:20) does not imply disregard for ethically responsible and vocationally oriented living. "In Christ" means living in the explicit context of the fundamental relationship with Jesus Christ that determines everything else. The priority and grace of the indicative is the ground of the imperative, which is no less gracious—it is also "in Christ." Any weakening of the imperative, however, would be to advocate a practical theology of cheap grace, grace without obligation or discipline or cost.

Mention of cheap and costly grace brings to mind Dietrich Bonhoeffer's teaching on discipleship.[22] For to live "in Christ" is to follow a call to discipleship, as it is also an awakening to conversion and a fulfilling of vocation.[23] Discipleship is the call to follow Jesus; conversion is the turning to God and the turning to others; vocation is the daily living in all things to God's glory. Discipleship, conversion, and vocation refer to the same reality—to life "in Christ"—but from three distinct perspectives. Discipleship reminds us of our being bound to Jesus Christ. Conversion reminds us that we are always in process of being turned back to God. Vocation reminds us that discipleship and conversion are not merely pious states or abstract theological concepts, but actual conditions of Christian existence, the truth of which is expressed through human work day by day.

Living out our vocation is to be understood in such a way that there is congruence between who we are in Christ and our life. According to Ray Anderson, "being Christian is a calling that is fulfilled in and through that which becomes one's destiny here on earth. . . . The Christian calling does not lead us away from our life and destiny here on this earth, but is a gracious calling to live with the knowledge that our life is a fulfillment of 'Christ in us.'"[24] Calling or vocation is not something that we do over and against meeting responsibilities to our employer, family, or friends. On the contrary, vocation is lived precisely in and through our lives in such a

---

22. Dietrich Bonhoeffer, *The Cost of Discipleship*, trans R. H. Fuller (London: SCM, 1959).

23. Thus Barth, *Church Dogmatics*, IV.2, 533–34.

24. Ray S. Anderson, *Christians Who Counsel: The Vocation of Holistic Therapy* (Grand Rapids: Zondervan, 1990), 162.

way that we are integrated people, people who live out a harmony between identity and purpose, faith and life.

Christian faith is transformational in nature, concerned with a way to truth that is experienced in living as God's saints. To put that less formally, God in the power of the Holy Spirit changes and charges people when they are brought into union with Christ. The transforming work of God is seen in lives that are turned around. Paul, for example, illustrates this with his distinction between the "natural" person (*psychikos*) and the "spiritual" person (*pneumatikos*) (1 Cor. 2:14–15). This change, which is both an event and an ongoing process, leads to a charge, a way of life in which the goal of living for God in all things becomes the means by which we continue to grow in knowledge of and love for God. This kind of action, in which we come to know the purpose of action through the action itself, is what Aristotle called "praxis." Again, according to Ray Anderson, "Christian praxis is encountering the reality of God through the actions in which that reality becomes manifest. Praxis does not bring the reality of God into the situation through applying a procedure, but discovers and makes manifest the reality of God through action."[25] To live vocationally is to live as a whole or integrated person; it is also to live theologically in and through our daily activities. It is a way of life "in Christ" whereby the reality that constitutes our deepest inner truth is known ever more deeply in and through our living it. It is by doing the truth in our actions that we come more fully to know the truth that is within us.

The arenas in which we struggle for lived faithfulness and in which we come to know and love God more deeply are the family and the workplace, in our political and civic responsibilities as well as our economic relationships, in our relations with strangers as in our relations with friends, in our response to the powerful and in our compassion for the poor, the weak, the sick, and all who suffer. In all areas of life the Christian lives out his or her vocation to be a saint. Vocation is not then the preserve of the professionally religious, as holiness is not the attainment of only the celebrated few. All Christians are God's saints, by definition; all Christians are charged to live that holiness in every area of life day by day. Martin Luther once summed up the issue in a typically earthy image: "God himself will milk the cows through him whose vocation that is."[26]

Pastoral work that does not include the call to conversion, discipleship, and vocation leaves people passive recipients of service. They can never

25. Ibid., 137.

26. Cited by Gustav Wingren, *Luther on Vocation*, trans. Carl C. Rasmussen (Philadelphia: Muhlenberg, 1957), 9.

know the full power and experience of grace in their lives, for they receive grace in one dimension only. Such pastoral work is theologically stunted, being merely the provision of service, offering a diminished grace. This is the height of unfaithfulness in ministry. It does not give the whole Christ, who comes not just "pastorally" with grace for us, but also with the call to live graciously for others. Jürgen Moltmann, we discovered earlier, is critical of what he calls "the pastoral church," the church that just looks after people.[27] He appreciates the need to relate pastoral ministry and the wider mission of the church as that is given by the gospel. All too easily the church slips into playing a role in society in which the question of God is allocated to a personal and private realm of existence in which pastoral work serves as a vehicle of inner unburdening, while external conditions are left as they are and in which the call to vocation goes unspoken and therefore unheeded. When Christian faith and pastoral work give up the eschatological imperative to anticipate in action the coming of the promised kingdom of God, society remains untroubled by Christianity, and pastoral work becomes a means of helping people to adjust to present conditions.

The call "Follow me" comes to every Christian from Jesus Christ himself. Karl Barth, in typical fashion, notes that grace here takes the form of command.[28] The grace that unites us with Christ requires that we are to do something, namely, share in his mission from the Father in some regard. We can only do as we are bidden (Matt. 14:28). But we are bidden by Christ, to whom we are bound. That is why it is grace, and that is why the yoke of Christ is easy and his burden light (Matt. 11:30). We could not do it otherwise, but that we must do it is the truth of our life hidden with Christ in God (Col. 3:3).

27. Jürgen Moltmann, *The Church in the Power of the Spirit*, trans. Margaret Kohl (London: SCM, 1977), xvi.

28. Barth, *Church Dogmatics*, IV.2, 534–35.

Chapter 9

The Ministry of the Presence of God

There was a Levite, a native of Cyprus, Joseph, to whom the apostles gave the name Barnabas (which means "son of encouragement").
Acts 4:36, NRSV

Lord Almighty, which hast endued thy Holy Apostle Barnabas with singular gifts of thy Holy Ghost: Let us not be destitute of thy manifold gifts, nor yet of grace to use them always to thy honor and glory.
Collect for St. Barnabas the Apostle, *Book of Common Prayer*, 1559

Glory to God whose power, working in us, can do infinitely more than we can ask or imagine; glory to him from generation to generation in the Church and in Christ Jesus for ever and ever. Amen.
Ephesians 3:20–21, JB

Through union with Christ we are bearers of the presence of God—receiving the mission of Christ, the one who sends the Holy Spirit from the Father and sharing in his life as a responding human being who lives in the power of the Spirit. What does Christ give us, or mediate to us, in his Spirit? And in what aspects of his ministry to the Father for the sake of the world do we participate? This chapter takes us into the heart of the ministry of Jesus as Emmanuel, in and through the gift of the Holy Spirit, by way of three related issues that pertain to the essence of pastoral work: (1) comfort and empowerment in the midst of suffering, which will include also asking for help, calling to one's side, and exhortation; this involves ministry with strength in a specific regard as we will be concerned with our sharing in God's ministry of presence as that is expressed in the New Testament by the words *parakaleo* and *paraklesis*; (2) power through weakness as God is present in strength in, with, and through us; and (3) presence with one another in the fellowship of suffering and comfort as the body of Christ, and the work of the Holy Spirit as Paraclete.

Ministry with Strength

There is no more hopeful word in pastoral care than "comfort" (*paraklesis*). In our afflictions, comfort is what we need, and the action of comforting suggests everything that is caring and gracious. "Comfort" derives from the Latin words *com* and *fortis*, which mean "with strength." The Greek *parakaleo* joins together two words, *para* (beside, nearby) and *kaleo* (calling out) so that *parakaleo* incorporates the idea of addressing another in response to a specific contingent situation.[1] Comfort is ministry near at hand, and as such reflects directly the ministry of the presence of God in, through, and as Jesus Christ. A ministry of comfort is both a strength-giving ministry and a ministry of address. As such, it is a ministry of the Word of God.

The idea of comfort has a profound biblical and theological reality that takes us deeply into the ministry of the presence of God and by means of which we claim the power of comfort for pastoral theology and ministry in three ways. The first is that God comforts us in our afflictions, an obvious thing to say, perhaps, yet filled with the power of the gospel. Second, receiving this comfort, we have a ministry of comfort now for others. Third, this comfort is understood to come to people within the communion of the congregation, for it is a *paraklesis en Christo*.[2] Thus, receiving God's gift of comfort leads immediately to the responsibility for pastoral vocation in order to share what we have received, work that expresses the love of one for another.

I begin with a discussion of 2 Corinthians 1:3–7, where these themes are concisely stated. Then I examine the term *parakaleo* in the New Testament, where it is expressed as both appeal—asking for help—and a calling to one's side. Finally I reflect upon urging, exhorting, or encouraging, that is, when God uses us as mediators of his comforting presence.

---

1. See Jacob Firet, *Dynamics in Pastoring*, trans. John Vriend (Grand Rapids: Eerdmans, 1986), 70.
2. Ibid., 71.

2 Corinthians 1:3–7

This passage is the great treatment of comfort in the New Testament.[3] It is the blessing part of the introduction to the epistle (or, more accurately, the fragment given as chapters 1–9) in which Paul sets forth the major themes that will reappear in the body of the letter.

> Blessed be the God and Father of our Lord Jesus Christ, the Father of mercies and the God of all consolation, who consoles us in all our affliction, so that we may be able to console those who are in any affliction with the consolation with which we ourselves are consoled by God. For just as the sufferings of Christ are abundant for us, so also our consolation is abundant through Christ. If we are being afflicted, it is for your consolation and salvation; if we are being consoled, it is for your consolation, which you experience when you patiently endure the same sufferings that we are also suffering. Our hope for you is unshaken; for we know that as you share in our sufferings, so also you share in our consolation.

Paul uses key terms of tribulation that directly affect pastoral care: *thlibo*, to be afflicted (1:6); *thlipsis*, affliction/distress (1:4); *pathemata*, sufferings/misfortunes (1:5, 6, 7); and *pascho*, to suffer (1:6). Positively, Paul sets over against these tribulations the reason for blessing God: God is the "Father of our Lord Jesus Christ, the Father of mercies and the God of all consolation" (1:3), here introducing the word that is emphasized throughout the passage, *paraklesis*, comfort or consolation.[4] He links this good news directly to Jesus Christ, a point he marks at verse 5b. He thinks of comfort also as the basis for our ministry of consolation. Within the Jewish tradition upon which Paul relies, "comfort" refers to God's faithfulness; and in

---

3. The following discussion has drawn from J. Paul Sampley, "The Second Letter to the Corinthians: Introduction, Commentary, and Reflections," in *The New Interpreter's Bible*, ed. Leander E. Keck et al., vol. 11 (Nashville: Abingdon, 2000), 40–41; Margaret E. Thrall, *A Critical and Exegetical Commentary on the Second Epistle to the Corinthians*, vol. 1 (Edinburgh: T. & T. Clark, 1994), 98–99; and Ben Witherington III, *Conflict and Community in Corinth: A Socio-Rhetorical Commentary on 1 and 2 Corinthians* (Grand Rapids: Eerdmans, 1995), 356–57. Reference has also been made to O. Schmitz and G. Stählin, "*parakaleo, paraklesis*," *The Theological Dictionary of the New Testament*, ed. Gerhard Friedrich, trans. Geoffrey W. Bromiley, vol. 5 (Grand Rapids: Eerdmans, 1967), 773–99.

4. *Paraklesis* is found 11 times in 2 Corinthians 1–8, and 7 times in the other recognized letters of Paul. It is used 6 times in 2 Cor. 1:3–7.

a Christian context it means God's faithfulness to us and through us through our union with Christ. This comfort/consolation is abundant (*perisseuo*, overflows; see also 2 Cor. 7:4, where Paul writes of being filled to overflowing joy, and Rom. 5:15, 17, and 20, where the reference is to God's overflowing grace). Clearly this is the stuff of pastoral work.

In the New Testament, the verb "to comfort" has strong associations with the Hebrew word *naham*, which is generally rendered in the LXX by *parakalein*, and in noun form as *paraklesis*. In the Old Testament, true comfort comes only from God and is God's proper work.[5] Divine comfort is expressed in Isaiah, for example, by two powerful pastoral metaphors for God: shepherd and mother. God is the shepherd who will feed his flock, gather in his lambs, carry them close, and lead them (Isa. 40:11). And God is the mother: as a mother comforts her child, so God will comfort his people (Isa. 66:13).[6] Comfort is also great theme in Isaiah 40:1, when Israel's time of punishment and exile is over; Israel remains God's elect; God has forgiven their sins.[7] Interestingly, the announcement of God's comfort is followed immediately by the cry to prepare to go out, for in order for the people to be comforted, a way must be prepared in and through the wilderness. God's comfort apparently does not leave people passive, but calls them forth into a divinely appointed vocation.[8] Further, in Deutero-Isaiah, as implied in Isaiah 40:1, for example, *naham* refers to the dawning time of salvation when God will comfort his people. Thus the "comfort" words of the New Testament likely refer to messianic deliverance and hope.[9] This is an important point for the interpretation of 2 Corinthians 1:3–7. That is, we need to insist upon the christological specificity that is embedded in the passage.

Second Corinthians 1:4 gets to the heart of the matter. The verse has two parts. The first refers to the reason for blessing God, "who consoles us in all our affliction (*thlipsei*)." The plural "our" suggests three interpretative possibilities: an editorial plural, the inclusion of those who minister with Paul, and the inclusion of those who will receive the letter. The flow of the passage suggests that the second option is the most likely, for at verse 6 the Corinthians are the recipients of Paul's comfort, which is

5. Schmitz and Stählin, "*parakaleo, paraklesis*," 789.

6. Ibid., 790.

7. Donald E. Gowan, *Theology of the Prophetic Books: The Death and Resurrection of Israel* (Louisville, Ky.: Westminster John Knox Press, 1998), 149.

8. Claus Westermann, *Isaiah 40–66: A Commentary*, trans. David M. G. Stalker, Old Testament Library (Philadelphia: Westminster, 1969), 32–33.

9. Thrall, *Second Corinthians*, 103.

given for all kinds of affliction. *Thlipsis* generally refers to tribulation, though the New Testament refers often to the affliction of believers, which has an eschatological overtone of suffering prior to the end.[10]

The second part of verse 4 emphasizes the consequence of receiving comfort: "so that we may be able to console those who are in any affliction with the consolation with which we ourselves are consoled by God." Comfort is not a personal possession.[11] Paul, comforted by God, has the ability—the responsibility, even—to comfort others when necessary, as the mediator of God's comfort.[12] There is a theological and spiritual logic here that moves toward *koinonia* and ministry, as we will see more clearly below. Something of the meaning of this in contemporary terms may be seen in the core philosophy of the various "Anonymous" groups, whose operating view is that those who are themselves recovering are best equipped to encourage and hold accountable others who wish also to recover. In a sense, then, there is a power for ministry in those who are themselves wounded, who have received the comfort of God, and who now minister to others in the strength of healing.[13]

The truth for pastoral work is that there is a direct relationship between woundedness, being comforted, and becoming empowered to a ministry of consolation. However, one exception modifies this as a general rule for Christian ministry, and it concerns verse 5, which leads us into theological subtleties that are important for pastoral theology: "For just as the sufferings of Christ are abundant for us, so also our consolation is abundant through Christ." The apostle's sufferings or misfortunes (*pathemata*) are *Christ's* because Paul lives in ever-deeper conformation to the life of Christ. Living in Christ his life imitates in some sense the life of the Lord. The *participatio Christi* is the ground for and leads to *imitatio Christi*. This relationship between participation and imitation is not reversible. Axiomatically, a person living in Christ will expect to share in Christ's sufferings, yet sharing in Christ's sufferings, we share also in his abundant consolation. The comfort amid tribulation comes through the instrumentality of Christ—*dia Christou*.[14] This instrumentality must, however, be understood precisely as our sharing in Christ's life. A pastoral theology of comfort cannot be understood independently of the person of Jesus

10. Ibid., 104.
11. Sampley, "Second Corinthians," 41.
12. Thrall, *Second Corinthians*, 104.
13. I have discussed this point at length in *The Search for Compassion Spirituality and Ministry* (Louisville, Ky.: Westminster John Knox Press, 1989).
14. Thrall, *Second Corinthians*, 110.

Christ, as if it might be something apart from him. This leads to the caveat or exception: unless we share in Christ's life through union with him, we do not participate in his comfort. Positively stated, through union with Christ we receive his consolation amid our sufferings, and as such, we share also in his continuing ministry of comfort for the world. We receive from Christ the *paraklesis* of God; but we share also in union with Christ his ministry of comfort. Aside from this participation, our ability to receive and give comfort is bereft of the power of the comfort that is abundant for us and for others.

This is apparently the conclusion Paul comes to in verse 6, where the general assertion of verse 4 is specifically applied: "If we are being afflicted, it is for your consolation and salvation; if we are being consoled, it is for your consolation, which you experience when you patiently endure the same sufferings that we are also suffering." The affliction Paul experiences as a result of his ministry, and which is the prior condition for receiving comfort, is for the consolation *and* salvation of the Corinthians.[15] Those who preach the gospel will be afflicted (2 Cor. 4:7–12).[16] (We return to this theme later in the chapter.) Yet it is for the salvation of his hearers that Paul preaches the gospel in the first place. Consequently, he is consoled in order to have a consolation for them when they too suffer, a consolation that gives them strength to endure their tribulations. This injunction, in effect to stay the course, is a common theme in Paul's writing. Again, then, there is the connection of those who live and minister in the Lord both receiving the comfort of God *and* giving that comfort to those who are afflicted.

Importantly, in verse 7, Paul refers to his congregation and himself as those who share in suffering and in consolation. The reference here is to *koinonoi*, fellow participants. Paul has a sure hope that by sharing in the fellowship of suffering they will share also in the fellowship of consolation, about which he has personal and incontestable knowledge.

Thus Paul expressed his pastoral theological conviction that amid affliction, comfort is a means of God's grace for his congregation and cause therefore for giving thanks to God. The gift of God's comfort is not a prescription for feeling good; rather, it is the active engagement of God by which God draws near through the ministry of Jesus Christ. There are three correlations for pastoral work.

1. Ministers can have the confidence that it is God's will to comfort and console those persons who are afflicted. This can be announced—it is a

15. Ibid.
16. Ibid., 111.

ministry of the Word of God—in the sure knowledge that God does not abandon those who suffer; even more, God acts in and through Jesus Christ (in the power of the Holy Spirit) to bring consolation. This is not pious rhetoric; it is the gospel of consolation and the expression in a concrete way of Christian hope. It is the basis for pastoral boldness.

2. For the Christian person, affliction is neither meaningless nor purposeless. Rather, in and through Jesus Christ, God assumes our afflictions into the divine work of care. We might say that God co-opts our suffering, redeeming it for good. In the context of God's consolations, afflictions become transformed into empowerments for ministry. Affliction, consolation, and vocation are bound together in this work of divine grace. Even as we say this, however, we are confronted with a terrible mystery that piety may tend to mask. We are aware of the almost unnameable depth of suffering in the world and in history for which there appears to be little or no consolation. There is little sign of empowerment for ministry. As we face the irresolvable theological pain of the problem of evil, we do so with an eschatological "nevertheless," believing that even as we must protest against the suffering in the world, so God is also redeemer at a depth of transformation that is beyond our mind's grasp. We hope for that which is not yet seen.

3. Affliction and consolation are experienced within the *koinonia* of the body of Christ, where comfort is given to those who have already received the kerygma.[17] In Christ, no one suffers alone. This suggests that there are evangelistic and ecclesial dimensions to comfort, for apart from relationship with Christ one will not receive the *paraklesis en Christo*. This will become clearer as we reflect further on the use of *parakaleo* in the New Testament.

Paraklesis *as Appeal*

Pastoral work is rightly thought of as giving care, and the emphasis is appropriately placed on the giver as the primary actor in the pastoral care relationship. Yet pastoral care is not about the caregiver, and there is a dangerous confusion of boundaries if it becomes so. Pastoral care is about God and God's care for persons. In the New Testament we read often of people asking for help, especially asking Jesus for healing. Here, then, is an initiative for the person in need to which pastoral theology must give attention. The possibility of receiving help, and the confidence to ask God

17. Firet, *Dynamics in Pastoring*, 71.

for it in the first place, have everything to do with the actuality of God's presence and the conviction of faith. Were God remote from us, a *Deus absconditus*, both hidden and unapproachable, we would not know to whom to cry out or have any confidence that the one to whom we cry out would hear or respond in healing love to our cry. It is in virtue of the gospel fact that God has drawn near; has come among us and become as we are; and, in the Spirit, remains among and with us as the presence of Jesus Christ, nearer to us than we are to ourselves, that we can address the living God whose will is to bless, heal, and comfort.

Amid affliction the cry of faith to God is not a speculative plea into the vast cosmic unknown, to a deity whose name and will remain a divine secret. Our cry to God is a response to the God who has already spoken to us.[18] Theologically, "Then God said" (Gen. 1:3) corresponds to "In the beginning was the Word" (John 1:1), for God's word has priority. Most remarkable of all, "the Word became flesh" (John 1:14). It is as those whom God has spoken into being and to whom God has spoken through his covenantal faithfulness with Israel, and universally and savingly in, through, and as Jesus Christ, that we answer respondingly to God through our appeals for God's help. Encouraging people to cry out to the God who has already drawn near and addressed them in redeeming love and grace is a most significant part of pastoral work, one that draws close to the piety of lamentation. The prayer of supplication has an important role in the pastoral piety of the faith.

It is on this basis, then, that we can apprehend in some depth the second meaning of *parakaleo*—beseeching or calling upon Jesus for help. Representative accounts from the New Testament will help:

> Matthew 8:5 // Luke 7:4: the healing of a centurion's servant at Capernaum. In Matthew, the centurion himself begs Jesus for help (*parakalon auton*); in Luke, the centurion sends elders of the Jews, who beg for help on his and the servant's behalf.
>
> Matthew 8:31 // Mark 5:10, 12 // Luke 8:31, 32: the exorcism of the two demoniacs according to Matthew, and of the one man in Mark and Luke. The demons beg to be sent into a herd of pigs. In an epilogue to the story, Mark's account (5:18) has the healed demoniac beg to follow Jesus.
>
> Matthew 14:36 // Mark 6:56: the people of Gennesaret beg Jesus to allow the sick to touch the hem of his outer cloak and be healed.

18. Thus Eugene Peterson, *Answering God: The Psalms as Tools for Prayer* (San Francisco: Harper & Row, 1989), 5.

Mark 1:40: the leper, kneeling before Jesus, begs for healing.

Mark 5:23 // Luke 8:41 (// Matthew 9:18–26, though no form of *parakaleo* is used): Jairus, falling at Jesus' feet, begs for the healing of his daughter.

Mark 7:32: people bring a deaf man to Jesus, begging for Jesus to lay his hands upon him.

Mark 8:22: a blind man is brought to Jesus for healing.

The points to be drawn from these texts are basic to pastoral need: (1) The focus in each appeal is Jesus; these are not general appeals to God. (2) There was a particular need for healing in each case; each passage is marked with a specific illness. (3) There appears to be a sense of desperation in the appeals, illustrated at Mark 5:10 by the use of *polla*—Jesus was implored *greatly*, and at Luke 7:4 by *spoudaios*—the elders of the Jews begged Jesus *earnestly*. (4) Often people interceded with Jesus on behalf of others.

The applications to be drawn from these points are obvious. Jesus, in the power of the Spirit, is the healing presence of God, who has drawn near. Those who are sick are to be encouraged to cry out to Jesus for healing. We too are to be encouraged to cry out on their behalf. Again we see that the ministry of *paraklesis* presses us toward an appreciation of the responsibility of the community of faith for those who suffer.

Parakaleo *as Summoning*

Parakaleo also means to summon or call to one's side. Commentators tend to bypass this dimension, observing that the usage carries little religious significance. Yet four texts from Acts seem to contain an important lesson for us.

In Acts 8:31 the Ethiopian eunuch "invited" Philip to accompany him and guide him in his understanding of Scripture. Acts 9:38 occurs in the midst of the story of Peter's raising of Tabitha from death. On her death, two disciples were sent to Peter "summoning" him to come to minister without delay. In Acts 13:42, after Paul's sermon in Antioch of Pisidia, the people "urged" him and Barnabas to speak again about the gospel on the next Sabbath. Acts 16:9 recounts Paul's vision of a man of Macedonia "pleading" with him to come to proclaim the good news to them.

These four passages all relate in some way to the message of salvation. Three are directly evangelistic in nature. The fourth occurs in an account of eschatological power. From them, we may conclude that where need is expressed—for the gospel or for pastoral presence—the Holy Spirit summons or calls out people to acts of ministry, specifically in these texts Paul, Peter, and Philip.

Ministry has a "from—to" aspect; one is called from one place or activity to another place or activity, there to minister alongside those who have called out to the Lord for help. This is illustrated in the now rather outmoded Christendom-centered notion of the parish, which derives from two Greek words, *para* and *oikos*, meaning "beyond the house." The pastor goes from his or her house to the places of the parishioners, and the parish is that area traditionally marked out for reasonable travel.

Deeply embedded within Reformed theology especially is the notion of "calling" a minister rather than a minister being appointed by an ecclesiastical superior. While one may be called to ministry in general, this branch of the church holds that a call is not yet worthy of ordination until one is called out by a people to a specific pastoral task *in their place*. Only when a person is called alongside a congregation, as it were, is a person rightly in pastoral ministry. The apostles were called to take the gospel to the people; their agenda was set by the gospel. They, like their Lord, had nowhere to lay their heads (or offices in which to hang their hats), and thus birthed a ministry that took the gospel to the people. What this might mean today in practical terms for each person in ministry is surely a matter worthy of much thought.

Parakaleo *as Exhortation and Encouragement*

"The Lord God has given me the tongue of a teacher, that I may know how to sustain the weary with a word" (Isa. 50:4). This Old Testament epigram introduces an important theme within the biblical understanding of *parakaleo:* the meaning as exhortation of the Word of God by the one who speaks in the name of God. Exhortation is both a missionary address and a word of admonition urging those who are already in Christ to a more faithful life. As the Dutch theologian Jacob Firet explained:

> It would certainly not be correct to conclude . . . that there is an absolute distinction between paraklesis on the one hand and kerygma and didache on the other. But for paraklesis this specifically focused address to the situation is typical. The fact, then, that the coming of God in his word also takes place in the manner of paraklesis means that God is present, reveals his name and truth, actualizes salvation, not in abstraction from the situatedness of human beings, but in

direct connection with it and with a view to it. Were God to come to me only in the mode of kerygma, that could mean: God has come; be silent before him—my realities and interests do not matter. The reality of the Kingdom takes precedence over them. Were God to come to me only in the mode of didache, that could mean: God has come; the road on which life has brought me is no longer important, he has another way for me. When God comes to me in the mode of paraklesis, it dawns on me: God has come and he wants to live in my house and my situation—my situation is important to him. God enters my situation in its concrete "thus-and-nowness," and he appears in it for that very purpose.[19]

All of this can be summed up thus: the ministry of the presence of God through the speaking of his Word through us is for the blessing and encouragement of another.

Paradigmatically, 2 Corinthians 5:20 states that God is making his missionary appeal (*parakalountos*) through us. God exhorts others through us, who have the ministry of exhortation. At stake here is the authority behind the exhorter's word (*hyper Christou*, on behalf of Christ).[20] God, through Christ, appeals to those who hear the exhorter. Thus, when Paul or anyone standing within the apostolic tradition and authority speaks, God speaks.[21] And their plea is, "be reconciled to God." This word is not to be accepted "in vain" (2 Cor. 6:1). When the exhortation is used to proclaim salvation, supplication and consolation are always interwoven in the plea, so that exhortation is entreaty, implying an obligation of response inherent in the proclamation of salvation.[22] Similarly, the "word of exhortation" (Acts 13:15) called forth from the apostles at Antioch of Pisidia carries with it the summons to believe.

The missionary appeal blends into pastoral admonition to live the Christian life. Luke 3:18, a summary of the Baptist's preaching, makes the point: "So, with many other exhortations, he proclaimed the good news to the people." Notice that this occurs in the context of calling forth conduct worthy of the gospel, as Luke 3:10–14 illustrates. The "word of exhortation" at Hebrews 13:22 is directed to those who have long had faith in the gospel, but who have grown weary. The later sections of Paul's letters refer

19. Firet, *Dynamics in Pastoring*, 70.
20. Schmitz, "*parakaleo, paraklesis*," 795.
21. Thrall, *Second Corinthians*, 437.
22. Schmitz, "*parakaleo, paraklesis*," 795.

frequently to exhortation: Romans 12:1, 2 Corinthians 10:2, and 2 Thessalonians 4:1 may be cited as examples. Such admonition to Christian life is *paraklesis en Christo* (Phil. 2:1), or *parakaloumen en kyrios Iesou* (2 Thess. 4:1). Thus the "Parakletic Formula," according to Firet, comes to those who have already received the gospel, not as a moral appeal, but in the name of the Lord Jesus and on the basis of what Christ has done. Salvation is its presupposition. The call is ultimately for fruit bearing.[23]

Whether as missionary admonition or as exhortation to live the Christian life, the appeal is based on the divine aid that is given in, through, and as Jesus Christ to those who suffer beyond the boundary of Christ or who need encouragement within it.

> "Exhortation," being effected by the Spirit, is based on the salvation already accomplished, and "comfort" or "consolation" takes place through the present and future act of God Himself to salvation. Hence it is hardly too much to say that, as defined by the NT act of salvation, *parakalein* and *paraklesis* may be traced back to the saving work of the triune God which leads those in need of help as suppliants to the Son of God, which is preached as exhortation in the power of the Spirit of God, and which carries with it already in this time the eternal comfort of God the Father.[24]

God draws near through the ministry of the Word of God to exhort people to accept the good news of salvation and to encourage them in faithful living. As noted, this is not moralism, but an appeal on the basis of a salvation already won for us. The power for help belongs to God and comes to us through the preaching of the Word. Thus there emerges a responsibility for pastoral care that is often forgotten: the guidance of people in terms of Scripture and the tradition that guards Scripture, that is, the doctrinal heritage of the Christian faith.[25] To put that in different terms, pastoral care is not just concerned with mediating God's comfort amid affliction, but is charged also with a ministry of guidance according to the admonitions of the Lord given through the apostles. For example, 1 Peter, with its call to holy living, is written as a letter of encouragement (1 Pet. 5:12). Jude 3 appeals to Christians to contend for the faith in the context of false teach-

---

23. Firet, *Dynamics in Pastoring*, 71, also citing Schmitz, "*parakaleo, paraklesis*," 795.
24. Schmitz, "*parakaleo, paraklesis*," 799.
25. Ellen Charry has demonstrated this point quite beautifully in *By the Renewing of Your Minds: The Pastoral Foundation of Christian Doctrine* (New York: Oxford University Press, 1997).

ers. Philippians 2:1 makes an appeal for unity of belief, doing nothing from selfish ambition or conceit, and looking only to the interests of others. Romans 12:1 is an appeal to Christians to offer themselves in appropriate, that is, coherent, worship (*logiken latreia*). At Ephesians 4:1 the apostle begs the people to lead a life worthy of the gospel. And so on. Clearly, pastoral admonition is not "value free." It urges people to live within a framework or boundary, and it identifies behaviors and attitudes that are not acceptable, and others that are to be expected and encouraged. The Scriptures teach that right believing will lead to right living; but right living must be taught and people must be guided.

The related practical points for pastoral care are quite obvious. Those committed to pastoral work are called upon to be exhorters of the gospel of salvation—there is no legitimate pastoral care that cares for people without, on the one hand, calling them to faith in Jesus Christ and, on the other, guiding the people accordingly.

Power through Weakness

As I have done throughout, I consider our ministries in terms of sharing in Christ's ministry to the Father, in the power of the Holy Spirit, for the sake of the world, but I specifically focus now on this as a ministry of God's presence. We who are weak share in Christ's strength because he dwells with and within us: "I can do all things through him who strengthens me" (Phil. 4:13). The remarkable thing, of course, is that God's power is veiled in human frailty. It was in Christ Jesus; it is so also with us. God's power in, through, and as Jesus Christ is power at work in those who are united to and in Christ and who share thereby in his life to the glory of the Father for the sake of the world.

The issues with which we are concerned are raised in two passages from 2 Corinthians, 4:1–15 and 11:16–12:10. Both passages contrast the weakness of the apostle with the strength and power of Christ, in union with whom alone is ministry possible. Both texts instruct us in the practice of ministry.

The contemporary context for reflection on ministerial weakness and God's power is the enormous fascination among many in ministry with both contextual awareness and programmatic competence, evidenced in, for example, the acquisition of therapeutic skills, training in development and management of programs, and marketing strategies as evangelism in order to grow congregations. A "missional" ecclesiology is admirable and is indeed theologically necessary. But is there not a danger abroad today of a ministerial programmatic triumphalism, in which God's salvation and blessing are tied to a special kind of pastoral competence and seeming contextual and contemporary relevance? Pastors now have coaches to train them in renewal ministry; congregations apparently have life cycles and an ecclesial DNA. Many contend that traditional seminaries and the classical theological curriculum are obsolete, and some so-called mega-congregations argue that they can train their ministers more effectively than mainstream seminaries for transformational ministry. Much of this may be appropriate insofar as the liberal mainstream theological curriculum is out of touch with the thrust for renewal.

Both a missional ecclesiology and a needs-directed pastoral emphasis are always appropriate in view of human suffering, and evangelism is an imperative of the faith. And there can be no argument against the need for a critically appropriated contextuality, without which we end up with a *logos asarkos*, a disembodied word that is contrary to the gospel. The dialectic may be put this way: the gospel is always embedded in a culture; Christ is always transforming culture. The question, of course, is: When are we responding to the culture in a biblical and theological way, and when might we be uncritically selling out to the mores and needs of the culture?

The danger is that in the drive to bring people to Christ and to know his comfort we might be in the process of being disconverted (to coin a word): pastoral competence and the drive for contextual relevance may become the pragmatic operational necessities with little serious and intelligent theological constraint. I fear that the dominant assumption in many church circles today is that the content and practice of the *consensus fidelium* can no longer be trusted to carry the power of the gospel, and that it is now up to ministers to compensate for this apparent weakness by developing a kind of hyper-contemporary, initiative-driven response of needs-directed competence. Thus we live in the time of the entrepreneurial pastor who understands ministry according to business practices that are focused on marketing and selling a product.

Paul's theology of ministry in 2 Corinthians, however, does not imply ministerial incompetence or lack of purpose; there is never any lack of imperatives in Paul's practical theology, and there is no lack of contextuality. But it is all predicated upon a profound awareness that whatever he does or says, it is God who converts and brings people to Christ, not Paul; it is God who comforts and blesses, not Paul; it is Christ in whom we live and through whom we come in worship to the Father, not Paul's programmatic or liturgical or homiletical giftedness. Thus the emphasis is on

God's power, and with this the humbled awareness of Paul's human weakness to accomplish anything of value for God's kingdom.

If one would live within the tradition marked out by the teaching of the apostles, one must grow in knowledge by being instructed in that tradition as interpreted and lived out in and by the church through two thousand years. Is it too harsh to suggest that theological, ecclesiastical, and liturgical traditions are increasingly now largely unknown or forgotten or just simply discarded by many today who advance the merit of what have come to be called "transformational ministries"?[26] Our present fascination with transformational process, contextuality, and programs of renewal, while laudable in that renewal is always necessary and we must reach the unchurched, nevertheless also suggests the presence perhaps of a deep crisis of confidence in the power of the electing love and grace of God, a power that does not depend on the stimulation of our receptivity,[27] or the adaptation of the gospel to cultural trends. The so-called new paradigm expressions of ecclesiology, ministry, and worship may be in danger of forgetting that the propagation of the gospel and the faithful worship of God are at the behest of God's gift and power. They are not ours to manipulate according to psychosocial fads or schemes of revitalization. The question once again is, can we trust that because the church through many centuries has been guided by the Holy Spirit, there is a tradition to receive, and we must receive it if we would be the faithful people of God? One part of that tradition is the awareness of God's power at work precisely through human weakness rather than ministerial competence. With this context in mind, Paul presents us with a theology and practice of ministry that grounds us in God's ministry and strength.

Paul introduces the theme of power through weakness first of all with the provocative metaphor that those in ministry are as earthenware containers (2 Cor. 4:7).[28] So great a treasure, so weak and frail a vessel. The contrast is startling in order to indicate that the power belongs to God and does not come from us. The treasure is the new covenant to which

---

26. For a classic statement of the importance of tradition, see Basil the Great, *On the Holy Spirit* (Crestwood, N.Y.: St. Vladimir's Seminary Press, 1980), 100, where he noted that unwritten traditions handed down through generations from the apostles were to be accepted as authoritative for the practice of faith.

27. The language here is from Thomas C. Oden, *The Rebirth of Orthodoxy: Signs of New Life in Christianity* (San Francisco: HarperSanFrancisco, 2003), 43.

28. For the following again see Sampley, "Second Corinthians," 62ff.; and Thrall, *Second Corinthians*, 320ff.

Paul has been called and empowered by God to minister: it is God "who has made us competent to be ministers of a new covenant" (2 Cor. 3:6). Ministerial competence is both charismatic and covenantal: it is a gift given by God, and it operates in such a way that attention is directed away from the minister to its ground and source in the promise, faithfulness, and act of God that are given in, through, and as Jesus Christ. In 3:6 the verb translated as "made us competent" (*hikanoo*) means to make someone sufficient or fit for a task. "Competent" (*hikanos*), used at 3:5, means sufficient or able. God is also *hikanos*, "the Sufficient One," now used as a divine title.[29] We are competent only insofar as we are given the gift and share in that which is Christ's. Paul has "no self-generated capacity for his apostolic task. . . . His 'sufficiency' comes from the one who was sometimes termed '[the] sufficient one.'"[30] This is the ground of Paul's confidence and competence, and it operates as a primary conviction in his practical theology.[31] To put this into the language I have used throughout this book, it is in union with Christ that we share in Christ's competence and thus in his ministry. We share in his being as the one alone who ministers the things of humankind to God for the glory of God and for the sake of humankind. To think and act otherwise, on the ground of our own supposed competence for ministry, is to be prideful indeed and casts aside the true basis for ministry, substituting in its place our own self-assertion.

The theme introduced here, God's power through ministerial weakness, is strongly represented as a second instance in the fragment given as chapters 10–13 of 2 Corinthians. Second Corinthians 11:16–12:10 especially illustrates Paul's profound awareness, and indeed celebration, of human weakness in view of this charismatic and covenantal competence. The interpretative key to the so-called fool's speech is Paul's presentation of weakness, understood by Paul now specifically as weakness in the Lord. Weakness in this context does not exclude his strengths, for he has indeed overcome potentially devastating trials.[32] It would be wrong to think that ministry is an invitation to passivity, for that would be a misunderstanding of human weakness as intended by Paul. The point is that left to ourselves and relying upon our native vitality and ability, we are not able to minister the things of God, but that does not mean that God does not give us strengths and abilities.

---

29. Thrall, *Second Corinthians*, 230 n. 287.
30. Ibid., 230.
31. Sampley, "Second Corinthians," 63.
32. Thrall, *Second Corinthians*, 720.

Second Corinthians 10–13 will help us to understand more deeply the idea of God's strength and human weakness. The passage is complex, both in its context within Paul's claim to apostolic authority over against the outsiders who have come among the Corinthian congregation proclaiming another Jesus, another gospel (11:4), and in its content, dealing as it does with the highest mystical experience and the most profound theology of ministry as a grace gift amid human adversity and weakness. Seeking to beat his opponents at their own boastful game—did they, we wonder, claim to have had visions and mystical experiences, which they then asserted as a basis for authority in ministry?—but with hesitation,[33] Paul recounts, albeit allusively, his own experience of rapture in the third heaven. His account seems to refer to an experience some seven years after his conversion. J. Paul Sampley sums up thus:

> If the intruders are boasting of their visions and revelations, Paul one-ups them with this extraordinary heavenly journey and then, irony of ironies, refuses to build a case for his authority upon that, choosing instead to let the matter be decided by what they have seen and heard in him. What they have encountered in him all along is the gospel lived in their midst, with the power clearly being God's and with Paul the menial earthenware vessel through which God has made this treasure present (4:7).[34]

In a stunning contrast with the intruders, Paul then writes of the thorn in his flesh (12:7), perhaps better translated as the stake (*skolops*) in the flesh, given to him by an angel of Satan, to keep him from being too elated. Satan is seeking to bring Paul down. Paul knows from Scripture that Satan attacks precisely those whom God has called to important ministry. Paul is an apostle of great power and influence, thus Satan has sent a messenger to destroy him. It does not matter that we remain ignorant of the attack or its particulars. Something profoundly difficult and dangerous happened, and continues, that Paul theologically interpreted. The attack is only partially effective, however; it keeps him from being too elated, but does not destroy his ministry. Three times he asked the Lord that the attack go away. In response Paul received a twofold assurance: the Lord's grace is sufficient, and the Lord's power is made perfect in weakness (12:9). The sufficiency of God's grace and power amid the attack of evil

33. Ibid., 772.
34. Sampley, "Second Corinthians," 164.

and the fact of human weakness sums up the hope of the gospel and pro-vides the sole basis for ministry. The power that Paul receives is the power of Christ (12:9), or the power that comes through Christ, the one who himself was helpless in weakness on his cross, yet who was raised in glory by God's power. Paul asks that that power may live in him. This is surely the meaning of our union with Christ, sharing with him in his death, and rising with him in his resurrection.

This passage raises a profound and troubling issue: Satan is after God's own, seeks to bring us down, rendering us faithless (see 2:11—Satan has his wiles and plans for us). This is not an abstract theology, but a dread-ful and dangerous reality. Days before my surgery, my colleague Dr. Martha Robbins visited me at home. Under her direction, in the peace of my basement, she led me on an imaginative prayer journey. She asked me to enter a safe place. To my surprise I found myself in the ancient, now rebuilt, abbey on the island of Iona, off the west coast of Scotland. I have visited that holy island many times, and worshiped often in the abbey, which has a spiritual power for me. I saw myself sitting alone, off by the side, hiding amid the ancient stones, seemingly shrunken and afraid. Slowly I became aware of the saints of the Scottish church praying for me. It was a near palpable experience of the communion of saints. I began to weep from the immense and intense emotional power of my awareness. Gradually—I have little sense of the time that passed—I was guided by the praying saints toward the huge green marble Communion table. Standing in front of it was Jesus. I have the sense of his height and of me kneeling or at least being below him. Two things he said: your cancer is the attack of evil, but I have the victory. (This parallels, I think, the verse at John 16:11: "The ruler of this world has been condemned.") This is the paradigm I use for thinking through the meaning of my illness: Satan wants to close me down. Be clear: I am not saying I am exemplary; but I am cognizant of the fact that my call to ministry is unambiguous.

I draw the conclusion that anyone who answers God's call to serve and who has a clear gospel message to proclaim will be under satanic attack. The sole hope is the power of Christ, who indeed has the victory. There-fore, whenever we are weak, whatever calamities we face, God through our union with Christ, in which he dwells within us, and we in him, turns the attacks to his own advantage, co-opting Satan's schemes we might say, not only to help us keep things in perspective, but to reveal and manifest God's own power working in and through us precisely in and through our weakness. I confess that I am not yet with Paul, for I am not able to thank God for the illness that afflicted me. But in spite of this, God uses what is evil for good, for ministry, and for the building up of the church. Much here cannot be explained, for we approach the limits of what can be humanly known. One can only say that it is so! This is indeed part of the great mystery of our sharing in the ministry of the presence of God.

The Body of Christ and the Gift of the Paraclete

We share in the ministry of the presence of God both in and by the power of the Holy Spirit, and within the communion of the church. My focus in this chapter is the ministry of the presence of God. It is precisely the ministry of the Paraclete to make Jesus present to, for, and within the community.

The Paraclete is peculiar to Johannine writings. On four occasions in John the Spirit is the Paraclete (*parakletos;* 14:16–17, 26; 15:26; 16:12–15). At 1 John 2:1 the exalted Jesus is described as *parakletos,* probably meaning advocate or helper in pleading our case before the Father. The noun derives from the verb *parakaleo,* the meanings and significance of which we examined above. The range may be recalled: to comfort, exhort, encourage, cry out for help, appeal. Various English translations indicate the variety of meanings given to translate the "Paraclete" in John: Comforter (KJV), Advocate (NRSV), Counselor (NIV).[35] Two points are important to note regarding the gift of the Paraclete: (1) The Paraclete binds us to the person and message of Jesus; this is the only ground for ministry, as I have argued throughout. (2) The Paraclete binds the community together as it gathers around Jesus.

1. The historical context of John's Paraclete theology is the immediate crisis provoked for the community around Jesus by his death.[36] The overarching question was: Does Jesus' death mark the end of the incarnation? The Paraclete carries forward the believer's relationship with Jesus so that those who follow after the historical relationship with Jesus may also participate in his risen life. By using the term "another Advocate," *allon parakleton,* John 14:16 tells us that Jesus is a Paraclete. As the "Spirit of truth," the Paraclete shares in the paracletic work of Jesus, who is the truth (14:6). The Paraclete has no work independent of Jesus, and the significance of this for today's so-called spirit theologies can hardly be overstated. As with Jesus in his incarnation, the Paraclete comes from the Father (14:16, 26); yet at

---

35. Gail R. O'Day, "The Gospel of John: Introduction, Commentary, and Reflections," in *The New Interpreter's Bible,* ed. Leander E. Keck et al., vol. 9 (Nashville: Abingdon, 1995), 747.
36. Ibid., 774.

15:26 and 16:7 it is Jesus who sends the Paraclete. Thus the Father, the Spirit, and Jesus are bound together. Gail R. O'Day sums up the point thus: "As with the unity of God and Jesus in their work, the relationship between Jesus and the Paraclete is also identified by the unity of their work."[37]

Of significance for my argument is the connection between Jesus' teaching that he abides in the believers and they abide in him (15:4), and the Paraclete as the Spirit who abides in them (14:17). This is both the ontological and experiential basis for Christian faith. As the Advocate who will teach the community of the future everything that Jesus has said (14:26), the Paraclete *is* the presence of Jesus whereby he comes to them as the living Word of God and, uniting them to himself through the Spirit, they henceforth share in his present and future ministry for the sake of the world. The theology of the Christian life and ministry is not primarily concerned with the Christian's life as such, but with Jesus Christ, in relationship to and with whom singularly the Christian has a life and ministry at all. That this is so is the ministry of the Paraclete.

2. The Paraclete is sent to the community. John 14:17b teaches that the Paraclete abides with and within the believing community: the Paraclete "abides with you, and he will be in [or among] you." The enspirited presence of Jesus with us and within us is certainly personal, but it is primarily a gift to, for, and known by and within the community of believers. There is a distorted theology today that tends to advocate that the gift of the Spirit means only the believer's relationship with Jesus, perhaps as a kind of private possession.[38] In John the presence of the Paraclete continues the mission of the beloved community gathered around Jesus as a believing, worshiping, and serving community through its union with him. Thus one important form of the ministry of the presence of God is the formation and continuance of this community. Its very existence and perseverance depends upon this gift of the Paraclete.

It is of interest to note that the doctrine of the perseverance of the saints in Reformed theology tends to refer to the saints individually, which of course has its place. Nowhere, for example, does the Westminster Confession refer to the perseverance of the community of faith, and its continued faithfulness in worship and ministry. This point is of great importance for pastoral care, negatively, because much recent teaching and practice has been highly individualistic, and positively, because one primary goal of all pastoral work is to deepen people's life within or to

---

37. Ibid., 747.
38. Ibid., 776.

bring people into the beloved community. One form of this critique is expressed thus: care that does not come from Word and sacraments and return to Word and sacraments is ultimately constricted and diminished. It is within Christian community that we experience ever more fully and rightly (as opposed to distortedly) the gift of the Paraclete: relationship with Jesus, the ground of all healing.

Chapter 10

The Ministry of the Reign of God

Those who hope in Christ can no longer put up with reality as it is, but begin to suffer under it, to contradict it. Peace with God means conflict with the world, for the goad of the promised future stabs inexorably into the flesh of every unfulfilled present.

Jürgen Moltmann, *Theology of Hope*

When I was a theological student in the early 1970s, hope was the theological word of the moment. One wit at Edinburgh used to say that the Bultmen had been replaced by the Moltmen, for Jürgen Moltmann's brilliant *Theology of Hope* had not long before been published in English, and was the dominant theological book of the time, Moltmann replacing Rudolf Bultmann as the radical theologian of choice. It was Moltmann's conviction, following Calvin, that faith depends on hope for its life, for it binds a person to the future of Jesus Christ. But without faith, hope becomes a utopia, something left hanging in the air.[1] According to John Calvin, hope is the expectation of those things that faith has believed to have been promised by God. Take hope away, faith dies.[2] In the mid-twentieth century, Emil Brunner also echoed Calvin: "Faith is the foundation of hope, hope is that which gives content to faith."[3]

---

1. Thus Jürgen Moltmann argues in *Theology of Hope*, trans. James W. Leitch (London: SCM, 1967), 20.
2. John Calvin, *Institutes of the Christian Religion*, ed. John McNeill; trans. Ford Lewis Battles; 2 vols. (Philadelphia: Westminster, 1960), 3.2.42.
3. Emil Brunner, *Eternal Hope*, trans. H. Knight (London: Lutterworth, 1954), 28.

Does it make sense to talk about hope today? The context of late modernity poses special problems for speech about hope.[4] We face the intellectual and moral problems characteristic of late modernity: the passionate but rather nihilistic sense of the immediate, and with it the loss or at least the constriction of our memories regarding the past and our imaginations regarding the future. Without the past, there is no promise, and without the future, there is no fulfillment. Perhaps a holdover from mid-twentieth-century existentialism, our contemporary sense of time has become conflated into an urgent, though somewhat timeless, sense of "now," in which all meaning is concentrated. The need for instant gratification and the emotional disturbance created by postponement mean that future fulfillment is that which must be avoided rather than anticipated, while the past simply holds little interest. The past is gone and the future is the sphere of dread. J. Christiaan Beker calls this an attitude of "apocalypse now."[5]

This attitude is seen most clearly in younger people today who feel there is less and less ground for hope in view of the decay of civilization all around us. Is hope reasonable when two world wars and two Gulf wars, holocausts and ethnic cleansings, revolutions that devour their own children, AIDS and SARS, famine, urban decay, and so on are all within recent or present experience? Life remains life unto death, and for many if not most of the world's population it is a life without redemption from the crushing weight of torture, war, poverty, disease, ignorance, systemic neglect, and pain. Can Christians speak cogently about hope in history amid such terrible human devastation? How can one hope for a future in God when there appears to be so little personal or public sign of God's blessing for so many people, when God appears to be incognito on the blighted landscape of the present?

Secular hopes have rushed to fill the vacuum left by God's apparent withdrawal to the sidelines of a wrecked history. Marxism is to be characterized accurately as a materialist and teleologically oriented basis for hope—and as a failed system at that. Free market and corporate capitalism, while they have produced wealth in abundance for some, have nevertheless not found the ethical vision or the pragmatic means to bring hope to the great mass of people around the world or to increasing millions who live in hopelessness in the decaying cities of the West. Moral collapse—personal, corporate, and political—rampant crime, widespread drug abuse,

---

4. For a trenchant analysis of the problems faced by a contemporary theology of hope see Jacques Ellul, *Hope in Time of Abandonment*, trans. C. Edward Hopkin (New York: Seabury, 1973).
5. J. Christiaan Beker, *Suffering and Hope* (Philadelphia: Fortress Press, 1987), 17.

the sense of a civilization with its increasingly coarsened behaviors: is it cogent to place one's hope in the capacity of, for example, Western society to find a moral power for renewal once again?

How we talk of God today compounds the problem of religious speech concerning hope. Agreed public discourse tends to be limited to so-called empirical facts, while theology, at least on the popular level, tends to be a matter either of psychology or personal opinion. Biology can be taught in public schools, but not God. Faith is allocated a space in the private realm of experience, and when it breaks out into public life, much apparent distress seems to result, with agitated talk of separation of church and state. God, apparently, is best kept at home. One assumes an implied ontological reference beyond the self when people talk about God, but it is a reference for most people that appears extremely fuzzy and nebulous. One result of the positivist or materialist temper of our times is the difficulty we have in giving intelligible form to and speaking rationally about spiritual and moral matters. There is no agreed ground on which to appeal concerning talk of either God or ethics.[6] What is Christian hope's possibility in a public, social, and moral cosmology in which God is either bracketed out altogether or restricted to a private compartment of human experience? Can we speak cogently about hope today in any way other than as a branch of psychological inquiry?[7]

Over and against these tendencies, the gospel properly understood nevertheless provokes a disruption in present thinking. On the ground of a past work of God, it anticipates a future work of God—*adventus Dei*, a final redemption in the future, a life beyond the grave, and a fulfillment of history beyond death.[8] For faith, this is a future opened up by the promises of God contained primarily in the resurrection of Jesus, promises out of the past that create a horizon of openness for the future. Promise creates an eschatological horizon of expectation as the faithful await the coming fulfillment with hope.[9] If this is true, it means that the loss of hope is not a thing in itself, but is rather the loss of faith in

6. For a rigorous criticism of modernity insofar as we are unable to find a common basis for moral discourse, see Alastair MacIntyre, *After Virtue* (Notre Dame, Ind.: University of Notre Dame Press, 1981).

7. Donald Capps has criticized Moltmann precisely because in trying to give hope an objective reference, he failed thereby to deal with the self, or the subjective dimensions of hope. Capps sees despair, apathy, and shame to be the obstacles to hope—each a negative affective disposition vis-à-vis the positive disposition of hope, in *Agents of Hope: A Pastoral Psychology* (Minneapolis: Fortress Press, 1995).

8. Brunner, *Eternal Hope*, 214.

9. See Moltmann, *Theology of Hope*, 191.

both the past of God's promises and the future of God's fulfillment. The twofold loss means that the present has neither any foundation nor any basis for expectation. Perhaps the loss of hope in this sense is now the characteristic expression of atheism today. Loss of hope, in the Christian sense of hope, and faithlessness certainly belong together.

The church is charged to give an account for the hope that is in it (1 Pet. 3:15). First, it will have to be an account of hope that has a transcendent ground beyond the self and in God, or it will be no hope at all. Without an objective reference that grounds it in reality, in past promise and coming, announced fulfillment, hope is merely wishful thinking, an affective disposition resting in our own capacity to "hope for the best" in spite of present experience. Second, it will have to be an account of hope that enables people to live with vitality and creativity in openness to the future in the face of the struggle for meaning, the experience of evil, and the fact of death. Such an account will recognize that there is a self who hopes. Third, it will have to be an account of hope that empowers people for personal, political, social, and economic transformation in the face of need on an historical and world scale. As Moltmann rightly saw, a theology of hope will be a theology of public transformations. The reason, quite simply put, is that the hope is for a new heaven and a new earth; it is hope in the promised and coming reign of God. One cannot live in the present under the announcement of this reign and remain passive in the face of everything that contradicts it. The challenge in all of this is to find the theological language that will be able to expand the spiritual, metaphysical, and moral imaginations of modern people so that such a hope is more than wishful thinking in the face of terrible deadly despair. This is surely a primary and urgent pastoral responsibility.

Employing the framework of the twofold ministry of Jesus Christ, in whose risen and ascended life we participate, we have a way of speaking about hope that has power for life. Pastoral theology may build on three points: the ground of hope, the liveliness of hope, and the transformations of hope.

The Ground of Hope

In the New Testament, Christian hope is based on the resurrection of Jesus.[10] The classic text is 1 Peter 1:3: "By his great mercy he has given us

---

10. "The ostensible basis for Christian hope in the New Testament is the resurrection of Christ." G. B. Caird, "The Christological Basis of Christian Hope," Caird et al., *The Christian Hope* (London: SPCK, 1970), 9. For a masterful theological treatment of the resurrection see Thomas F. Torrance, *Space, Time and Resurrection* (Grand Rapids: Eerdmans, 1976).

a new birth into a living hope through the resurrection of Jesus Christ from the dead." Or again: "God raised the Lord and will also raise us by his power" (1 Cor. 6:14). In John 14:19 Jesus says "because I live, you also will live." More generically, perhaps, Acts 23:6 reads that Paul is on trial concerning hope and the resurrection of the dead.[11] The early Christians believed that the resurrection was not only a sign that Jesus was alive, but a guarantee that they would live also.[12] If Christ is not raised, in other words, the whole edifice of Christian faith and life collapses (1 Cor. 15:14) because hope is without content or ground.[13]

As the resurrection of Jesus is the ultimate basis for Christian hope, that event itself cannot be understood apart from the events that lay three days before it in the Christian story, on the day Christians call "Good Friday." In a seemingly curious observation, Karl Barth notes that Good Friday is the day of the Father, Easter the day of the Son, and Whitsunday or Pentecost the day of the Spirit.[14] Is this not an unexpected allocation, for surely Good Friday is the day of the Son, the day of the death of Jesus; and Easter is the day of the Father, when Jesus was raised by the power of God? Commenting on Barth, John Macquarrie thinks, however, that Barth got it right. The cross casts a dark shadow over God, affecting God and, as it were, giving an inner meaning to the resurrection. The cross is not just a Jesus event, but even more so a God event, as Moltmann explained:

11. The NRSV here seems to miss the connection between hope and resurrection, reading "hope of the resurrection," although the footnote makes mention of the Greek, which reads *peri elpidos kai anastaseos.*

12. Caird, "Christological Basis of Christian Hope," 16–17.

13. Is resurrection credible? This chapter is not directly on the theme of resurrection, but this at least should be said. There seem to me to be three answers to this question. First, resurrections do not happen, and we expect some day to find the bones of Jesus. The resurrection is then to be interpreted as a metaphor for a symbolic system of ethical and religious value that gives life meaning and orientation up to but not beyond death. Second, the resurrection was a corporate spiritual event, rather like Bultmann's notion that Christ was resurrected into the kerygma, into the proclamation of the early church. In this case, resurrection is an existentially appropriable experience of meaning obtained through participation in the hearing of the sermon or some such liturgical variation. This is really a form of the first answer. Third, it was an historical event, but as such it was unique, being an event that defines history on its own terms, and that opens up a hitherto undisclosed future for history. Options one and two involve rearranging New Testament descriptions into alternative systems of meaning that are congruent with modernity. Option three involves calling into question contemporary assumptions of meaning on the basis of the Gospel accounts.

14. Karl Barth, *Church Dogmatics,* I.1, trans. G. W. Bromiley (Edinburgh: T. & T. Clark, 1986), 381. I found this reference in John Macquarrie, *Christian Hope* (New York: Seabury, 1978), 68.

To understand what happened between Jesus and his God and Father on the cross, it is necessary to talk in Trinitarian terms. The grief of the Father here is just as important as the death of the Son. The Son suffers dying, the Father death of the Son. The Fatherlessness of the Son is matched by the Sonlessness of the Father, and if God has constituted himself as the Father of Jesus Christ, then he also suffers the death of his Fatherhood in the death of the Son. Unless this were so, the doctrine of the Trinity would still have a monotheistic background.[15]

The consequence of this is that the resurrection has to be interpreted in the light of the cross—for the resurrection is the future of the crucified Christ. This means too that the cross is the history of the resurrected Jesus, for his identity is one in and through cross and resurrection.

The Christian hope is based on the faith that God did not deal with Jesus *ex machina*, acting as an untouched outside agent. The cross is not only an event that ended Jesus' life; it is also a God-event, for the cross reached into God's inner experience in such a way that God in Christ has experienced at firsthand, as it were, life unto death. The cry of dereliction from the cross, "My God, my God, why have you forsaken me?" is, as Moltmann notes, a cry from within God that can be understood properly only on the basis of the Trinity: "My God, why hast thou forsaken *thyself*"?[16] God has entered into solidarity with the abandonment and dereliction of the human plight, and from within it, in the resurrection of the crucified Jesus, given it a new future. This is the ground of Christian hope.

One additional point needs to be made regarding sin. The redemptive power in history is not hope itself, but that for which one hopes. It is a part of Christian hope that the past has been dealt with, a past that had to be dealt with because of sin. Hope for the future does not make sin or its consequences obsolete.[17] Atonement is not reducible to at-one-ment, or divine solidarity with human suffering, for human evildoing is still a factor. God's solidarity with our plight in the humanity of Jesus is not the same as God's expiatory bearing of our sins in that same humanity. The event of God in Christ means both that our sin is borne, and thereby borne away, and that God has entered into our plight and made it God's

15. Jürgen Moltmann, *The Crucified God*, trans. R. A. Wilson and John Bowden (New York: SCM, 1974), 243.

16. Ibid., 151.

17. It is precisely George Hendry's contention that Barth, Moltmann, and Pannenberg have attenuated sin. See "Is Sin Obsolescent?" in *The Princeton Seminary Bulletin* 8, no. 3 (1986), 256–67.

own. We must speak therefore of both atonement and at-one-ment. The resurrection means that there is a future for our pasts in our sinfulness as well as a future for our presents in our despair.

Clearly, then, we cannot jump to an Easter-based hope by way of jumping over the cross. To do so would evacuate hope of significance at that point where life is really experienced in its desperation and terror as life unto death in the contexts of the deepest experience of abandonment and the burden of sin that remains part of our existence. Whatever else Easter hope means, it means it is precisely our suffering unto death and our sinning unto deadliness that have been dealt with. The hope of the gospel, in other words, lies not only in a hope for the future, but also in a hope for the past, our pasts and our coming pasts of sinfulness, disobedience, and faithlessness. In the dying humanity of Jesus Christ, God has as an act of *God* gathered up our history and present experiences of fear, wantonness, violence, death, and so on into himself, and given humankind a hitherto undisclosed future that is now announced in the event of the resurrection of Jesus Christ from the dead.

The ground of Christian hope is twofold. It lies first in who was resurrected, for as truly God, Jesus took our deadliness into the divine self and gave us life, and as truly human, Jesus shared our real humanity and gave us a new future. But there is a second and often missed point: resurrection is not just something that happened to Jesus, but something that, through our union with Christ, we affirm will also happen to us. Sharing in his life as the Word of God to and for us, we share also therefore in his destiny as the resurrected one. Resurrection, then, must be thought of not just as a doctrine of faith to be believed, but also as a personal apprehension of faith through hope.

The pastoral implications are enormous. Two stories may make the point.[18] Nicole was a lovely baby, so full of life, an icon of hope for her parents. As a first-year student of theology I met Nicole when her belly had already grown to be huge with the tumor that was soon to kill her. Her dying was drawn out, painful for her and her very young parents. At Nicole's death, her parents were wrung out with failed hopes for a medical miracle.

On the outskirts of San Salvador lies the Catholic parish of Calle Real, astonishingly misnamed the "royal road," for it is a place of truly amazing dereliction and neglect. One is overwhelmed by the acrid smoke, the unre-

---

18. These two accounts were used also in Andrew Purves and Charles Partee, *Encountering God: Christian Faith in Turbulent Times* (Louisville, Ky.: Westminster John Knox Press, 2000), 153.

paired damage of war, the ragged children playing soccer on scrubland, and the yapping mongrel dogs everywhere. On first glance it is hell. The Catholic priest there is American, and we attended Sunday morning mass, a festival of life celebrating the meager harvest. In the midst of grinding poverty the people brought gifts to lay before God. They sang and danced and laughed. The patron saint of the parish was paraded around the church, with banners and streamers in abundance. Afterward, outside, women of the church prepared lunch over huge open fires. I wrote in my journal: "The image which has emerged for me at Calle Real is 'fruit of the Word.' This is hope, God is here, life in the midst of death."

What can Christian faith say to Nicole's grieving parents that might give them hope in the face of death? What is the nature of the hope that empowers the people of Calle Real, who danced for joy in praise of God in the face of poverty and political despair? An account of the hope of the gospel must meet the challenge of these questions head-on or else be rendered worthless, and even worse, become an offense in the face of the terrible suffering it seeks to address. It is the challenge of hope, I think, that it compels us to speak of life in the face of death. Hope affirms that life, not death, has the last word. How is this possible?

For Christian faith, to speak of hope is to speak of Jesus Christ. Perhaps that point can be made most strongly by rewording just slightly the introduction to John's Gospel. "In the beginning was the hope, and the hope was with God, and the hope was God. The hope was in the beginning with God. And the hope became flesh and dwelt among us." Putting it this way we can see clearly that while the Christian's hope has to do with the Christian hoping, it has much more to do with who God is, what God does toward us, and the fact that we share in that. To put it differently, in thinking about hope we do not just think about hope as such, as an affective state, but about Jesus Christ, and of our union with him, for he is our hope, even whether we feel hopeful or not.

Jesus is the subject matter of hope, just as our union with him is the agency that makes hope personal and powerful in our lives. This does not mean that no value is placed on hope as a subjective experience. On the contrary, hope as a human experience in the face of suffering and death is a blessed experience and a miracle of our union with Christ. There always remains a hoper who hopes. But hope is not its own subject, at least not first of all, because Jesus and our union with him, not our hoping, is the hope of the gospel.

Pastorally speaking, the ground of hope that must be proclaimed and celebrated is the resurrection of Jesus. This is the ground and truth of all Christian worship. Without it, worship becomes religious self-actualization. A hope in a vague sense of God, a hope that is not christologically specific, a hope that turns the resurrection into a metaphor or a social experience, is a hope that will dissipate in the face of blunt, deadly reality, leaving us with a hope only in our own resources. This is a recipe for despair. If Christ is not raised, not only faith but also hope is in vain. Pastoral work is always in one way or another a ministry of hope that because Christ is risen, we too will share in his life. This word of assurance, on the basis of this ground, must ever be on pastors' lips. The ultimate word, the decisive word that is ever and always announced is: Christ is risen! Life!

The Liveliness of Hope

Donald Capps has correctly commented that the theologians of hope—arguably Barth, Moltmann, and Pannenberg—in the attempt to ground Christian hope objectively in the life, death, and resurrection of Jesus, gave insufficient attention to the experience of hope. A hope that is not experienced in some kind of interior process, that is only a proposition commanding assent, is no hope at all. One could argue, however, that Capps falls prey to the counterfault, of considering hope largely as a psychological experience. Clearly we should not fall into the trap of thinking in terms of an either-or.

John Calvin was aware that objectivity in faith had to have a corresponding subjective or personal dimension. "As long as Christ remains outside of us, and we are separated from him, all that he has suffered and done for the salvation of the human race remains useless and of no value to us. Therefore to share with us what he has received from the Father, he had to become ours and to dwell within us."[19] The liveliness of Christian hope, that is, hopefulness, is based on the belief and indeed the experience that Jesus is not just raised but also present in the power of the Holy Spirit: Christ in us, the hope of glory (Col. 1:27). If Christ is our hope, it is nevertheless we who have hope and who live hopefully.

Only God gives the gift of Christian hope, and there is a certain sense in which there is little else to say. The matter is God's responsibility. Even so, this Jesus, raised from the dead, is, as Emil Brunner rightly noted, "a living creative experience through faith and the Holy Ghost."[20] In the New Testament, and so also for Christians in their experiences through-

---

19. Calvin, *Inst.* 3.1.1.
20. Brunner, *Eternal Hope*, 143.

out subsequent history, the resurrection does not stand isolated from the presence of Jesus, the hope that that presence engenders, and, as we will see, the ministry that the liveliness of hope calls forth. Jesus' promise in Matthew is this: "remember, I am with you always" (28:20), and especially is this true, presumably, where Christians gather in small communities (Matt. 18:20). Moltmann calls this the church of the apostolate.[21]

From within the Reformed tradition, the presence of God in Christ—the experience of the covenant of grace—is administered in the preaching of the Word of God and in the administration of the sacraments of baptism and the Lord's Supper.[22] The tradition's reluctance to step outside the dominically ordered and ecclesially prescribed administration of grace is salutary amid a culture and a church struggling with too much emphasis placed on subjective authority and privatism in matters of faith and life. Thus content and experience, the gospel as objectively grounded and offered and subjectively received and participated in through Christian community, and especially in the ministry of the Word and sacraments, are profoundly held together as the one action of God's saving and transforming grace. Not the least of what this means today with regard to hope is the church's call to preach the Word of God and administer the sacraments faithfully as the only tools at our behest. This carries with it the responsibility to nurture Christian community, especially through renewal of worship. While hope must encompass all of life and is therefore not reducible to Word and sacraments, there can be no experience of Christian hope aside from Word and sacraments and, therefore, Christian community.

As to the hope itself, announced in sermon, sealed in baptism, in which we participate in the Eucharist through a physical union with Christ in bread and wine, it comes to a sharp focus with the ultimate question: What happens when we die? With Paul, the church asserts, rather honestly, that "if for this life only we have hoped in Christ, we are of all people most to be pitied" (1 Cor. 15:19). Yet even as we try to answer the question, we recognize that we see in a mirror, dimly (1 Cor. 13:12), and faith is neither without doubt and ambiguity, or incognizant of a need to keep a certain modesty regarding its proposals at this point, for we draw near to matters of great mystery and delicacy. There comes a point in theological

21. By virtue of his identifying assurance, Christ is present in the apostolate. On the same assurance, this is to be laid alongside the church of the least of the brothers and sisters (an ecclesiology based on Matt. 25:31–46) and the church of the reign of God (an ecclesiology of the Parousia), in Jürgen Moltmann, *The Church in the Power of the Spirit*, trans. Margaret Kohl (London: SCM, 1977), 123–24.

22. "The Larger Catechism," *Book of Confessions*, Presbyterian Church (U.S.A.), 2002, 7.145.

reflection where metaphysical speculation is just theological dilettantism. The short answer is that as nothing will be able to separate us from the love of God in Christ (Rom. 8:39), our future beyond death is locked into the future of Jesus Christ. His life is our life. In some sense or other, then, Christian hope is for life in Christ and through Christ after death.

What that might mean is the subject of enduring and probably irresolvable debate,[23] and at the end of the day the how is not as important as the who in whom hope trusts. It is interesting to note in passing that the funeral service is not called the Service of Christian Hope, as if now, at the last, everything is to be cast back upon ourselves, our faith, our hopes, and our theories of eternal life. Rather, the funeral service is called the Witness to the Resurrection, where everything is cast back upon Jesus Christ, into whose future we trust ourselves and pray God for the faith to rest in that. Hope does not point back to itself but away from itself to the risen, present Christ.

In the commendation at the end of the funeral service we read:

> All of us go down to the dust;
> yet even at the grave we make our song:
> Alleluia, alleluia, alleluia.[24]

What, then, does the liveliness of hope mean for pastoral work? How might this affirmation of the objective and subjective dimensions of hope shape day in and day out what pastors do? The connection has already been made between hope and worship. Pastoral work that does not seek, as a defining task, to bring people into and encourage them in participating ever more deeply in worship becomes a pastoral work that separates its ministry from the sustaining ground of hope. It is ultimately worship that orients us regarding God and ourselves, that gives a perspective on life that is true and not ephemeral and merely self-indulgent fancy. It is worship that keeps God's promises and hope for future fulfillment before us. It is in worship that we participate in the Word delivered in sermon and sacrament and share thereby in Jesus' response to the Father, which is lived out as gratitude and thanksgiving.

I noted in passing that there is a connection between the liveliness of hope and the work of the Holy Spirit. One of the most amazing verses in

---

23. For a useful review of issues and how contemporary theologians have addressed the matter see Stephen H. Travis, *Christian Hope and the Future* (Downers Grove, Ill.: InterVarsity Press, 1980), chapter 6.

24. *Book of Common Worship* (Louisville, Ky.: Westminster John Knox Press, 1993), 925.

Scripture is surely the opening to the long hymn of praise that begins the Epistle to the Ephesians. "Blessed be the God and Father of our Lord Jesus Christ, who has blessed us in Christ with every spiritual blessing in the heavenly places" (1:3). On this work of the Holy Spirit two things can be said for our purpose. First, consider your blessings. A blessing is meant here to mean real changes effected among and within people. This is not some vague sense of well-being, but God's actual work within us. Second, the blessings we receive are empowerments given from heaven. Heaven is not a place, of course; heaven is best understood dynamically, meaning the power of God's reign, and is thus directly related to the ground of Christian hope. So the verse that opens this great theological treatise reminds us that we have been changed and charged by the power of God's reign at work within and through us in Jesus Christ. God has chosen us in Christ to bless us with blessings that are uniquely the gift of heaven. In pastoral work we remind people of their blessings, helping them to put their life in the context of God's promises and acts.

But the liveliness of hope is not a passive disposition. Jesus said, "I chose you. And I appointed you to go and bear fruit, fruit that will last" (John 15:16). In other words, one will know Christians by their fruit, by the power of God's blessing that flows in and through us through union with Christ. Christians empowered by the Holy Spirit are marked as fruit bearers, as kingdom-powered people, as generative, productive, creative people, people who birth the good works of the blessing that are given as empowerments. Christians are cosmically endowed to be fruit bearers. Christians are a fecund people.

Perhaps the pastoral implications may be helpfully expressed in a homiletical mode. There is nothing the devil likes more, I suspect, than Christians playing "poor me" and "Ain't it awful." The evil one rejoices surely when Christians have pathetic attacks. These are dull, old games; they seduce us into thinking that we have nothing much to contribute, that we are not really of much use. Our minds and talents are just too meager. Our sense of the possible lacks vision. We stumble around in the fog of our own feelings of inadequacy. While we have every possible blessing given to us from God, we tend to get caught up in an all too present awareness of our failings. The liveliness of faith and hope are squashed by despair.

Thomas Merton, the monk and spiritual teacher, used to speak about the battle between true and false self. Our true self is our self in Christ, baptized and blessed with every blessing from heaven. It is who we really are. Our false self is that bit of us, in spite of the truth of who we are, that refuses to believe and to live out the empowerment we have from God. In spite of our being elect in Jesus Christ from the foundation of the world, in spite of the fact that nothing can separate us from the love of God in Christ Jesus, in spite of having every blessing in the heavenly places, a bit of us refuses to believe it or live in its power. Merton called this living a lie, but it exercises its demonic work over us. We stand before the mirror in the morning and insist that we do not see a saint but a pathetic excuse for a Christian. And the devil rejoices, laughing all the way to hell. Pastoral work confronts this lie with words of hope, promise, and the call to move forward in the light of the gospel.

First Corinthians 12:7 teaches that "to each is given the manifestation of the Spirit for the common good," following Acts 1:8, "You will receive power when the Holy Spirit has come upon you." The meaning here is that each Christian has a gift from the Holy Spirit, a blessing from God, that is open to sight, that is visible, and is given for a missional purpose. The Greek word that we translate as "manifestation" was frequently associated with the idea of something or someone "significantly shining." Just imagine it: Christians significantly shining! This is the liveliness of hope. After all, Christians are the light of the world. A city set upon a hill cannot be hidden. Our light is not to be hidden under a basket. Rather our light shines before others—"so that they may see your good works and give glory to your Father in heaven" (Matt. 5:14–16). Practical Christian renewal has to find a space for helping the people of God discover and accept their giftedness and blessedness and then to hold them accountable for its suitable employment and enjoyment.

There is a children's song in the *Church of Scotland Hymnbook*, though I have not been able to find it in an American hymnbook. It is a bit individualistic, but may still have its appropriate place in Christian piety as it holds together both the power of Christ within us and our response to live as persons with a mission.

> Jesus bids us shine with a pure, clear light,
> Like a little candle burning in the night.
> In this world of darkness; so let us shine,
> You in your small corner, and I in mine.
>
> Jesus bids us shine, first of all for him;
> Well he sees and knows it, if our light grows dim:
> He looks down from heaven to see us shine,
> You in your small corner, and I in mine.

Jesus bids us shine, then, for all around;
Many kinds of darkness in the world are found—
Sin, and want, and sorrow; so we must shine,
You in your small corner, and I in mine.

The Transformations of Hope

The transformations of hope are based on the coming of the reign of God that we are called to anticipate in time. Hope is not, as Karl Marx once suggested, a fleeing from the earth and a longing beyond history, but a way of life on earth and in history. Dietrich Bonhoeffer once reminded the church that "only those who cry out for the Jews may sing Gregorian chants." For our part, we have no right either to speak of God or reflect on Christian hope if we do not do so in the midst of the political and social realities that confront us.[25] All theology is by necessity political theology in the sense that it is written, read, and debated in the context of wars, murders, torture, starvation, sickness, and death. Jesus Christ did not live and die in an ivory tower, religiously removed from the murk and grime of savagely cruel existence.

"Those who hope in Christ," wrote Moltmann, "can no longer put up with reality as it is, but begin to suffer under it, to contradict it. Peace with God means conflict with the world, for the goad of the promised future stabs inexorably into the flesh of every unfulfilled present."[26] This is a trenchantly important statement for a theology of hope. If we fail to grasp its point and do not follow its counsel, hope slides into privatism and individualism. Rather, hope must draw the mind into opposition to those experiences of reality where no truth or justice is found, provoking within us a peculiar and specifically Christian incongruence with the status quo, thus setting loose powers that are critical and transformative of it.[27] The person of faith suffers under the difference between hope and reality, remaining unreconciled to present experience and no longer willing to put up with it. "If the promise of the kingdom of God shows us a universal eschatological future horizon spanning all things . . . then it is impossible for the [person] of hope to adopt an attitude of religious and cultic resignation from the world."[28] This, be it noted, is not an appeal for liberal

25. Thus Jürgen Moltmann, *The Experiment Hope* (Philadelphia: Fortress Press, 1975), 102.
26. Moltmann, *Theology of Hope*, 21.
27. Ibid., 118–19.
28. Ibid., 224.

political perspectives, but an admonition to be faithful to the eschatological indicative of the gospel that creates its own imperative for action and
life. The question is: What does it mean for how we must live and act *today*
that we have hope in a promised new heaven and a new earth?

It was a feature of Calvin's thought that the whole world belongs to the
reign of Jesus Christ, has come under his redemption, and that the triumph of Christ will be manifest among all nations.[29] The missionary
impulse of the gospel is compelled by an inner necessity to reach forth
into the present condition of humankind. It assumes as the highest priority but is not to be limited to the reconciliation of souls to God, for God's
grace in and through Jesus Christ extends over the whole world.[30] All creation is the arena of the *regnum Christi*, and that means that Christian hope
has to be thought through in terms that include political, social, and economic hope, as well as personal hope, that is, salvation, in the light of the
reign of Christ. The full meaning and range of the lordship of Jesus Christ
is at stake here. Again one might ask of the church: How radical is your
Christology?

Christian hope, then, does not dissolve hope into politics. Rather, it is
in obedient hope that Christians place themselves into situations that call
out for transformations, for the hope of the gospel must be seen as hope
for the hopeless, wherever they are to be found and in whatever form that
hopelessness is found. We have no right in the gospel to limit the hopelessness to which Christian mission and ministry responds to a personal
sphere of existence. Such a broad situating of Christian ministry means
that expressions of hope by necessity get bound up with contingent
processes, with political party issues and contemporary political debates,
for there is no other way to engage in history. A ministry of hope that does
not take the risk of concrete engagement ultimately fails to be a ministry
of hope and is instead faithless, sitting on the sidelines for fear of contamination. Christians in hope will seek rather to anticipate the future of
Christ according to the measure of the possibilities available to them.[31]
Even so, a politics of Christian hope will also be a sociocritical theology
of hope that refuses to ratify any contingent process, political or national

29. Thomas F. Torrance, *Kingdom and Church: A Study in the Theology of the Reformation* (Edinburgh: Oliver and Boyd, 1956), 161. For an earlier and briefer form, see idem, "The Eschatology of the Reformation," in *Eschatology: Four Papers Read to the Society for the Study of Theology*,
Scottish Journal of Theology Occasional Papers no. 2 (Edinburgh: Oliver and Boyd, 1953),
36–62. Calvin arguably makes it clearer than Torrance that there is a political dimension to this.
   30. Calvin, Sermon on 1 Timothy 2:5–6, cited by Torrance, "Eschatology of the Reformation."
   31. Moltmann, *Crucified God*, 329.

ideology and identity, as in itself the will of God. To do otherwise is idolatry. Even while working within the possibilities of politics, a theology of
hope is a theology that demythologizes all absolute statements concerning state and ideology.

Hope is the place where the personal cry of pain for freedom and
release merges with the cry of the oppressed and misused for redemption
and justice. There can be no real separation between work for social righteousness, evangelism, and pastoral care. To divide them into discrete and
forever separated categories is a misuse of Christian hope, and, in effect,
a serious and erroneous reduction of the gospel. It limits its scope and
denies the inclusive nature of the reign of God. It says that the lordship
of Jesus is limited to human hearts only in some delimited personal sphere
of existence and has no rule over the systems of commerce and banking,
over health care and schooling, over political discourse and economic policy, over foreign affairs and the use of military power. To say this, as I noted
earlier, is not to sanction theologically any particular policy, for that is
idolatry, something that politically active people on all sides of political
debate may be prone to do. Christian eschatology must always point to a
gap between history and salvation, for present experience is not yet the
reign of God. Nevertheless, the propensity to sin is not an excuse for political idleness. To refuse to risk contamination by being involved in the
often murky processes of the political, social, and economic engagements
amounts to a denial of the gospel's eschatological claim that all life in every
respect is under the one reign of God through Jesus Christ.

A sociocritical pastoral theology of hope is required to cover many
issues. The theological insight that should govern our thinking is the doctrine of Irenaeus that has been helpfully co-opted by Moltmann: *ubi Christus—ibi ecclesia*, wherever Christ is, there the church is found. What forms
of mission with regard to the social and political aspects of hope, then,
may be identified to illustrate our participation in Christ's mission to the
Father for the sake of the world? The following programmatic statement
from Moltmann is helpful in outlining the calling of Christians in society
in the light of the hope promised by the gospel:

> This mission is not carried out within the horizon of expectation pro-
> vided by the social roles which society concedes to the Church, but
> it takes place within its own peculiar horizon of the eschatological
> expectation of the coming kingdom of God, of the coming right-
> eousness and the coming peace, of the coming freedom and dignity
> of man. The Christian Church has not to serve mankind in order that

the world may remain what it is . . . but in order that it may transform itself and become what it is promised to be.[32]

Community

To belong to Jesus means that we belong within community. The priority
properly given to the kingdom or reign of God means, among other things,
that human life is lived with liveliness within relationships that form us into
communities. Some of these relations are primary. Some are less intimate,
but not thereby of little importance, for example, belonging to associations
connected with employment, recreation, and shared perspectives or goals.
At yet wider and more inclusive levels, we are members of nations that have
distinct characterizations, as well as what is now called the global village.
None of us lives or dies alone, for him- or herself. Everybody is in some
sense connected to others at many levels of experience and involvement;
we live as interconnected persons. In fact, our being as persons in the first
place is relational before we are personal individuals. Apart from relationships we are more akin to things than to persons. The relationship between
the contemporary formulation of the social Trinity and theological anthropology makes the point: belonging to God through union with Christ, thus
personhood in an ontological sense, we also belong to one another, without which relationships our Christian life as a life of personhood disinte-
grates.

   Christian hope leads us to give priority to the things that make for community, to make our lives within community, and to see sin as those behaviors and structures that make for broken relationships or to no possibility
of relationships in the first place. Sin is that which destroys personhood,
for it has its root in a broken relationship with God, in relation to whom
we are persons in the first place. Pastoral care in the light of the hope
promised by the gospel is defined by a primary concern for relationships,
to help mend what is broken and inaugurating what is not yet manifest.
To this end, pastoral care must operate at many levels. At the interpersonal level, pastoral work is a ministry of reconciliation—between men
and women, husbands and wives, children and parents, friend and friend,
and, of course, enemies. It is also involved in educating people into those
things that make for enduring and person-building relationships, and
where necessary even creating them in the first place. But it cannot remain
there. For pastoral care must also be concerned with restoring and creat-

---

32. Moltmann, *Theology of Hope*, 327.

ing relationships of love, justice, and respect at the wider community and national levels. Pastoral work is rightly involved in issues of racial justice and equal rights, of access to health care for all, of adequate schooling, housing, and so on. The point here is not to prescribe public policies, but to say that pastoral work includes ministries at every level of relationship, from the interpersonal, to the community-wide and national, and to the international. In all things, Christians bear witness to the coming reign of God as relationship restorers, as builders of intimate, local, national, and international relations that in purpose, structure, and functioning anticipate the coming reign of God.

Concrete Works of Liberation

We cannot avoid commitment to specific goals. Moltmann's comments above highlight righteousness, peace, freedom, and dignity. To repeat: these gospel imperatives are not to be dismissed as merely liberal social or political agenda items. They have a deeper significance, for they reflect aspects of the nature of the reign of God. The gospel pushes us, at it were, to points of commitment, to perspectives and positions that may indeed serve the world to "become what it is promised to be." Christians cannot remain neutral before the great issues of national and international life. Christians, too, may disagree on means to an agreed end, but the gospel presses upon us as by the Spirit we are brought into an ever-deeper conformity to the mind of Christ. Christian life means that we are ever involved in repentance and the ever-deeper conversion of our minds so that we have more fully the mind of Christ. Such conformity means surely a transcending of personal and national self-interests. It means the liberation of the mind and will from sectarian perspectives, but no less so it entails an advocacy of policies, attitudes, and behaviors that are congruent with the reign of God, even as these policies, attitudes, and behaviors are not the reign of God.

It does mean that advocacy against social righteousness—accepting implicit institutional racism in criminal justice through advocacy of the death penalty, for example—is to be countered on the grounds of Christian social ethics. It does mean that advocacy against peace—through a national "might is right" attitude that leads to a disregard of just war ethics, for example—is to be countered on the basis of the peacemaking imperative of the gospel. It does mean that advocacy against freedom—through trapping people in the prisons of poverty through unemployment and an inadequate social security safety net or through unjust labor policies, for example—is to be countered, for Christ came to free the prisoners, those trapped in systems of inhumanity through no fault of their own. It does mean that advocacy against the dignity of all—through demonizing people whose behaviors are deemed to be against the will of God, homosexuals, abortionists, and so on, for example—is to be countered, because Christians are called to love the sinner even as they denounce the sin. Christians are to be advocates for social righteousness, peace, freedom, and dignity, though on gospel terms, not on terms of personal or national self-interest. The Christian church, Moltmann reminds us, has not to serve humankind in order that the world may remain what it is, with its petty allegiances and sectarian patriotisms (I add as commentary), but in order that it ever more fully corresponds to the promised, announced, and coming transnational, interethnic, multilinguistic reign of God.

The prayer of the church is "Thy kingdom come." This is the prayer for God to do what only God can do. All things finally are cast back upon God. Like a navigator scanning the horizon, Christians look beyond the present and short-term field of vision to the new heaven and the new earth of God's kingdom. That we are called to play our part in its coming is a gift of God. So we do not despair over the slim pickings that seem to result from our ministries. Trying to be faithful in every way, we trust God to bring in the sheaves. We do not lament our meager talent. We trust God to prosper our work in ways we cannot even begin to imagine. We do not collapse into a slough of self-pity over our spiritual poverty. We believe that God is doing a new work even with us. We put our hands but lightly to the plow, and we are amazed even then that the furrow is straight, to discover at a much later time that some seeds of God's Word have been planted by us in unexpected places. We did not recognize good soil even when we walked upon it. It is all God's doing. We rejoice, therefore, in the hope that is within us. We give thanks to God for that little faith we do have, even if it is only the size of a mustard seed. We celebrate the acts of faithfulness, and even surprise ourselves with moments of sacrificial love that can have no other source than God. We press on, following Christ of the upward way, trusting in him to keep using cracked pots like us, vessels of clay, as his instruments of blessing and healing and grace for a work that will prosper. We remember the words of the Lord: "I have chosen you, and appointed you, to go and bear fruit, fruit that will last."

Index